The Dieppe Raid

The Dieppe Raid

The German Perspective

By Graham Anthony-Thomas

Pen & Sword
MILITARY

An imprint of
Pen & Sword Books Ltd
Yorkshire – Philadelphia

Pen & Sword
MILITARY

First published in Great Britain in 2023 by
PEN & SWORD MILITARY
An imprint of
Pen & Sword Books Ltd
Yorkshire – Philadelphia

ISBN 978 1 52678 606 7

A CIP catalogue record for this book is available from the British Library

Typeset in Chennai, India
by Lapiz Digital Services.

Printed and bound by CPI UK

Pen & Sword Books Ltd incorporates the imprints of Pen & Sword
Archaeology, Atlas, Aviation, Battleground, Discovery, Family History, History, Maritime,
Military, Naval, Politics, Social History, Transport, True Crime, Claymore Press,
Frontline Books, Praetorian Press, Seaforth Publishing and White Owl

For a complete list of Pen & Sword titles please contact

PEN & SWORD BOOKS LTD
47 Church Street, Barnsley, South Yorkshire, S70 2AS, England
E-mail: enquiries@pen-and-sword.co.uk
Website: www.pen-and-sword.co.uk

Or

PEN AND SWORD BOOKS
1950 Lawrence Rd, Havertown, PA 19083, USA
E-mail: Uspen-and-sword@casematepublishers.com
Website: www.penandswordbooks.com

Contents

Author's Note

Growing up in Canada in the late fifties and early sixties for most people the Dieppe Raid held a kind of morbid fascination. It was Canada's greatest military disaster where so many lives had been lost. There is much Canadian literature that has been devoted to the subject as scholars and historians have tried to come up with a definitive answer as to what went wrong. Why did the raid take place? Why did so many brave Canadians die on the beaches that day? What was it all for?

One could say that Dieppe is ingrained still in the Canadian psyche although fewer and fewer young Canadians today have any idea of what the Dieppe Raid was and just how bad the loss of life was.

It holds a special place in my heart because it reminds me of my father. He fought in the British Eighth Army in the desert, Sicily, Italy and finally in north-west Europe. Though he never spoke much about his time in the British Army he did guide me in my love of military history. It was my father who first told me about the Dieppe Raid and while I had heard bits and pieces of it I never really understood it. As a young teenager I began to research the events that took place on that infamous day, 19 August 1942.

When I left Canada back in the 1990s talking about the Dieppe raid or discussing it was becoming unfashionable. It was not politically correct. It was seen by the legacy media as glorification. Yet, across Canada there are many memorials to the men who fell at Dieppe. Indeed, in the province of New Brunswick, there is a city named Dieppe, in honour of that battle. So, while, the government and the media look with disdain upon Canada's military history there are still many who keep the memory alive for all generations. Despite this, I doubt if many young people, not just in Canada but also in Britain, know much, or anything, about the Dieppe Raid.

There is a wealth of material that has been written about the Dieppe landings from the perspective of the Allies but not much has been written about the German perspective of the Allied operation. The Germans were, after all, the victors in that operation according to most sources. Their losses were far fewer than the Allies, the materiel that they lost was far less and they managed to stop the Allies from advancing beyond the town of Dieppe. Yet, even to this day, very little has been written about the German perspective of the raid by the English-speaking academic and historical communities. Perhaps, this is because the Allied historians, shortly after the raid took place and certainly right after the war, put a positive spin on the raid. It was an experiment to see if amphibious landings on the coast of Europe could be achieved, for example, or, could Hitler's Fortress Europe really be broken? However, the reality is that the battle cost the Germans far less than it did the Allies.

If, as most people might think, that history is written by the victors, then this book is designed to shed some light on the German perspective on the Dieppe raid.

The Germans thought the landings were a failed invasion attempt to break Fortress Europe. The Allies looked upon it as a testbed for later, much larger amphibious operations on the beaches of North Africa, Sicily and north-west Europe (the D-Day landings). The influence that the Dieppe raid had on D-Day cannot be ignored. Lessons were learned on both sides but which side was able to implement those lessons with a greater degree of success when the time came? This, perhaps, is where the Allies were the victors of the battle after all because of what they learned for future operations?

Most of the information for this book comes from German sources, war diaries, combat reports and so forth, that were collated by Canadian historians just after the war. The Canadians were very meticulous about creating historical accounts of the exploits of their troops and military operations, the British less so.

Other sources have also been used to create this book in order to try to provide the reader with a balanced and accurate view (so far as can be determined from the source material) of the Dieppe operations.

Like the Somme, Dieppe is still part of Canadian heritage, whether it was a failure or a success. Hopefully, by the information presented within these pages the reader will be able to come to an understanding of what the Germans thought of the Allied landings at Dieppe, if the Germans really were the winners of the battle or, ultimately, the losers. In addition, the reader will also hopefully come to his or her own conclusions about the success, failure and even necessity for the Dieppe Raid.

Graham Anthony-Thomas
Wiltshire, January 2023

Part 1

Chapter 1

Introduction

Perhaps the best way to provide the reader with a brief background to the landings is to look at the situation just prior to the operation.

Dieppe was probably one of the largest combined arms operations up to that point in the war. Two infantry brigades and large numbers of other troops were involved in the raid along with a tank battalion. It was the first time that Canadian tank units engaged the enemy.[1]

> Both in preparation and in execution, DIEPPE was an extraordinarily complicated operation, and the mass of documentary material relating to it is proportionately large. The operation was preceded by a very long course of detailed planning and training, and it seems essential to take note of these matters as well as of the actual events of the raid.[2]

Of course the landings were not entirely a Canadian affair and the story cannot be told solely from that perspective. British and other Allied forces were involved and of course both the Royal Navy and the Royal Air Force played crucial roles in the Dieppe landings. The events of the raid extended over a large area and while our main focus of this book is the German perspective of the raid, the defences they created and how they countered the Allies, we cannot really discuss this side of the operation without looking at the lead-up to the landings, and the landings themselves.

In the summer of 1942 the German Army occupied the whole of the western coastline of Europe, an area that stretched from the Pyrenees to

---

1   This information is from Report No. 100, Canadian Military Headquarters, Operation Jubilee, The Raid on Dieppe, 19 August 1942, Part 1 The Preliminaries of the Operation.

2   Ibid.

the North Cape. At the same time in Britain the Allies were building their army, which included a growing Canadian contingent supported by strong and continually growing United States forces. Since the collapse of France in 1940 the Allies had been building up the equipment, training troops and making preparations initially for a German invasion of the United Kingdom.

However, on 22 June 1941 Hitler kicked off Operation Barbarossa, the invasion of the Soviet Union. This operation pulled away much, but by no means all, of the German war machine then in France and with it went the threat of an invasion of the United Kingdom.

> In these circumstances the apprehension of a German invasion of the United Kingdom which was current during the twelve months following DUNKIRK has very largely ceased to exist.[3]

With the reduction of the threat of invasion of Britain the thoughts within the public as well as many Allied commanders turned to the possibility of a second front in Western Europe, that is turning the tables on the Germans and mounting an invasion of the continent from Britain by Allied forces, thus creating the second front.

> The British Government has allowed it to be known that such a development is a definite part of the Allied strategy; though in the nature of things it is not proposed to announce times and places in advance, and it is intended to base decisions upon the facts of the military situation rather than of public demand.[4]

According to the *Daily Express* of 5 October 1942, the Soviet Government made no secret of its desire for the Allies to create a second front in north-west Europe to relieve the pressure on Soviet forces in the east. In the *Daily Express* article, Stalin, premiere of the Soviet Union, stated that a second front in north-west Europe was very important to Soviet strategy.[5]

---

3   Ibid.
4   Ibid.
5   *The Daily Express*, London, 5 October 1942, as cited in Report No. 100, Canadian Military Headquarters, Operation Jubilee, The Raid on Dieppe, 19 August 1942, Part 1 The Preliminaries of the Operation.

This is reflected in a speech Prime Minister Churchill gave in the House of Commons on 11 November 1942 that outlined the situation in the summer of the same year. The speech laid out the massive preparatory work for creating the second front as so desired by the Soviets:

> The attack which will be made in due course across the Channel or the North Sea requires an immense degree of preparation, vast numbers of special landing craft, and a great army trained, division by division, in amphibious warfare. All this is proceeding, but it takes time.[6]

In that speech, Churchill noted that the German Army in France, despite the fact that most of it was engaged in the monumental struggle on the Eastern Front, was as large as the British Army in England was, excluding the Home Guard. The Germans had built huge fortifications along the Channel and North Sea coasts, known as the Atlantic Wall, thus making an invasion of mainland Europe especially difficult.

> It would have been most improvident for us to attempt such an enterprise before all our preparations were ready. They have very greatly advanced. Enormous installations have been and are being brought into existence at all our suitable ports, but no one would have been justified, nor indeed would it have been physically possible, to have made an effective invasion of the Continent during the summer or autumn of 1942.[7]

Churchill went on to say that in June 1942 a joint communique had been issued by the UK, the USA and the Soviet Union about creating a second front in Europe the same year. The main objective of this communique was to lead the Germans into thinking such a front was to take place; that a landing on French soil from England by the Allies would happen. Churchill stated that it was highly important for the Soviet Union that the Germans would believe the Allies were going to land in 1942, thus forcing them to keep 33 divisions in the west, which would relieve the pressure on the Soviets.

---

6   Ibid., the speech was reported in *The Times* of 11 November 1942.
7   Ibid.

With the American entry into the war and after the German invasion of Russia in 1941 the Allies wanted to break Germany's grip on Europe while also ensuring that the supply lines to Russia were secure. To do this, it was decided in July 1942 to mount amphibious landings in French North Africa, which would prove to be a mammoth undertaking.

> General Marshall, the head of the American Army, with which is included the American Air Force, paid two visits to this country, the first in April, the second in July; and on the second occasion he was accompanied by Admiral King, the Commander-in-Chief of the American Navy. It was decided on this second occasion to hold the enemy on the French shore and to strike at his southern flank in the Mediterranean through North Africa. In this decision the British and American Staffs were wholly united, and their views were shared and adopted by the President and the British War Cabinet . . . Orders for the North African expedition were accordingly issued at the end of July.[8]

However, plans for the Dieppe operation were already well under way as early as April 1942 before the decision was taken to attack the enemy in North Africa. This means that preparations and planning were moving forward at a time when Churchill openly stated that it was not yet certain that an invasion by sea of Western Europe would take place in the summer of 1942.

> Investigation, however, had proved that a large-scale cross-channel operation would not be feasible in 1942. The best that could be devised was a series of raids on an increasing scale. These had culminated in the fine exploit at St Nazaire on 28 March 1942.[9]

Therefore, part of the Allied reasons for the Dieppe raid can be seen, in the light of Churchill's statement and knowing also that the Germans would be monitoring British radio communications, as pinning the Germans to the

---

8   This speech was reported in *The Times*, 12 November 1942, cited in Report No. 100, Canadian Military Headquarters, Operation Jubilee, The Raid on Dieppe, 19 August 1942, Part 1 The Preliminaries of the Operation.

9   *The Dieppe Raid: The Combined Operations Assault on Hitler's European Fortress August 1942*, An Official History, Frontline Books, ISBN 978-1-52675-291-8.

French shore. Another reason was that the Dieppe raid was a practice run for launching operations on a much larger scale later on, as with the North African landings in November 1942, and ultimately Operation Overlord, 6 June 1944.

Indeed, in September 1942, Churchill stated that the Dieppe raid was 'a reconnaissance in Force,' and that it was 'an indispensable preliminary to full-scale operations'.[10]

There is a document that supports this observation that is dated prior to the Dieppe landings. The document is a letter from Lord Louis Mountbatten to the Chiefs of Staff Committee dated 11 May 1942 asking for approval of the plans for the operation. Part of the response from the Committee is as follows:

> Apart from the military objective given in the outline plan, this operation will be of great value as training for Operation SLEDGEHAMMER, or any other major operation as far as the actual assault is concerned. It will not, however, throw light on the maintenance problem over the beaches.[11]

And so we have some justification from the Allies for mounting the Dieppe landings. This operation was also the first time the British had attempted landing armour from tank landing craft onto beaches under fire.

> This was the largest raid actually carried out, and the only one in which the landings of tanks was attempted, and in which more than an hour or two was allowed for military operations on shore; it was also the last, because the available landing craft were soon afterwards required for use in the North African expedition, and subsequently the strategic policy regarding raids underwent a change.[12]

---

10 As reported in *The Times*, 9 September 1942, according to Report No. 100, Canadian Military Headquarters, Operation Jubilee, The Raid on Dieppe, 19 August 1942, Part 1 The Preliminaries of the Operation.

11 Ibid.

12 See *The Dieppe Raid: The Combined Operations Assault on Hitler's European Fortress August 1942*, An Official History.

As this book is primarily about the German perspective of the Dieppe landings perhaps it is time to provide a brief overview on what the Germans thought of the raid. The best source for this overview comes from Field Marshal von Rundstedt's observations of the Allied operation.

At the time he was Commander-in-Chief West and his initial view was that the expenditure in men and materials was far too great for the operation to be classified as a raid. 'One does not sacrifice 29 or 30 of the most modern tanks for a raid.'[13] Von Rundstedt felt that by employing such a large force, the British wanted to quickly seize the 'Dieppe bridgehead', after its defences had been destroyed, in order to use the excellent port facilities for landing 'floating and operational reserves'.

> For with the floating reserve alone there were 28 tanks, certainly of the same types. An expenditure of 58 such tanks cannot be reconciled with a short destructive raid. Nor, however, can it be established without contradiction by the captured operational order, whether the operation was of a local character or – in the event of success – was to be the beginning of the 'Invasion'.[14]

Von Rundstedt knew that after the completion of their tasks and re-embarkation, Nos 3 and 4 Commando were ordered to wait before returning to England to see if they were to take their place in the reserve force due to land behind the main force if the landings had been successful. They were to return to England without delay only in the case of not succeeding in their tasks.

> Also the hint in the captured order that the troops are not to destroy the gasworks at Dieppe, but to leave them going until the Engineers arrive, leaves open the possibility of issuing new orders at a given time. It appears certain that, had Dieppe fallen, these orders would have been given.[15]

---

13   From Report No. 10, Historical Section, National Defence Headquarters, Operation Jubilee, The Raid on Dieppe, Information From German War Diaries, Report of the Commander-in-Chief West, (Field Marshal von Rundstedt) on the Dieppe Raid, 19 August 1942.

14   Ibid., Paragraph 2.

15   Ibid., Paragraph 4.

Von Rundstedt's Chief of Staff, Kurt Zeitzler, visited 302nd Infantry Division at Dieppe on 20 August, the day after the landings and the battle. When he returned to headquarters he gave his impressions to his Commander-in-Chief. His main impression was that the Allied losses were high and that bodies still lay everywhere despite the clean-up process from the day before. He stated that: 'The English fought well. Canadians and Americans not so well, the latter quickly surrendered under the impression of high bloody losses.'[16]

Overall, Zeitzler stated that the German forces involved in the battle had prevented the Allies from penetrating in force deep into Dieppe and establishing a beachhead.

If nothing else, this opening chapter has provided some differing points of view about the Dieppe landings. As we delve deeper into the German defences, preparations, actions and views of the landings; in addition to the Allied operations, we hope that a picture of the operation will emerge that will provide the reader with a different perspective from the German point of view of the Dieppe raid.

---

16   Ibid., Section II, Evaluation, 1945hrs.

Chapter 2

German Defences

Dieppe was not altogether an easy target for a surprise landing.[1]

For the Allies there were several tempting military targets within the town of Dieppe and its port. These included the radar station at Caude Côté, the Saint-Aubin fighter airfield situated on the western outskirts along with railway yards, shipping yards, stores and docks. The Allies also believed that the town was weakly defended because second-rate troops were stationed there. This should have made the raid relatively easy and successful for the Allies. Dieppe was also well within reach of fighter airfields in the south-eastern part of England.

> It lies in a stretch of chalk cliffs which extend from Cap d'Antifer to the town of Ault, 56 miles to the north-east. In the vicinity of the port these cliffs are fairly high and present an almost unbroken front to the sea.[2]

Cliffs extend along the coast for several miles in a fairly solid line with the exception of Dieppe, the town and the port, the only gap in this part of the coast. The River Arques enters the English Channel at Dieppe. Save for a few ravines and openings along the cliffs there were precious few other areas that had major gaps that would enable a large number of troops and equipment to be landed and moved inland.

However, the beaches were narrow 'and rocky with occasional ledges which render landings almost impracticable at or near low water'.[3] According

---

1 See *The Dieppe Raid: The Combined Operations Assault on Hitler's European Fortress August 1942*, An Official History.

2 Ibid.

3 See *The Dieppe Raid: The Combined Operations Assault on Hitler's European Fortress August 1942*, An Official History.

to the Official History of the Dieppe Raid, in order to undertake the landings smooth water was required otherwise the swells that would normally be created by the wind blowing into shore would have made such an attempt untenable. Under these conditions the Allied Combined Operations Headquarters believed that there were only a few days per month in the summer that would provide the necessary smooth water for the landings to take place.

Yet with the drawbacks outlined above, Dieppe was still seen by the Allies as a viable target because of its defences, beaches and the distance from England. The German 302nd Infantry Division had, in preparation of their coastal defences, made allowances for the coastline, the width of the Divisional sector, and the various slopes and ravines of the coast that led directly down to the sea. As a result, the Germans did not use continuous defences, instead they concentrated these around key focal points such as ports and other places where it was possible for the Allies to carry out an amphibious landing. The Germans did not have enough resources to set up defences of every ravine and they knew that they could not prevent the Allies from landing at Berneval-le-Grand and Varengeville-sur-Mer, nor stop them from gaining localised successes using specialist troops.[4]

The Germans created two major coastal gun emplacements; one battery of six 5.9in naval guns at Varengeville known by the Allies as the 'Hess' Battery, while at Berneval they had installed a battery of four naval guns of the same calibre that they code-named the 'Goebbels' Battery.

The main German strategy was to create strong defensive points near ports, enabling them to beat off any attacks by land or sea. However, key to their strategy was to have as many mobile reserves on hand as possible in order to strengthen the strongpoints at the ports and mount immediate counterattacks wherever they were needed. That would generally mean attacking Allied troops that landed between the German strongpoints. 'It is all the more important to withhold strong reserves as in any large-scale assault the enemy will certainly launch a simultaneous Air and Sea attack against our coastal defences; the air attack consisting of strong airborne and parachute forces.'[5]

---

4   Report No. 116, Operation Jubilee, The Raid on Dieppe, 19 August 1942, Additional Information from German Sources, Directorate of History, National Defence Headquarters, Ottawa, Canada.

5   See Report No. 116, Operation Jubilee, The Raid on Dieppe, 19 August 1942, Additional Information from German Sources, Directorate of History.

Within the Dieppe area, the Germans deployed the 571st Infantry Regiment and HQ with two infantry battalions, HQ Engineer Battalion and two engineer companies, eight beach defence guns and three 47mm anti-tank guns manned by infantry troops. They also deployed the third battalion of the 302nd Artillery Regiment, which was made up of two batteries of light howitzers and two batteries of only equipment and supplies, plus, for coastal defence, the 265th Infantry Howitzer Battery.

> Three field batteries each of four guns either 4in or 5.9in., were thought to be situated on the east headland commanding the harbour, behind the town near Arques la Bataille, where divisional HQ was believed to be located, and near Appeville, not far from the fortified position 'Quatre Vents' Farm.[6]

In addition, anti-aircraft units that consisted of one 75mm heavy AA battery, sections of 50mm, 37mm and 20mm guns respectively with 200 troops from different naval units were added to the defensive mix including 60 police and one experimental unit.

As for Corps reserves, the Germans deployed the Regimental Headquarters of 676th Infantry Regiment at Doudeville, while in the Hericourt area they deployed the 1st Battalion, 676th Infantry Regiment, the 3rd Battalion around Yvetot and in the Bacqueville area they also deployed the 3rd division of the 570th Infantry Regiment. The 81st Tank Company was also deployed in the Yvetot area.[7]

These reserve units proved to be extremely useful as they were able to rapidly reinforce the areas of the 302nd Division as well as units of the 332nd Infantry Division. The reserve units as outlined above were highly adaptable and proved to be very effective in countering the Allied landings at Dieppe.

In addition, the Allies had considered bombardment from the air and from the sea. As a result, large fighter and bomber forces were assembled that were within relatively short flying distances from the Dieppe area. The Germans had set up machine gun emplacements (pillboxes) and gun batteries along

---

6   See *The Dieppe Raid: The Combined Operations Assault on Hitler's European Fortress August 1942*, An Official History.

7   See Report No. 116, Operation Jubilee, The Raid on Dieppe, 19 August 1942, Additional Information from German Sources, Directorate of History.

the cliffs and around the harbour, particularly the mouth of the harbour. The guns on the cliffs and in the houses along the coast enfiladed the western coastline. However, 'built-up areas near the main landing beaches constituted a serious obstacle to naval or aerial bombardment during an actual landing'.[8]

Another consideration that made this type of bombardment difficult for the Allies was that shell bursts from large-calibre naval guns would have put the lives of the troops landing on the beaches in great danger. Also, if the houses were to be attacked from the air by heavy bombing the distance between the streets and buildings of the town and the sea was much too narrow and again would have put the landing parties in serious jeopardy. 'There was, of course, that alternative of heavy protracted bombing to flatten the houses along the sea front prior to the raid but it was considered that such action would probably warn the enemy of the impending assault . . .'[9]

---

8 See *The Dieppe Raid: The Combined Operations Assault on Hitler's European Fortress August 1942*, An Official History.

9 Ibid.

Chapter 3

The British Plan of Attack

It had originally been intended to use ten drifters to create a smoke-walled 'sanctuary', in which the landing and other craft would lie while the troops were ashore; in the final plan these were dispensed with, as it was considered that the same result could be produced by smokescreens laid by destroyers, landing craft and from the air. Smoke carrying aircraft, too, were to mask the defences on the east cliff at the moment the main landing touched down.[1]

The intention of the British plan of attack was clearly laid down in the documents the Germans captured from British and Canadian prisoners they took after the battle. The Germans discovered that the British planned to put the coastal batteries near Berneval and Varengeville out of action. Two commando units of 250 and 350 men respectively were to be used for this purpose. This was to ensure these two batteries could not shell the initial landing as well as the evacuation, which was scheduled to be completed by 1530hrs in the afternoon of 19 August 1942.

As far as the Germans were concerned, from the captured documents they had their impression was that the main Allied objective was to be the strongpoint area of Dieppe, where seven battalions, supported by special troops and one Army Tank Battalion (58 tanks), were to be deployed. Near the village of Puys one of those seven battalions, with one Light Battery (Br. Troop) and one Light Anti-Aircraft Assault Section were to land in the first wave and another battalion in the second wave.

One detachment was to attack the anti-aircraft emplacements at Cap Romain, which meant that they were to swing east after landing. Another detachment was to penetrate into Puys as well to attack all anti-aircraft

---

1   See *The Dieppe Raid: The Combined Operations Assault on Hitler's European Fortress August 1942*, An Official History.

emplacements along the coastal road from Puys to Dieppe on the hill to the east of the port.

The remainder of the Allied battalions were to swing south from Puys, attack 'A' Battery (unmanned) at the Neuville crossroads, then occupy the Dieppe gasworks or electrical works that were to be destroyed by a special engineer detachment.[2]

Near Dieppe one battalion with one platoon of tanks was to land due west of the port with their right flank on the Rue Duquesne. At the same time, another Allied battalion had the task of occupying the rear areas of the port and the Basin of Kanda, and was to advance up to the racetrack, which they were to prepare for use as a landing ground. Simultaneously, two warships were to enter the port: the destroyer HMS *Locust* and a cutter. Two more battalions with an Army tank battalion, less one platoon, were to land on the Dieppe Beach west of the Rue Duquesne.

One detachment supported by one tank platoon was to attack the hill west of the casino, push on in the direction of the coast road leading to Pourville and roll up the various German battalion headquarters located in that area.

Another detachment, also supported by a single tank platoon, was to advance through the town in order to take the anti-aircraft positions and the positions of B Battery on the main road to Le Havre. The remainder of the two battalions, supported by one tank company, was to advance along the main road to Rouen to the HQ of the engineer battalion on the southern edge of the town and make contact with Allied troops, which by this time would have been on their left near the anti-aircraft positions east of the engineer HQ.

In Pourville, another Allied battalion was to land in the first wave. From this, one company was to move from Pourville along the coastal road to Dieppe and was to roll up from the west the enemy anti-aircraft and air force positions along the coast. The second company was to attack the Four Winds Farm (Fermes aux Quatre-Vents or Quatre-Vents Farm) positions on the east bank of the River Scie. The third company was to advance along the west bank of the Scie up to the southern edge of Pourville, while the fourth was to move from Pourville along the coast up the high ground in order to take the machine gun position situated up there.

---

2   Ibid.

The final Allied battalion was also to land at Pourville behind the previous one, which should have established a bridgehead. (The perimeter of this bridgehead was formed by the company objectives mentioned above.). Elements of this final Allied battalion were then to advance along the west bank of the Scie in a south-westerly direction towards the airfield at Saint-Aubin. Subsequently it was to proceed north-east and take the positions of the 265th Battery North of Arques-la-Bataille, where the division HQ was presumed to be located.

However, it was not apparent to the Germans if more units were to land should this attack have been successful.

The Germans believed that the maps the British were using were excellent as all the information on them had been obtained by aerial reconnaissance. This included the smallest detail of the German positions, and even the Dieppe anti-tank walls, which separated the streets from the harbour and the promenade, were shown. However, the maps provided no information as to how well the local French and Allied espionage activities had worked. Indeed, the Germans discovered that the maps did not have the locations of their regimental or other HQs. The German Divisional HQ was, for example, believed to be in Arques-la-Bataille where it had been situated many months previously but at the time of the raid was no longer there.[3]

Just before Operation Jubilee kicked off, changes in the Allies' command structure took place. Replacing the original overall commander for the Army, Lieutenant General Montgomery, was Lieutenant General H.G.D. Crerar, commanding 1st Canadian Corps. This was due to the fact that the large majority of troops were Canadian: 4,963 officers and other ranks combined.

> On the naval side, Rear-Admiral Baillie-Grohman, and his Chief of Staff, Commodore Back, were no longer available, and at the suggestion of Lord Louis Mountbatten two members of Combined Operations Headquarters – Captain J. Hughes Hallett and Commander (acting Captain) J.D. Luce – were appointed as Naval Force Commander and Chief of Staff on 17th July.[4]

---

3   Ibid.
4   Ibid.

The 17 August 1942 saw the preliminary order for the expedition to sail on the night of 18–19 August issued such that the main assault was to take place at 0520hrs and the flank attacks to take place earlier at 0450hrs. At the final conference on the operation between the CCO and the force commanders, heavy bombardment of the town was again brought up but the decision not to use heavy saturation bombing was officially agreed upon and confirmed.

Chapter 4

The German Response

The Germans derived a considerable amount of information from numerous documents, which they captured including the operation order of the 2nd Canadian Division and the Orders of the Naval Force Commander.[1]

In this chapter, we look at the German responses to the Allied landings at Dieppe. To put this into context it is necessary first of all to provide a brief narrative of the action. A much more detailed narrative of the German reaction has been laid out in Part 2 of this book.

In June and July 1942, the Germans mounted several aerial photographic reconnaissance flights over the southern coast of England. In June, these flights showed a growing concentration of small landing craft on the Kent coast, which by July had increased substantially. This, and information from their agents, indicated to the Germans that the Allies were mounting some sort of attack against the French coast.

However, other than the photos and the information from German agents in England the facts about an impending invasion by the Allies could not be checked. This meant that by 15 August the Germans could not be sure what the Allies were planning. However, German headquarters did believe that a large-scale Allied operation along the French coast was imminent. Submarine bases, defence establishments, defensive positions and so forth were reinforced to full complement, with supplies, ammunition, resources and personnel. 'The defence organisation was continually exercised to make certain that all the local reserve sections, air and army, should be ready to come quickly into action.'[2] German Army Group West ensured that the motorised reserve units 'were stationed near enough to the coast to be able to

---

1   See *The Dieppe Raid: The Combined Operations Assault on Hitler's European Fortress August 1942*, An Official History.

2   Ibid.

come into action en masse on the first day of a landing'.[3] This was crucial to the Germans' successful defence of Dieppe.

Just prior to the landings at Dieppe on 19 August, at 0500hrs the British naval force, which had set sail after a slight delay, engaged a German convoy that alerted the German coastal defence system. While the German defenders were still unsure as to the whether the ships in front of Dieppe were friendly or enemy, the answer came with a series of Allied air attacks by the Royal Air Force that began at dawn. These attacks were directed at defensive positions on both sides of Dieppe. These bombing and strafing attacks were meant to pin down the German defences and while that was taking place swarms of landing craft in waves of 40 to 50 headed for the shore, coming out of the protection of the morning fog and smokescreens laid down by the attacking aircraft and naval fire from the destroyers offshore. German artillery fire was unable to destroy the British landing craft due to the smokescreens. The only time that artillery and heavy weapons hits were registered on the landing craft was as they touched down on the beach. Yet fog and smoke made visibility on the beaches difficult as well.

The main German defensive force became aware of the full scope of the attack a little after 0600hrs, when it became apparent that no attacks were taking place at the mouth of the River Somme in Le Tréport or in the area under control of the 532nd Infantry Division. As a result, the division dispatched the Bicycle Troop and the reinforced 3rd Pioneer Company to Berneval from Arques-la-Bataille. These forces were commanded by Major von Blucher and were ordered to relieve the Berneval battery then under attack.

The First Battalion of the 571st Infantry Regiment, then in Dieppe, was ordered to leave Quiberville around 0710hrs and move to Hautot in order to counter the British attack in the direction of Pourville.[4]

AT 0730hrs the 3rd Battalion of 570th Infantry Regiment came under command of 302nd Infantry Division and was ordered to Offranville, while the remainder, 676th Infantry Regiment HQ, its 1st and 3rd Battalions, 1st Battalion of the 332nd Artillery Regiment, and the 81st Tank Company, were ordered to move to Bacqueville, 14km south-east of Dieppe.

In the Hautot area, around 1000hrs, the 1st Battalion of the 571st Infantry began preparing for a counterattack on British positions in Pourville.

---

3   Ibid.

4   See Report No. 116, Additional information From German Sources.

However, because of the close country, fighting would be difficult and unfamiliar. To remedy this, the battalion mounted a reconnaissance in the direction of Pourville and Varengeville, opening its attack on Pourville around 1130hrs. The result of this attack enabled it to clear the hill west of Pourville of British and Commonwealth soldiers, where 200 prisoners were taken.[5]

In the meantime, all the corps reserves were now under command of 302nd Infantry Division in order to mount an attack out of Offranville towards Pourville supported by tanks from the 81st Tank Company. However, this attack never took place because the 1st Battalion of the 571st Infantry Regiment had already cleared the British and Commonwealth troops out of the area west of Pourville.

In the afternoon, the 676th Infantry Regiment was deployed to the Pourville–Saint-Aubin, sector where it committed two battalions and held one in reserve. At this time there were several messages reporting large formations of ships arriving from England and the Germans believed there was a possibility that the British attack would be renewed.

The 10th Armoured Division, now nominally under the command of LXXXI Corps, was ordered to move its advanced units as quickly as possible up to an area 14km south of Dieppe. The rest of the division was then ordered into the Neufchatel–Londinières area. According to the German sources, the intention of the German commanders was to position the 10th Armoured Division west of the River Argues to attack the British and Canadian units that had landed at Pourville. However, the decision to commit the 10th Armoured into this area depended on whether other German forces had been successful in pushing the enemy at Pourville back into the sea. If that was the case, the 10th Armoured were to be deployed to the east.

The following orders were issued to the 10th Armoured Division and the 302nd Infantry Division at 1200hrs:

a) The 10th Armoured Division with its advanced elements and those units already committed from the 302nd Infantry Division and Corps Reserves, first attack the heights west of Pourville. It is to destroy the enemy, and then join in the attack from the west of, and in, Dieppe, if this is necessary.

---

5   Ibid.

b) Boundary between the 302nd and the 10th Divisions: from the western edge of Pourville to Janvall to the Scie Valley.

c) Those parts of the 302nd Infantry Division and Corps Reserve that have already advanced to the west of this line will be attached to the 10th Armoured Division.

d) One reinforced Panzer-Grenadier Regiment at the disposition of Corps remains to the south and in the vicinity of Londinières.

e) The divisions will make mutual arrangements for the time at which 10th Armoured Division assumes tactical control.[6]

However, the 10th did not go into battle on that day but was, instead, ordered to stand by in the area of Torcy-le-Petit–Neufchatel–Londinières areas at 1345hrs. They remained there throughout the day and into the night. At the same time the 10th Armoured Division remained in the combat zone during the night of 19–20 August.[7]

At Berneval, east of Dieppe, the British Army landed a Commando force numbering 250 men, who took up positions in a defile. Their task was to seize and destroy the 2nd Battery of the 770th Army Coast Artillery Battalion. Using rope ladders and guylines, the British Commandos climbed up the ravine to the top of the cliffs, avoiding the minefields that had been placed in the ravine. They managed to attack the battery located in a fortified strong-point. One German machine gun patrol was dispatched from the battery and moved to the ravine, where it was able to take part in the local defence. The battery managed to ward off a series of unco-ordinated British attacks helped by their army anti-aircraft gun platoon. The Germans repelled the British attacks using direct fire at close range and by machine gun and rifle fire. The German special Air Force installation (radar) and its crew of 100 men, in permanent support of the battery, was also attacked by the British, though in a lesser degree and all the attacks were driven off.

In the course of the day the first information about our losses which, even if they are not to be considered exact until hospital

---

6   Ibid., Report No. 116, Additional information From German Sources

7   Ibid.

returns etc., are confirmed, show that those of the Army have been moderate.[8]

Major von Blucher, commander of the German 302nd Anti-Tank Battalion, was ordered to launch an attack on Berneval by HQ 302nd Infantry Division. In addition to his existing command he was also given command of the Bicycle Squadron from Saint-Nicolas and the attached 3rd Pioneer Company, both of which were later reinforced by the 3rd Company of the 572nd Infantry Regiment.[9] The battery at Berneval had managed to send messages via wireless regarding the disposition of the nearby British attacks, enabling von Blucher to launch a successful counterattack against the British Commandos that resulted in two officers and 80 men being taken prisoner.

West of Dieppe, the German 813th Army Coastal Battery was situated at Varengeville. Against this target the British launched an attack with 300 Commandos. They landed on both sides of Varengeville at the base of the cliffs under the cover of a smokescreen. Elsewhere, another company of Commandos landed near the fortified strongpoints at Quiberville, against a platoon from the German 3rd Company, 571st Infantry Regiment. However, the Germans frustrated this attack with concentrated machine gun and rifle fire. While these forces were pinned down, the attack at Varengeville was going well and turned out to be a success for the British. Here the Commandos climbed the cliffs aided by small, wooded, rugged ravines stretching down to the sea.[10]

Once they had reached the top of the cliffs, the British Commandos attacked the German battery from all sides using machine guns, sub-machine guns, rifles, mortars and grenades. At the same time, RAF fighters and fighter bombers pounded the battery with bombs and cannon fire, stopping the defenders from mounting a real defence against the Commandos. The German losses amounted to 28 dead and 29 wounded (according to German sources).[11] The German battery commander who was directing fire from

---

8   See *The Dieppe Raid: The Combined Operations Assault on Hitler's European Fortress August 1942*, An Official History.

9   See Report No. 116, Additional information From German Sources.

10   Report No. 116, Operation Jubilee, The Raid on Dieppe, 19 August 1942, Additional Information from German Sources, Directorate of History, National Defence Headquarters, Ottawa, Canada.

11   These figures are according to Report No. 116.

the observation post was one of those wounded during this action. 'Later, accompanied by the observation section, he fought his way towards the fighting Battery.'[12] Shells stored in the ammunition pits, the battery emplacement and in the guns themselves ignited from the aerial bombing and mortar fire, causing several explosions and setting the guns on fire, making them unusable. The British re-embarked at approximately 0900 hours taking their wounded and dead with them, including some German prisoners.

> Both operations, at Berneval and at Varengeville, obviously had as their mission the destruction of the two heavy coastal batteries. This would have facilitated further debarkations and embarkations at Dieppe.[13]

The Germans knew that both coastal batteries were vulnerable but the lack of available troops meant that both could not be given special protection by the infantry. In addition, the Germans realised that the main British attack on Dieppe was developing on a broad front with three main thrusts at the village of Puys, at Dieppe itself and at Pourville.

At Puys the Allied landings collapsed under heavy concentrated fire from the German defences, with heavy losses. Indeed, not one Allied soldier managed to penetrate these defences and move forwards. 'The flanking fire in front of the obstacles, on the high sea wall, and on the beach itself decimated his attacking lines. Aside from the numerous prisoners, over 150 dead were counted at this point.'[14]

The Allied battalion that landed at the Rue Duquesne just west of Dieppe did not do much better. The battalion came under heavy fire and was destroyed along with its tanks. HMS *Locust* moved into the harbour approaches at 0700hrs and was hit by artillery and anti-aircraft fire. Having received several direct hits, the destroyer turned back into the fog and was never seen again. She was 'presumably sunk, since the stern of a large sinking ship with some 200 or 300 men on board was observed during a moment when the fog had lifted'.[15]

---

12   Ibid., Report No. 116, Additional Information From German Sources.
13   Ibid.
14   Ibid.
15   Ibid.

Two Canadian battalions landed, reinforced by tanks, and tried to make their way off the beach up to the promenade. The tanks were either destroyed as they landed or, as a few of them managed to get to the beach promenade, they were then hit by heavy artillery fire. Only a few patrols managed to penetrate into Dieppe itself.

> There are still British dead everywhere, especially in front of our heavy gun positions. In front of one machine-gun post which flanked the narrow strip of beach between the sea and the cliffs, there are piles of dead (more than 100 only in this spot); much booty in equipment and infantry weapons, light and heavy.[16]

The Allied battalion that attacked Pourville in the west managed to move into the town and overpower the German garrison stationed there. They then tried moving forward with two companies that advanced west out of Pourville along the coastal road towards the Scie valley, where they successfully attacked several German positions. 'They succeeded in getting as far as the anti-tank position, which they disabled temporarily by direct hits, and possibly by hand grenades.'[17] Some Allied (Canadian) patrols managed to get as far as the Scie dam but when they attempted to advance towards the northern part of Four Winds Farm, a heavily defended German strongpoint, they were wiped out. As such both companies, while having advanced the furthest, were unable to penetrate the main line of German resistance. 'The main Dieppe defences really began at this anti-tank position. Pourville was only a lightly held advanced outpost.'[18]

Two other companies from this Allied battalion had advanced towards positions west of the River Scie, where they managed to attain their first objectives. They seized the southern edge of Pourville and the machine gun position on the hill west of Pourville, where they established a bridgehead.

The last Allied battalion to land (Canadian) was to push forward towards the west bank of the Scie and capture its main objective, the airfield at

---

16   See *The Dieppe Raid: The Combined Operations Assault on Hitler's European Fortress August 1942*, An Official History. This comes from a report sent to General Jodl, which included the personal impression of the action of the operation by the German Chief of Staff for Army HQ.

17   See Report No. 116.

18   Ibid.

Saint-Aubin. This battalion also reached Pourville and managed to advance in close wooded country on the hills west of the Scie as far as Hautot, where it was caught in the flanking fire from Four Winds Farm. 'It then encountered the forward Bicycle Platoon of the Regimental Headquarters of the 571st Infantry Regiment and some patrols from the 1st Battalion of the same Regiment.'[19]

Up to that point this Allied battalion had not encountered real German opposition as there were very little defences set up in the area. However, it wasn't until they came within range of the German defences at Four Winds Farm that they came under real concentrated fire. Nevertheless, the Germans, in their report on the raid on Dieppe, were at a loss to understand why the Allies halted at Hautot 'and were unable to carry out their mission, which was to push on towards the Saint-Aubin airfield. Presumably, it was halted by the commander of the English Forces, because the frontal attacks on Dieppe and Puys had failed.'[20]

In the papers that the Germans retrieved from captured Allied soldiers and officers they discovered that the operational orders were, after landing, for the troops to reach their assigned objectives by 1230hrs, then march back to the beaches for re-embarkation from 1230hrs onwards. Re-embarkation was to be completed by 1530hrs. Yet, 'up until midday, many more boats kept landing on the beaches at Dieppe. In the smokescreen, it could not be seen whether they were bringing up more troops or loading up with soldiers already landed.'[21]

The main German strategy was to create strong defensive points near ports, enabling them to beat off any attacks by land or sea. However, key to their strategy was to have as many mobile reserves on hand as possible in order to strengthen the strongpoints at the ports and mount immediate counterattacks wherever they were needed.

However, it was not apparent to the Germans if more units were to land should the first wave have been successful. 'It is possible that the convoy of 26 large boats which left Portsmouth about noon and which later on turned about, was to be the second wave, should the operation have been a success.'[22]

---

19   Ibid.
20   Ibid., Report No. 116.
21   Ibid.
22   Ibid.

This is also supported by the fact that several Allied prisoners said they had expected support or relief from 1700hrs onwards.

For the Germans, the British plan of attack was a failure. They believed the British miscalculated the strength of the German defences and tried to 'grab the bull by the horns' by landing the main body of their invasion forces, particularly the tanks, directly in front of the town of Dieppe. Although they were aware of the street defences in the town in the form of concrete constructions, anti-tank walls, machine gun positions and coastal guns, the Allies persisted with this plan of attack, landing where the defences were strongest, which baffled the Germans. They found it difficult to understand why the Allies did not support the battalions that landed near Pourville with armour. An attack with tanks from Pourville against the hill west of Dieppe and against the Four Winds Farm might have been successful, although it would have been most difficult to overcome the anti-tank walls, the pier and the Scie dam.[23]

In addition, the Germans did not understand why the British did not employ airborne troops. Had they attacked Puys simultaneously with airborne troops and from the sea, the position of the German troops defending Puys could have been catastrophic.

The Germans knew that the British massed employment of the air force against the coastal defences of Dieppe should have shattered their defences to such a degree that it would have enabled the assault battalions to break through the coastal defences. Yet, the British employed a heavy smokescreen over Dieppe that effectively diminished the accuracy of aerial bombing and ultimately the overall effect of the air attacks. In short, the smokescreen, as far as the air attacks were concerned, was a factor in the overall failure of the operation, in the Germans' view.

The Allies did land light and heavy mortars but their entire combat order mentioned only one light battery and one light anti-aircraft section to be landed near Puys. However, this landing failed, so the artillery was not employed. 'A few light assault guns would probably have been of more use to the British in their first attack, than the tanks.'[24] The landing force had no artillery support whatsoever due to the smokescreen, which made the fire control observation on the big ships virtually useless.

---

23   Ibid.
24   Ibid.

It is astonishing that the British should have underestimated our defence as they had details of most of it from air-photos; equally striking is the short time in which they expected to carry out the operation.[25]

The operational order, almost 100 pages long, fixed every detail of the action for each unit of the invasion force. 'This method of planning made the failure of the whole raid inevitable in the event of unexpected difficulties.'[26]

The Germans captured 95 Allied officers and 2,122 men.[27] By 24 August the Germans had buried 475 men with the tide continuing to wash corpses ashore. 'A high percentage of enemy losses, which cannot, however, be estimated, was incurred at sea through our artillery fire and aerial bombardment, and through the sinking of landing craft, flat-bottomed boats, and destroyers. Total enemy losses probably amount to at least 60 to 70% of the landing force.'[28]

---

25   Ibid.

26   Ibid.

27   These figures are according to Report No. 116, Additional information From German Sources and may not be as accurate as other sources.

28   Ibid.

Part 2
The Narrative

Chapter 5

Crossing the Channel and the German Convoy

> This encounter accordingly had a bad effect upon the fortune of the operation generally. . . . However, there is no evidence to suggest that this engagement 7 miles offshore gave definite warning to the enemy of the approach of the raiding force . . .[1]

The time has now come to look in detail at the events of that fateful day. By examining these events and how the Germans reacted to them we can get a good idea of how their High Command gained its view that the raid was a failed invasion attempt.

We will start this procedure at the beginning from the point when the Allied forces left England and began the passage towards Dieppe. Excluding minesweepers, the total number of ships and landing craft amounted to 252 vessels. Moving this armada across the Channel without being detected by the enemy on a timetable and without accidents was no small feat. The passage was nearly successful.

However, there were complications, not least of which was the minefield laid by the Germans in the English Channel through which the Allies would have to sweep two passages. These were swept by the 9th and 13th Minesweeping Flotillas on the night of 18–19 August. Both passages had been carefully realised in the plans for the operation and once they had been swept were marked by dim 'dan' buoys.[2]

There were 13 groups in the force[3] with the first four groups made up of infantry landing ships and small armed escort vessels. The following

---

1   Report No. 101, Operation Jubilee, The Raid on Dieppe, Part 2, The Execution of the Operation, Paragraph 15, Canadian Military Headquarters.

2   See Report No. 101, Operation Jubilee, The Raid on Dieppe, Part 2, The Execution of the Operation.

3   Ibid., Canadian Military Headquarters.

three groups, 5, 6, and 7, were made up of personnel landing craft and their escorts. Groups 8 to 12 were the tank landing craft and their escorts, while the final group, 13, included HMS *Alresford* and seven French Chasseur patrol craft.

The military and naval force commanders were in HMS *Calpe*, a destroyer, along with Air Commodore Cole, the representative of the Air Force commander. At HQ No. 11 Fighter Group Uxbridge Air Vice-Marshal Leigh-Mallory had taken up his position in order to best control the actions of his squadrons. Four other destroyers along with the infantry landing ships followed HMS *Calpe* through the swept western passage in the minefield.

A duplicated headquarters was set up in HMS *Fernie* in the event *Calpe* was destroyed in battle. Brigadier Mann was the senior military officer in *Fernie*. In the event that Brigadier Roberts became incapacitated or became a casualty of war, Mann was to assume command. The command would pass to Brigadier Southam, commanding 6th Canadian Infantry Brigade, in the event that Mann was to become a casualty. Should Southam become incapacitated the command was, according the operational plan, to fall on the shoulders of Brigadier Lett, commanding the 4th Canadian Infantry Brigade, and then if something happened to him command would go to Lieutenant Colonel Henderson.

The LCPs (landing craft personnel) and LCTs (landing craft tank) were successfully led by HMS *Fernie* through the Eastern channel of the minefield.

Although the minefield was successfully circumnavigated by the convoy, it was not without incident. *Queen Edna*, the infantry landing ship, lost touch with the destroyers it was supposed to be following and passed through the eastern channel instead of the western. It had Groups 1, 2 and 3 with it. HMS *Locust*, despite failing to find either channel, managed to pass through the minefield.

Once through the minefield the convoy then formed into a series of waves with Groups 1, 2, 3 and 5 in the front, followed by Group 4, then by Group 8. Groups 6, 7 and 9 followed in the next wave, with Groups 10 and 11 behind them. The final wave was made up of Groups 12 and 13. The destroyers *Albrighton*, *Berkeley*, *Bleasdale* and *Garth* covered the western (starboard) flank of the formation, while the eastern flank was covered by the Polish destroyer *Ślązak* and by HMS *Brocklesby*.

On the night of the operation the weather was 'fine and clear, and the sea absolutely calm.'[4]

According to the reports from the Canadian Military Headquarters, there were two small incidents that took place during the passage to the designated beaches. On board HMS *Duke of Wellington*, around 1710hrs, a grenade exploded amid the troops of the Black Watch of Canada, causing 19 casualties in total including one fatal.[5] A nearly identical incident took place at 2330hrs on board HMS *Invicta* when a grenade went off among C Company South Saskatchewan Regiment, causing 17 casualties.[6] This was put down to carelessness while grenades were being cleaned.

The detailed plan of the operation provided for the Navy to carry out a small demonstration off the coast of Boulogne[7] by three motor gunboats between 0330 and 0450hrs. These three vessels dropped smoke floats and depth charges but to no avail. 'No enemy ships were sighted and there were no searchlights or other activities observed on shore.'[8] The entire demonstration was ineffective.

About 7 miles from the coast of France around 0347hrs, nearly one hour before zero hour, Group 5 of the British flotilla suddenly came across a small convoy of at least five enemy ships. Group 5 were heading towards Yellow 1 and Yellow 2 Beaches and consisted of 25 troop landing craft, accompanied by SGB5, ML346 and LCP (L) carrying No. 3 Commando.[9] The German convoy consisted of a small tanker escorted by several armed coastal craft.[10] At 0535hrs the tanker was attacked by ML346 by gunfire, resulting in the crew abandoning ship and it subsequently drifting ashore. Had *Ślązak* and *Brocklesby* been in close proximity to Group 5 they would have been able to

---

4   Report No. 101, Operation Jubilee, The Raid on Dieppe, Part 2, Statement by Lieutenant F. Royal.

5   Report No. 101, War Diary, RHC August 1942, Appendix 10.

6   Report No. 101, War Diary, S. Sask. R, 18 August 1942.

7   See Report No. 100, The Raid on Dieppe, 19 August 1942, The Preliminaries of the Operation, paragraph 44.

8   Report No. 101, C.B. 04244, note to paragraph 28.

9   Report of Group 5 Commander D.B. Wyburd, Appendix 7 to Enclosure No. 13, Report of Naval Force Commander, Report No. 101.

10   The tanker is not mentioned in the reports of the Naval Force Commander or of Commander Wyburd, although he did later call the mysterious ship 'a small tanker of some 200 tons'.

intercept the German convoy and deal with it. However, they were nowhere near Group 5 at the time and did not get involved in the action.

> The Commanding Officer of *Slazak,* who was senior, believed, it
> appears, that the fire came from the shore, and this belief resulted
> in Group 5 being deprived of the protection which it should have
> received from the destroyers.[11]

The German convoy and SGB5, supported by LCP (L) 1, then became embroiled in a violent confrontation with each other that resulted in SGB5 suffering severe damage and the landing craft in the group becoming completely scattered. This meant, according to reports, that No. 3 Commando would not be able to launch its attack against the Berneval battery[12] with complete success.

From the shore, the Germans heard several heavy detonations coming across the water from a north-westerly direction around 0530 to 0540hrs. This was the German convoy that encountered the Allied landing craft heading for Dieppe.

> The Officer on Duty at GHQ West received the following mes-
> sage from Naval Group Command West at 0545hrs. 'At 0450hrs
> our convoy attacked by surface craft 4km off Dieppe. No further
> details yet available. In the opinion of Naval Group West custom-
> ary attack on convoy.'[13]

This naval engagement badly affected the operation as a whole. While it was only 7 miles offshore, the fighting alerted the Germans to the presence of the Allied raiding force. A great deal of tracer ammunition was fired during this

---

11   It must be noted that this senior officer's report merely states that tracer and starshell were observed firing from shore. Later, the Naval Force Commander stated that he believed the senior officer of *Ślązak* was guilty of 'an error of judgement' and stated that British officers in future should be in command of all detached units. Report No. 101.

12   The code name for the Berneval battery was 'Goebbels'.

13   Battle Report of German Commander-in-Chief West (GHQ Army Group D) on the English Landing Attempt at, and on Both Flanks of Dieppe, 19 August 1942, Historical Section, Army Headquarters, Ottawa, November 1946.

encounter, which was also very noisy so there is no doubt that the Germans were alerted.

German divisional command quickly established telephone contact with the Aircraft Reporting Centre at Dieppe and were informed that the convoy was under attack by Allied naval craft. This was around 0558hrs.

> G.H.Q. West received the following message from HQ 15th Army: 'According to a report of HQ 81 Corps English fast units attacked own convoy at 0500hrs 20km off Dieppe. Troops in a higher state of alert, Navy and Air Force have been informed.'[14]

Sub Lieutenant C.D. Wallace, RCNVR, Boat Officer for the Flotilla Officer of the 1st LCP. (L) flotilla, in LCP (L) 42, was killed during this engagement.[15]

---

14 Ibid. This report was received at 0600hrs at GHQ West.
15 See Report No. 101, The Raid on Dieppe, 19 August 1942, The Preliminaries of the Operation.

Chapter 6

Yellow Beaches
British No. 3 Commando

These batteries, if not silenced, would seriously endanger our ships and craft lying off Dieppe.[1]

At the north end of Berneval-le-Grand was a German coastal defence battery that No. 3 Commando, led by Lieutenant Colonel J.F. Durnford-Slater, was supposed to attack and put out of commission in order for the landings to take place without much defensive artillery fire from the Germans. Divided into two sections, No. 3 Commando was to land on Yellow 1 and Yellow 2 beaches. Yellow 1 was east of the battery at Berneval, while Yellow 2 was west of the battery north-east of Belleville-sur-Mer. While both beaches were narrow, Yellow 2 was particularly so being only 100 yards wide. The only way to gain access inland from Yellow 2 was by a narrow gulley in the shape of a chimney.

Here, along this part of the coast, the gorges that led into the interior were strewn with booby traps and heavily wired. The Germans had placed anti-personnel mines in the central gorge to try to stop anyone assaulting from the sea climbing up to the gorge and ultimately moving inland. The Germans had strengthened the natural anti-tank defences near the approaches to the beaches so they were sure that no tanks could get up the central gorge. An Army coastal artillery troop, an anti-aircraft section and a 'Gleiwitz' radar station were located near Berneval-le-Grand. The Germans felt the radar station would be of great importance to the Allies.[2]

Divisional HQ decided to send an officer's patrol to carry out reconnaissance in the area around Berneval. As such they ordered 1 Battalion

---

1   Ibid.
2   See Report of 302 German Infantry Division, Operations Section -1a, on the
      Dieppe Raid.

570 Infantry regiment, then on divisional reserve in the Touffreville/ Auquemesnil/Assigny area, to despatch the patrol. At 0650hrs a company from Assigny was ordered to move up to Saint-Martin-en-Campagne in order to carry out more reconnaissance in the overall area of Berneval.[3]

> Reports on enemy landing attempt as yet not clear. Must count on possibility of an alert.[4]

Division decided to give command of all troops engaged with the Allies in the Berneval area to Major von Blucher, who was then Officer Commanding 302 Anti-Tank reconnaissance battalion, which was at the time assigned to divisional reserve.[5]

The new command included the 302 Cyclist Squadron; 3 Company, 302nd Engineer Battalion; and the 302nd Anti-Tank Company, which had been ordered up to Saint-Nicolas and remained there as a divisional reserve.[6]

> Naval Group Command West reported at 0732hrs that 'according to a message received from Sea Commandant Seine-Somme at 0625hrs, a landing attempt of enemy units in progress at Berneval. Naval Artillery firing on enemy ships'.[7]

The action at sea against the German convoy had left Group 5 in complete disarray, making the task of No. 3 Commando difficult indeed. Out of the 23 landing craft of Group 5, four had never made it as far as the encounter with the German vessels due to engine trouble, while another four were damaged as a result of the fighting and turned back, steaming to England. After the encounter, five other landing craft of Group 5 attached themselves to SGB5 and another three to LCP (L) 1, 'while seven landed their troops'.[8] Out of these seven craft only four returned.

---

3   Ibid.

4   This is part of an order issued by GHQ West at 0700hrs to 10 Panzer Division, SS Division Adolph Hitler and 7th Air Force Division.

5   Report of 302 German Infantry Division, Operations Section -1a, on the Dieppe Raid.

6   Ibid.

7   Battle Report of the German Commander-in-Chief West (GHQ Army Group D) on the English Landing Attempt at, and on Both Flanks of Dieppe, 19 August 1942.

8   Commander Wyburd's report of the action as sited in Report No. 101.

The Senior Officer of Group 5 was supposed to break radio silence 'if by delays or casualties it is the opinion of the senior military officer that the success of the landing at YELLOW beach is seriously jeopardised'.[9] Unfortunately for Commander Wyburd, this did not happen as the radio sets on SGB5 had been damaged during the action against the German convoy along with the wireless sets of other landing craft. This meant that the other force commanders in HMS *Calpe* were not aware of the problems with Group 5 until 0610hrs. The headquarters ship did not get a full report of the action at sea until 0630hrs, when Lieutenant Colonel Durnford-Slater and Commander Wyburd arrived in an LCP (L).[10]

Some of the landing craft from Group 5 pushed on towards their objectives and managed to land on Yellow 1. Five landing craft, with a sixth coming in a little later, landed their troops at 0510hrs under covering fire from ML346. They were twenty minutes later than had been planned and immediately ran into heavy German defensive fire. Pounded by artillery and heavy machine gun fire, these troops were unable to get to the battery to carry out their tasks. At 0700hrs the British tried to withdraw the troops from Yellow 1 'but only the Naval Beachmaster and the Beach Signal party were taken off under heavy fire but no soldiers were seen'.[11] According to the reports it appears that initially these troops had been overwhelmed by the German defences.

The Germans began laying down harassing fire from the Army Coastal Artillery Troop as the second wave of Allied boats landed. 'All the personnel from the troop including the Gleiwitz radar station fired at the British and Canadian troops as the boats came in. Joining in the battle from the German side was the Officer's Reconnaissance Patrol from 3 Company, 570 Infantry Regiment. More units arrived to join the battle, including von Blucher's HQ composite force, the Cyclist Squadron and 3 Company from 302nd Engineer Battalion, along with 3 Company 570th Infantry Regiment.[12]

The first message is sent at 0800hrs to the High Command of the Armed Forces/Armed Forces Operations staff [German], '0605hrs

---

9   See Naval Operation Order No. 1, para 32, Report No. 101.

10   Commander Wyburd's Report, as cited in Report No. 101.

11   See Report No. 101, The Raid on Dieppe, 19 August 1942, General Outline of the Operation.

12   Report of 302 German Infantry Division, Operations Section -1a, on the Dieppe Raid.

enemy landing attempts at, and around Dieppe, battle in progress. Detailed report follows.'[13]

Meanwhile, just five minutes before zero hour on Yellow 2 beach, LCP (L) (landing craft personnel (large) managed to land its troops on the beach. Lieutenant H.T. Buckee, RNVR, was the Boat Officer of this landing craft, which carried three officers and 17 other ranks from No. 3 Commando. Major Peter Young was the senior officer on this craft of No. 3 Commando. The Beachmaster was Sub-Lieutenant D.J. Lewis RCNVR, who remained on the vessel while the Commandos disembarked. After the unexpected confrontation with the German convoy, Major Young and Lt Buckee discussed the best way forward, knowing that the rest of their troops had been dispersed in the fighting. They decided to continue on to their objectives and as such prepared for landing. As LCP (L) 15 touched down on Yellow 2 Beach the handful of troops led by Major Young stormed ashore and disappeared quickly up the ravine to the top of the cliffs above.

Because of their small size, an actual attack on the battery just outside of Berneval, No. 3 Commando's main objective, was out of the question. Split into sections of three, this small group of 20 men placed themselves in concealed positions and began sniping at the German positions on the battery. For more than an hour and a half the British Commandos sniped at the German gunners, keeping them off balance to the point where they traversed one of the large guns in the battery to try to use it against the snipers, but to no avail. So, while the battery was not put out of action it was ineffective against the landings for that period of time.

> During the time that the Commando party was in action, the fire of the battery against our shipping was certainly ineffective, and it is doubtful, indeed, whether it ever became effective. As Brigadier Mann noted, 'As far as I know, no effective fire from the battery at Berneval developed – due to the action of 3 Cdo. Their work was very good and probably vital.'[14]

---

13 Ibid.
14 Ibid., Section 40 to 41.

At 0930hrs a composite German force under Major von Blucher at Berneval attacked No. 3 Commando units. Fifteen minutes later 3 Company 302nd Engineer Battalion smashed through Berneval-le-Grand and fought their way through to join up with 2 Troop, 770 Coastal Artillery Battery. Once they'd joined up with the battery, 3 Company continued to pursue Allied infantry units, who were rapidly withdrawing towards the gorge north-west of Berneval. As the Germans continued to mount pressure on the Commandos, low-flying RAF[15] fighter-bombers dropped smoke and strafed the Germans, slowing them down and giving the Allies a chance to withdraw.[16]

> The Allies were pushed out of Petit Berneval around 1020hrs by the German Cyclist Squadron along with elements of 3 Company 570th Infantry Regiment. However, on Hill 101, north-east of Petit Berneval, Allied infantry units still held firm although 3 Company encircled them. While this was taking place two recce patrols from 1 Company 570 Infantry Regiment[17] had moved along the foot of the cliffs towards Petit Berneval to join in the counterattack on Hill 101.[18]

At 1020hrs a strange report came in to GHQ West:

> The following message arrived from HQ 15th Army, however it has not been confirmed by G-Ops HQ. It states: 'At Criel-Plage an enemy company has landed. Counterattack in progress, proceeding favourably.' Clarification of above by telephonic request of G-Ops GHQ West arranged immediately.[19]

Based on the reports coming in from the field by 1030hrs, German Divisional HQ considered the area around Berneval to be safe of further Allied attack,

---

15   Royal Air Force, most likely cannon-equipped Hawker Hurricanes.

16   Battle Report of the German Commander-in-Chief West (G.H.Q. Army Group D) on the English Landing Attempt at, and on Both Flanks of Dieppe, 19 August 1942.

17   One patrol consisted of one officer and 40 men of other ranks.

18   Report of 302 German Infantry Division, Operations Section -1a, on the Dieppe Raid.

19   According to the report, the so called landings at Criel-Plage were really supposed to be at Criel-sur-Mer, 10km north-east of Berneval. However, sometime later it was proved that near Criel-Plage there were no Allied units.

although they had not yet received a final report of the situation by this time. Division issued the following order: 'When the enemy defeated, composite force will be withdrawn and the task of pursuit assigned to 3 Company 570 Infantry Regiment.'[20]

While this was taking place, Major Young, leading a small party of Commandos, managed to withdraw back to Yellow 2 Beach, where they were met by Lieutenant Buckee, and they all managed to climb aboard LCP (L)15 at 0810hrs and sailed back to England. They suffered no casualties in this action.

> The bold action and extraordinary good fortune of this single craft and the Commando troops who were its passengers is a very bright spot in the general gloom of events on the eastern flank beaches. That 20 soldiers should land completely unsupported, should succeed in interfering effectively with the action of an enemy battery, and should subsequently be withdrawn without loss by the same craft which put them ashore, constitutes a truly remarkable episode.[21]

---

20 See Report of 302 German Infantry Division, Operations Section -1a, on the Dieppe Raid, Appendix B.

21 For this action, Major Young and Lieutenant Buckee both received the DSO. See Report No. 101, The Raid on Dieppe, 19 August 1942. A description of this action can be found in the Combined Operations Report C.B.04244 (held at the National Archives in Kew) along with the various naval reports of the day.

Chapter 7

Orange Beach
Varengeville: No. 4 Commando

The good luck of this Commando, which was the only military unit engaged in the operation to capture all its objectives, was in curious contrast with the ill luck encountered by No. 3 Commando on the opposite flank.[1]

The German battery at Varengeville on the western flank was the objective of No. 4 Commando, commanded by Lieutenant Colonel Lord Lovat MC. Before this operation he had distinguished himself in earlier raids, especially with the Canadians in Operation Abercrombie. This part of the Dieppe operation was an astounding success as opposed to the operation, less Major Young's action, by No. 3 Commando on the opposite flank that was an abysmal failure.

The battery was situated south-west of the village of Varengeville-sur-Mer and consisted of six 15cm coastal defence guns. The battery was code-named 'Hess' by the Allies. Orange 1 and Orange 2 were the two beaches allocated to No. 4 Commando. Orange 1 was a very narrow beach at Vasterival, while Orange 2 was the eastern part of a much longer beach near Quiberville. Indeed, at some point, the planners of the operation had looked at Orange 2 as a possible place for landing tanks.

The Germans originally believed that the defences at Quiberville would not hold against a heavy, sustained attack by the Allies. However, against a small lightly armed Allied attack they felt the defences would be sufficient. East of the River Saâne the area was defended on the high ground by nearly two thirds of an infantry company, two beach defence guns and half a heavy machine gun platoon. If the Allies broke through they would

---

1   See Report No. 101, The Raid on Dieppe, 19 August 1942.

then encounter 1 Battalion 571 Infantry Regiment stationed near Ouville. The Germans also believed that because they had dammed the Saâne and installed anti-tank obstacles on both sides of the river, the danger from tanks was minimal. So, for this moment in the landings, Quiberville did not need reinforcements.

> Around 0732hrs a message from HQ 15th Army came through stating 'C. of S HQ 81 Corps, reports enemy (Allies) on land at Berneval. Counterattack laid on with about three companies; details not known yet. Bombing attack on Dieppe continues, landing attempt at Pourville repelled. Situation at Quiberville still unclear!'[2]

At this point, GHQ West ordered 2 Battalion, 570 Infantry Regiment, on reserve at that time, to assemble near Saint-Rémy and to get there using whatever transport they could find. However, because the Germans at that time did not consider the Allied landings their sole endeavour, and believed that more Allied attacks would come at other points along the 75km divisional front, they decided to hold back the battalion and Regimental HQ of 570 Infantry Regiment and to keep them in reserve.

> Naval Group Command sent a report to GHQ West at 0740hrs stating that a message had been received from the Commanding Admiral France that telephone connection had been cut to the Port Commandant of Dieppe. 'English continue to land at Dieppe. Destroyers laying smoke on coast: up to now twelve tanks have landed one is on fire.'[3]

No. 4 Commando for the Dieppe Raid were made up of 252 all ranks including a small contingent of US Rangers.[4] For the Channel crossing they

---

2   See Report of 302 German Infantry Division, Operations Section -1a, on the Dieppe Raid.

3   The quote is from the Dieppe Naval Signal Station as cited in the Battle Report of the German Commander-in-Chief West (GHQ Army Group D) on the English Landing Attempt at, and on Both Flanks of Dieppe, 19 August 1942.

4   No. 4 Commando's operational order refers to '7 attached Allied personnel'. See Report No. 101, The Raid on Dieppe, 19 August 1942.

had embarked aboard HMS *Prince Albert* and then were put ashore using Landing Craft Assault (LCA) vessels. The craft heading towards Orange 2 saw some vessels in the distance, which they assumed were enemy and gave them a wide berth, touching down on the beach at exactly zero hour. Those disembarking on Orange 1 were approximately three minutes late.

Group 1, commanded by Major D. Mills-Roberts and composed of 88 all ranks, was to land at Orange 1 and then move swiftly to the north, where they were to engage the battery with 3in mortars. Group 2 meanwhile, commanded by Lord Lovat, was, after landing at Orange 2, to make a sweeping move and attack the battery from behind.

Two Bangalore torpedoes were used by Group 1 to clear barbed wire obstructions and mines in a gulley that led up to the top of the cliffs. Fortunately, these torpedoes were used during an Allied fighter attack on the battery and so the noise of the explosions was not heard by the Germans. Scrambling up to the cliff, the mortar party moved quickly to a spot as close to the battery as they dare get. Once positioned, they opened fire on the battery using small arms and a 2in mortar. The mortar's third shell smashed into the charges stacked beside the German guns, which exploded at 0607hrs causing enough damage that the guns never fired again. They then began firing with the 3in mortar and managed to keep the German positions in the battery site under heavy small arms fire.

Meanwhile, a German reconnaissance patrol of 3 Company, 571 Infantry Regiment, had reported to GHQ West that the high ground between Sainte-Marguerite and Varengeville was clear of Allied troops. This area housed the Army Coastal Artillery Troop.

Earlier, however, British commandos had attacked the Army Coastal Artillery Troop by landing at the feet of the steep cliffs between Pourville and Ste-Marguerite and, using mountain-climbing equipment, scaled the cliffs. At Sea-Gull Gorge, some 500 metres West of Pourville, this area of the cliffs was protected by a section of infantry and by the defended lighthouse locality at Phare D'Ailly (including 813 Artillery Troop observation post, Navy Signal Station, Radar and aircraft reporting team). In addition to this, those gorges that extended up the cliffs from the beaches or slightly inland had been heavily wired and mined.

However, due to lack of personnel Division was unable to provide a permanent covering force with the exception of a nightly patrol.[5]

The Germans realised that such a force could have been formed by denuding the Regimental Reserve Battalion that was already weakened by sending a detail to reinforce the infantry company at Quiberville and Saint-Aubin. Behind this coastal sector nearly 1.5km from Phare d'Ailly the Germans had deployed the 813 Army Coastal Artillery Troop (the German Varengeville gun battery), an objective that No. 4 Commando was to attack and destroy. This troop was, in fact, its own strongpoint, which meant that it was responsible for its own defence against land and air attacks. This position had been built with concrete gun emplacements constructed very close to each other along with dugouts and a command post, and due to the lack of tactical subordination, HQ had no say in how the guns were to be placed or indeed in the initial location of the troop itself.

> The construction of the gun emplacements came under the command of the German naval authorities. By the time the concrete emplacements were finished the control over the reinforced programme for field constructions for all branches of the German Armed Forces had been transferred to Division as outlined in the Fuhrer's directive No. 40. Since that time Division had repeatedly informed Artillery Coastal Commanders that it could not provide infantry protection for that particular artillery troop.[6]

> 'HQ 81 requests air effort against everything that floats but asks refraining meanwhile from any effort against the land. Will request land effort in due time.'[7]

---

5   See Report of 302 German Infantry Division, Operations Section -1a, on the Dieppe Raid, Appendix B.

6   Battle Report of the German Commander-in-Chief West (GHQ Army Group D) on the English Landing Attempt at, and on Both Flanks of Dieppe, 19 August 1942.

7   This message was sent by GHQ West to 3rd Air Fleet asking for air support after discussing the situation with 81 Corps HQ as cited in the Battle Report of the German Commander-in-Chief West (G.H.Q. Army Group D) on the English Landing Attempt at, and on Both Flanks of Dieppe, 19 August 1942.

On the day of the landings, at 0902hrs the commander of 770 Army Coastal Artillery Battery informed Division by telephone that 813 Troop was engaged in close-range combat. At this time Division was already aware that a landing attempt at Quiberville had been pushed back. They also knew that a platoon from 2nd Company 571 Infantry Regiment had been dispatched to the Varengeville-Pourville area to reconnoitre the situation there and report back.[8]

While Group 2's landing on Orange 2 Beach was opposed by German defenders, they managed to get through the beach wire and penetrate inland along the bank of the River Saâne. Turning left after advancing along the bank for approximately 1,600 yards, they headed into the wood of Blancmenil-le-Bas, where they quickly began organising for their attack on the battery from the rear. One troop from 4 Commando moved to the edge of the wood towards their concentration area and ran across a party of about 35 German soldiers who were getting ready to attack Group 1. This troop destroyed the Germans.

At 0620hrs on the dot cannon-armed Hurricanes roared in at low level and began shooting up the battery with 20mm shells. However, 'this was only partially successful because as the squadron came in, it was mixed up with Focke-Wulfs'.[9] As this was taking place Group 2 attacked, crossing 250 yards of open ground that was swept by enemy machine gun fire. Dodging bullets, they attacked the battery overrunning the German defenders and forcing hand-to-hand fighting with bayonets. The ferocity of Group 2's attack left most of the battery garrison troops dead with the exception of four men who were taken prisoner. During this action, Captain P.A. Porteous, wounded three times, took command of F Troop that had lost both its senior officers during the initial stages of the fighting and led them in the final assault on the battery.

With resistance now gone, both groups of No. 4 Commando blew up the six guns of the battery. Five were destroyed at 0650hrs, while the sixth was blown up a few minutes later. West of the battery near Sainte-Marguerite, A Troop (they landed with Group 2 and had moved into a position between the village of Sainte-Marguerite and the battery) spotted a German patrol

8   See Report of 302 German Infantry Division, Operations Section -1a, on the Dieppe Raid, Appendix B.

9   From Notes from Theatres of War, No. 11, p.15.

moving towards Group 2 now at the battery. A Troop quickly ambushed the patrol and shot them up using rifle and machine gun fire.

Now in complete control of the battery, the men of No. 4 Commando 'collected the bodies of those who had fallen on the battery site and ran the Union Jack above them'.[10] That done, they then withdrew back to Orange 1 and Orange 2 beaches under enemy sniper fire, which proved to be ineffective. At 0730hrs the Commandos began the re-embarkation procedure just as the Germans opened up with artillery fire. Fortunately, the shells from the artillery burst some 500 yards west of their position, caused no casualties and did not interfere with re-embarkation. Once aboard, Lord Lovat sent a signal to the headquarters ship about the success of his mission:

0850hrs: Every one of gun crews finished with bayonet. Ok by you.[11]

At 0900hrs HMS *Fernie* took on the Commando wounded while the rest of the detachment of No. 4 Commando sailed back to England in their LCAs.

In this very brilliant affair, a model of bold action and successful synchronization, No. 4 Commando lost two officers and ten other ranks killed, three officers and 17 other ranks wounded, nine other ranks wounded and missing, and four other ranks missing. As a result of the action of No. 4 Commando, heavy casualties and material losses were inflicted on the enemy. A most formidable German battery was completely destroyed and the safety of our ships lying off Dieppe during the remainder of the operation was thereby very materially enhanced.[12]

At Quiberville, the Germans had used a flanking attack on the left while maintaining constant communication with Saint-Aubin and Quiberville

---

10   See Report No. 101, The Raid on Dieppe, 19 August 1942.

11   This is in Ops 3-3-1-2 Div, Vol. II, from HQ 1 Cdn Corps, in Kew.

12   See Report No. 101, The Raid on Dieppe, 19 August 1942; Chapter X of this book for a much more detailed account of this action. The accounts of the Commando were also based upon statements made by Lieutenant Colonel Lord Lovat, Major Mills Roberts, Lieutenant Colonel Durnford-Slater and Major Young shortly after the actions took place.

posts and were able to report to GCHQ West that all was well by mid-morning. There would be no more surprises from the Allies in this sector.

However, the situation near 813 Artillery Troop was somewhat different. A report from German posts at Quiberville East reached HQ at 1010hrs that stated the artillery troop was surrounded by Allied units. This information came from the recce patrol that had been sent from Quiberville East earlier that morning who had just arrived back at HQ with the bad news.

However, as we have already seen, by the time the recce patrol returned to HQ the fighting around 813 Artillery Battery was over and the Allies had withdrawn. This information about the situation at 813 Artillery Battery was only received by GCHQ West at 1100hrs from 770 Army Coastal Artillery Battery HQ, some time after 4 Commando had departed. Upon hearing this news, German HQ decided to send a company from 1 Battalion, 571 Infantry Regiment, to advance on Varengeville right away. At this time, the entire battalion was positioned to the east of 813 Artillery Troop and its flank was north-east of the Château de Varengeville.

The defended lighthouse garrison near Varengeville was made up of three officers, eight NCOs and 66 other ranks from the observation and computing centre, Army Coastal Artillery Troop, Navy and Air Force. No reports or calls for help had come in from the lighthouse garrison so it was assumed by GCHQ West that the area there was under control. The reporting centre was in regular wireless communication with an aircraft observation post near the lighthouse garrison as well as with the Army Coastal Artillery Battery. Both of these were in the vicinity of the lighthouse garrison and would have been aware if there was any fighting in the area.

> Much of the Quiberville area had been cleared of Allied units and one of the German defensive positions there reported to Division that Allied ships were hiding behind a smokescreen and appeared to be withdrawing. Some had turned eastwards while many others had turned northeast away from Dieppe. At 1100hrs Division received a report from 770 Army Coastal Battery that 813 Artillery Troop was no longer under attack and was clear of the enemy, who had withdrawn back into their landing craft.[13]

---

13   Battle Report of the German Commander-in-Chief West (GHQ Army Group D) on the English Landing Attempt at, and on Both Flanks of Dieppe, 19 August 1942.

The shipwreck of the Dieppe operation had become clear to the enemy's Operational Command. To bring the precious shipping into an area rendered perilous by German aircraft did not seem advisable. But to move the convoy of transports near the strongly defended naval port of Portsmouth did not necessarily mean that the enemy had given up his intentions.[14]

14　This quote is from a further analysis by C-in-C West, von Rundstedt as cited in the Battle Report of the German Commander-in-Chief West (GHQ Army Group D) on the English Landing Attempt at, and on Both Flanks of Dieppe, 19 August 1942, that was sent to G.H.Q. West. The term 'shipwreck' is actually used in the German report.

Chapter 8

Assault on the Main Beaches: Dieppe

Initially, the landings at the main beaches in front of the town of Dieppe went with minimal resistance from the Germans at touchdown. However, that quickly changed.[1]

Behind the landing craft were the destroyers, which began their bombardment of German positions on shore as laid down in the Operational Orders. HMS *Locust* did not take part in this bombardment as it was some distance behind Group 4. Four destroyers did take part: HMS *Garth* opened fire on the eastern side of Dieppe harbour at 0519hrs, HMS *Bleasdale* pounded the casino and its outbuildings at 0513 up until 0520hrs, while HMS *Berkeley* began its bombardment at 0510hrs pounding houses at the back of Red Beach. Finally, HMS *Albrighton* began hammering the beaches at 0513hrs and stopped once the Very signal light had been spotted indicating the landing craft were running into the shore.[2]

In addition to this, the RAF laid down a smokescreen over the eastern headland at 0510hrs that lingered until approximately 0600hrs. RAF fighter-bombers tore in low over the beaches, neutralising German fire along the front of the landings from 0515 to 0525hrs.

This air action was corroborated by the troops as they went into shore. 'The Navy landed us dry at approx. 0520hrs, after we had witnessed the arrival of the Air Force who machine-gunned the coast before we went in.'[3] Other accounts describe similar sights, indicating that the RAF was on time and did its job effectively.

---

1   Report No. 108, Operation Jubilee, The Raid on Dieppe, 19 August, Part II, Execution of the Operation, Section 2, The Attack on the Main Beaches.

2   Reports of Destroyer Commanders, Enclosure No. 13, Report of Naval Force Commander.

3   Account by Colour Sergeant Major J Stewart, Royal Hamilton Light Infantry (RHLI).

Fighter-bombers bombed and strafed the high ground on both sides of the port. The fighters attacked, hammering the German defenders with machine gun and cannon fire while bombers dropped their ordnance on the same positions. Mixed in with this was fire from British warships firing regular rounds as well as smoke shells and smoke bombs. Despite this the Allies only managed to occupy the west beach, while the city and port remained firmly in German hands, as the following message indicates:

> Own convoy dispersed North of Dieppe during enemy landings. One enemy boat destroyed by ramming, several hits on S-Boats and 1 flotilla leader. Two aircraft shot down. Smaller part of convoy off Valery en Caux. Divisions in the respective coastal defence sector have been informed through Naval Group.[4]

From 0600hrs the sounds of battle had been increasing from the direction of Dieppe. Explosions could be heard from German Divisional Headquarters and the German 571 Infantry Regiment HQ reported that the Allies were attempting to land at Quiberville and dropping bombs on Dieppe itself. At 0622hrs, the German 770th Army Coastal Artillery Battery sent messages to Divisional HQ reporting that Berneval was being attacked from the sea. In the Dieppe sector telephone communications were being disrupted as the landings increased. At this time, divisional sector reports were unable to confirm Allied approaches despite the increasing signs of battle coming from Dieppe. At 0630hrs GHQ West (von Rundstedt's HQ) received a report on the situation that stated:

> According to a message from HQ 81 Corps of 0605hrs, 'bombs dropping on Dieppe, and enemy landing attempts at Berneval, Dieppe, Pourville, and Quiberville.' This resulted in the Chief of Staff GHQ West, G-Ops Branch, Army Administration Officer and Air Force Liaison officers being alerted to the danger. G.H.Q. West's first analysis of the situation stated:

---

4   This message came in to GHQ West from Naval Group Command West at 0845hrs, as cited in the Battle Report of the German Commander-in-Chief West (GHQ Army Group D) on the English Landing Attempt at, and on Both Flanks of Dieppe, 19 August 1942.

'It cannot yet be estimated whether the operation is of a local character and what strengths are involved. But because there have been simultaneous landing attempts at several localities (for the first time) on a front of 20–25km and in daylight it is possible that the landing is a major effort. Moreover, not known what is behind. The possibility of an attack at another point still open! Situation still unclear. For the resulting picture of situation at 0650hrs.'[5]

Lieutenant Commander C.W. McMullen, Royal Navy, in charge of navigating the landing parties into Red and White beaches (the main Allied landing effort at Dieppe) describes the landing at White Beach:

The flotillas started deploying and the smoke laying aircraft started dropping their smoke bombs on the East Cliff. The bombardment, bombing and cannoning of the beaches commenced, excellently timed, and although fire appeared to be coming at us from every direction (including astern) the boats touched down on the beach at 0523. Two of the White Beach boats were heavily damaged during the approach but all White Beach boats disembarked their troops. Red Beach boats appeared to do likewise.
I fired three red Verey [sic] lights as arranged when the leading boat was about 200 yards from the shore; the bombardment, however, had stopped some little time before this. The smoke mortar was used throughout and smoke bombs were lobbed onto the shore across the whole front of the flotilla in the last few hundred yards before reaching the beach.[6]

The flotilla carrying the Royal Hamilton Light Infantry (RHLI) beached at 0522hrs with the flotilla's centre boat coming in where it was supposed to be some 200 yards from the casino. While it was stated earlier that the landings on Red and White Beaches were predominantly unopposed, witness

---

5   See the Battle Report of the German Commander-in-Chief West (GHQ Army Group D) on the English Landing Attempt at, and on Both Flanks of Dieppe, 19 August 1942.

6   From Appx 5 to Enclosure No. 13, Report of Naval Force Commander, cited in Report No. 108, Operation Jubilee, The Raid on Dieppe, 19 August, Part II, Execution of the Operation, Section 2, The Attack on the Main Beaches.

statements seem to refute that claim. The Germans were indeed very active, as we can see from the report of HMS *Glengyle*'s Flotilla Officer, who stated that two boats of his flotilla became casualties from German fire.

HMS *Prince Charles*, carrying elements of the Essex Scottish, had a good run into the beach.

> Our fighter aircraft came into attack when the craft were about 300 yards offshore. The touch-down was made at 0520 and the disembarkation of the soldiers from the boats was facilitated by the steepness of the beach.[7]

The reports from both the Navy and the Army indicate that the touchdown on Red and White Beaches was a few minutes later than originally planned, arriving at approximately 0523hrs.

> As soon as the land could be distinguished it was found that the Flotilla was to the westward and the Flotilla Officer altered course so as to beach in the correct spot. This made rather a big space between HMS *Prince Leopold*'s and HMS *Prince Charles*' Flotillas at the touchdown, which was made a few minutes after schedule.[8]

A report from the German Sea Commandant of Seine-Somme Sector sent to GHQ West via the Naval Commander Channel Coast that stated:

> English still landing (at Dieppe). 17–20 tanks on the beach firing at the town. English destroyers laying smoke-screen. One troop transport has been sunk east of Dieppe. MG and cannon attack of enemy fighters (time not given.).[9]

---

7   Report of the Flotilla Officer on HMS *Prince Charles*, Appx 3G to Enclosure 13, Report of the Naval Force Commander.

8   Report of the Flotilla Officer of HMS *Prince Leopold*, Appx 2E to Enclosure 13, Report of Naval Force Commander.

9   See the Battle Report of the German Commander-in-Chief West (GHQ Army Group D) on the English Landing Attempt at, and on Both Flanks of Dieppe, 19 August 1942.

Another message from the same source followed immediately:

> 0735 English are landing units. Destroyers laying smoke. About
> 20 tanks on the beach. Four destroyers cruising 3 sea miles off the
> port entrance. English fighters guard the landings.[10]

At 0740hrs a report came into C-in-C West (von Rundstedt's HQ) from
Naval Group Command stating that:

> A message had been received from the Commanding Admiral
> France that telephone connection had been cut to the Port
> Commandant of Dieppe. The Dieppe Naval Signal Station
> reported 'English continue to land at Dieppe. Destroyers laying
> smoke on coast; up to now twelve tanks have landed, one is on fire.'[11]

C-in-C West Field Marshal von Rundstedt issued the first of his analysis of
the situation that stated in part 'operation has greater extent and seems to
aim at taking possession of Dieppe as bridgehead'.[12]

---

10   See Report of 302 German Infantry Division, Operations Section -1a, on the
        Dieppe Raid, Appendix B, Report on the British Attack on Both Sides of Dieppe on
        19 August 1942.

11   Ibid.

12   See the Battle Report of the German Commander-in-Chief West (G.H.Q. Army
        Group D) on the English Landing Attempt at, and on Both Flanks of Dieppe,
        19 August 1942.

Chapter 9

The First Wave of Tanks

While the infantry landing craft were close to their scheduled time of arriving at the beaches, this was not the case for the craft carrying the tanks. Their delayed arrival had an adverse effect on the rest of the operation, as we shall see. The first wave of tanks, nine in all, was supposed to touchdown around 0515hrs but did not arrive at the beaches until 0535hrs. The reason for the delay was a navigation problem by the leading LCT that could not get a prompt and accurate fix for several minutes on the area where it was to land its tanks.

> The craft gradually opened out into line abreast, and the 1st Flight
> [of tanks] was led in through the smoke at 0530.[1]

The LCT craft carried elements of the Essex Scottish and the RHLI as well as the tanks. Accounts from these units collected after the operation from those who made it back to England indicate that the air attack was over by the time they were approaching the shore.[2]

Why is this of importance? The delay resulted in a gap from the point when the air attack and naval bombardment ended and the time at which the 6pdr guns of the tanks could be brought to bear on the German defences.

> The two battalions landed on time but the LCTs were between
> ten and 15 minutes late owing to having been given a wrong fix for
> their position some distance from the Beach. This of course meant

---

1   Report from A, L.C.T. Appx 9 to Enclosure No. 13, Report of Naval Force Commander, cited in Report No. 108, Operation Jubilee, The Raid on Dieppe, 19 August, Part II, Execution of the Operation, Section 2, The Attack on the Main Beaches.

2   Account from Private J. Maier, Essex Scottish, B Coy on LCT 4, in Flight 1A, Report No. 108, Part II, The Attack on the Main Beaches.

that the immediate fire support of their six pounders and Besas was not available when it was most desirable that it should be.[3]

The main landings on Red and White Beaches took place punctually and according to plan, with the exception that the landing wave of three LCP approached from the too far to the Westward and were about 10 to 15 minutes late in touching down. The air support, and the smoke-making aircraft on the East cliff, were accurately synchronised, and the destroyers' fire, both on the houses along the front while the boats were going in, and subsequently on the East and West cliffs, appeared to be as effective as could be expected.[4]

Wave after wave of Allied boats had come in at Dieppe landing troops and tanks. Indeed, cannon-armed Hurricanes attacked defensive positions on both sides of the high ground at Dieppe.

By the time of the landings on the main beaches the assaults on Green and Blue beaches were already under way, which meant that there was no element of surprise for the advancing fleet of landing craft. The RAF air attack and the naval bombardment would also have alerted the Germans to the presence of the advancing flotillas. The key, therefore, was to ensure all activity was effectively synchronised and that there was sufficient force to overwhelm the German defenders so the Canadians could enter the town and possibly push on from there.

However, neither the naval bombardment of the beaches or the RAF fighter-bombers strafing the German defences with cannon and machine gun fire were sufficient to permanently subdue the Germans. 'Against concrete defences these expedients had little permanent effect, though doubtless they greatly reduced enemy action while they lasted.'[5] What is clear from the reports is that heavy and accurate German fire pounded the landing craft carrying the infantry and that this fire became murderous from the moment they touched down on the beaches.

Lieutenant Colonel McRae was with the Essex Scottish and he describes the reaction of the German defences to the landings:

---

3   Brigadier Mann, Lecture Notes, The Combined Service Raid on Dieppe, 19 August 1942.

4   Excerpt from Report of the Naval Force Commander, C.B. 04244, Paras 924–5.

5   See Report No. 108, Part II, The Attack on the Main Beaches, Section 30.

As we continued to move in, visibility grew better and we came under fire of the shore weapons about five o'clock (AM). The intensity of the fire increased and shells and long range mortar bombs were bursting in the sea among the advancing craft. Some of the craft were hit and sunk but the majority of them were able to carry on. There was no hesitation, flotillas retained their formation, and despite the heavy fire, the assault wave of craft touched down on the beach at 0525hrs.[6]

Evidence from the members of the RHLI is very similar:

As we neared the beach shells were falling close around us; we learned later that much of this was heavy mortar. Then we ran into MG fire. As we reached the beach and the door opened we could see the Casino and right in front of us was a MG post firing on us.[7]

There are other accounts of the German response to the landings from more members of the RHLI that suggest the defensive fire at the moment of touching down was not that intense but that it grew once they were on the beach and pushing forward towards the town. 'The enemy seemed to hold his fire until we were half-way across the beach and then opened up and were caught between crossfire,'[8] is an example of this.

German 571 Regiment had sent reports to Division about the Allies landing heavy tanks on the beaches immediately in front of the town against which 'our 2.5 and 3.7 anti-tank guns were ineffective.' This forced Division to move 302nd Anti-Tank Company with their 7.5 cm anti-tank guns under the command of the Regiment at 0900hrs.[9]

---

6   Report of Lieutenant Colonel D.F. MacCrae, SD&G Highlanders, extract from the Essex File of personal stories, cited in Report No. 108, Part II, The Attack on the Main Beaches, Section 31.

7   Report from Private V.C. Drury, HQ Coy, Signals, RHLI, Report No. 108, Part II, The Attack on the Main Beaches, Section 32.

8   Report of Private J. Telfer, C Coy, RHLI, Report No. 108, Part II, The Attack on the Main Beaches.

9   See Report of 302 German Infantry Division, Operations Section -1a, on the Dieppe Raid, Appendix B, Report on the British Attack on Both Sides of Dieppe on 19 August 1942.

Chapter 10

The RHLI on White Beach

Once landed the German fire became more intensified, including that from well-placed mortars. The source of enemy fire, although not visible, was definitely coming from the Castle, the Casino and points on the West Cliff.[1]

While earlier it was mentioned that the German fire was not intense at the moment of landing by the RHLI it very soon became extremely so. Indeed, the intensity of the German fire can be seen in the RHLI war diary:

On landing we were met by heavy German fire of all types from the Casino, the building and positions along the esplanade and from the headlands on both flanks. The entire battalion was pinned down by the weight of this fire. D Company (Coy) on the West of the Casino was almost wiped out. In front of us lay three rows of wire, a six-foot wall, and 150 yards across the esplanade, Dieppe itself. Many of the officers and men were killed or wounded in an attempt to cross the beach and scale the wall.[2]

One of the most important points for the RHLI in terms of capturing it and using it to their advantage was the large casino building. It was also hugely important to the Germans as a defensive position and as such it had a large 4in gun mounted in the north-east corner of the building, while outside the Germans had set up several strongpoints that surrounded the building, which included a heavy pillbox built in the north-east corner directly in front of the building. This pillbox had a gun similar to that of the British 40cm

1   Report from Sergeant F.B. Volterman, RHLI.
2   Report from Captain W.D. Whitaker, War Diary, RHLI August 1942, Appx 21.

Bofors. This alone was manned by a crew of five. The tower of the casino also housed several snipers.

By exploding Bangalore torpedoes against the wire obstacles on the beach, elements of the RHLI were able to move into the casino and begin clearing it of German defenders. But first they had to get past the pillbox at the front of the building. In an act of real courage, Private T.E. Greaves rushed the German position with a Bangalore torpedo, which he thrust into the loophole and set it off. The torpedo exploded, killing all the German occupants of the pillbox. However, Private Greaves was later listed as missing.

Before the Canadians could enter the casino, the wire around the front of the building and along the porch needed to be cut and subsequently was, enabling the Canadians to move inside. Sergeant G.A. Hickson, Royal Canadian Engineers, entered last after trying to extricate the 40cm gun from the pillbox but to no avail.

The clearance of the casino took some considerable time as it was a large building full of rooms and passages of varying sizes. 'Clearing it of enemy snipers was in consequence a long and complicated operation.'[3] Despite being well-equipped with charges, it took the Canadians almost an hour to clear the building. The Germans were either killed or taken prisoner as the troops moved through the structure.

Clearance was done by using plastic explosive charges. Sergeant Hickson and his team blew down walls inside the building with these charges, taking out several snipers in the process. Once the snipers had been killed or captured, Sergeant Hickson turned his attention to the big 4in gun in the northwest corner that was firing on British ships offshore. This gun emplacement covered two storeys, with the gun itself being on the upper floor, which was behind a locked steel door. Hickson attached several charges to the door, then blew it down. The explosion sent the door flying and either killed or stunned the German gun crew inside. Hickson and his team rushed into the room as the smoke cleared, took those left alive prisoners while Hickson planted a 1lb charge in the breach of the gun and set it off. As there was already a shell in the breach, the explosion from the charge destroyed the gun.[4]

---

3   See Report No. 108, Part II, The Attack on the Main Beaches, Section 39.

4   Ibid., Section 40.

HMS *Calpe* received a signal at 0712hrs that the casino had been taken.[5] Throughout the clearance of the casino several troops from the RHLI had remained on the beach, suffering heavy and intense German fire from defensive positions the Canadians could not reach. The Canadians were stuck in enfilade fire from the headlands and this is borne out in the following passage:

> I made a dash from the boats to about half-way up the beach. Lieutenant Baisley from then on took us forward over the wall. At this point Lieutenant Baisley was killed. Nobody else tried to go over the wall after that. We did not know exactly where the fire was coming from.[6]

Some of the men from the RHLI now on the beach took shelter along the sea wall, lying in positions west of the casino building, while others took up positions under the wall immediately in front of the building. Against the murderous crossfire they were pinned down and there was nothing much they could do.

Now stuck on the beach, Lieutenant Colonel R.R. Labatt, commanding the RHLI, tried his best to exercise some form of command via his No. 18 wireless set. He was east of the casino and ordered Sergeant F.V. Goodman, HQ Coy, to direct his team's Bren gun fire onto German positions on the high ground to the left.

Smoke concealed the high ground on both sides of the beach and the town of Dieppe itself, making the targeting difficult for German gunners.

> Anti-tank walls sealing off the streets running to the beach prevented tanks from reaching through into the city, but at the same time prevented our 7.6 cm Anti-Tank guns from taking up positions at close range. Only enemy recce patrols had succeeded in penetrating the city through buildings near the beach.[7]

---

5   This is in the HMS *Calpe* Intelligence Log, War Diary, GHQ 2 Canadian Division, August 1942, Appx 51.

6   Report from Sergeant J. Douglas, HQ Coy, War Diary, RHLI August 1942.

7   See Report of 302 German Infantry Division, Operations Section -1a, on the Dieppe Raid, Appendix B.

Chapter 11

Penetrating Dieppe

The Casino when occupied constituted what was in fact a covered avenue between the beach and the BOULEVARD DE VERDUN skirting the front of the town. Thanks largely to this fact, at least two parties of the RHLI and one party commanded by a sapper sergeant were able to penetrate into the town and remain there for some time.[1]

From the Boulevard de Verdun, which runs along the front of the town, to the casino is a flat, covered avenue from the beach. Once the casino had been captured by the RHLI this covered avenue was able to provide the necessary cover for two groups of these troops to move into the town and take up positions inside Dieppe. On the south side of the casino other groups of RHLI were able to take up positions in small buildings and slit trenches, from where they could continue to snipe at German positions fronting the esplanade.

At 0600hrs, while the casino was still being cleared, Captain A.C. Hill, second in command of B Coy, took a small group of 14 men and entered the town. He was determined to get as far into the town of Dieppe as he could. Hill ordered CSM J. Stewart to provide cover as they dashed across open ground toward the buildings along the front of the town.[2]

The Germans had set up defensive positions blocking the Rue de Sygogne with heavy wire obstacles, which made passing through this area of the town impossible for the small Canadian group as they had no way of cutting

---

1   See Report No. 108, Part II, The Attack on the Main Beaches, Paragraph 45.

2   Captain Hill's activities and the events that he and his party undertook was attested to by a number of individuals, some within his party and from others in the RHLI. See War Diary, RHLI August 1942 cited in Report No. 108, Part II, The Attack on the Main Beaches, Section 39.

through. However, on the east side of the street Captain Hill managed to break into a cinema, which they then passed through and entered into the town. From here they moved along Rue Courbonne, into Rue Saint-Rémy to Rue de Sygogne, where they came into contact with a German patrol and opened fire. After heavy fighting they retreated back along Rue Saint-Rémy towards the Rue de la Barre, where once again they engaged another German patrol. In order to get away from the Germans, the Canadians moved into the square surrounding the Church of Saint-Rémy. From the square they moved back into the Rue de la Barre, where they opened fire on a group of Germans with their only Bren gun. This German patrol was outside a headquarters near the Place Due Puys Sale. Under fire, the Germans took casualties but also inflicted losses on the Canadians.[3]

By this point the German opposition was increasingly lethal and Captain Hill decided to retire back to the cinema. En route they shot up the gun crew of an anti-tank gun near the intersection of Rue de Sygogne with the Rue Claude Groulard.

Between 0730hrs and 0800hrs Captain Hill and his men managed to get back to the cinema, where they remained for approximately two more hours. During this time they were joined by more troops from the RHLI. Captain Hill observed German infantry closing in on their position in the cinema at 1000hrs. At this point, he and Major H.F. Laxier decided the best course of action was to withdraw back to the casino. Sergeant Stewart then laid down defensive fire against the approaching Germans while the main body of the Canadians pushed out from the cinema along Porte du Port d'Ouest. Once they were joined by Stewart and his Bren team, they all rushed across the open ground to the casino, with only one man being hit.

At 0900hrs another party of troops from the RHLI managed to get out of the casino, cross the esplanade and move into the town. This party was under the command of Lieutenant L.C. Bell.[4]

Sergeant Hickson also managed to lead a small group of men into the town of Dieppe. This group was made up of 18 men and they moved through the south-east wing of the casino into the Boulevard de Verdun.

---

3   Ibid., Sections 48–50.
4   Report from Captain W.D. Whitaker, War Diary, RHLI August 1942, Appx 21.

That they crossed the open boulevard in safety was probably due to the cover provided by a tank which had stopped near the south-east corner of the Casino and engaged enemy machine-guns in and around the Castle, silencing much of the enemy fire at this point. This may have been the tank, 'Bert' which appears in German photographs in this vicinity.[5]

Hickson and his men managed to move through the building that faced the beach and took up a position north of the Church of Saint-Rémy near an inter-section, where they came under intense sniper fire. They could see people in civilian clothes moving in the streets despite the machine gun and sniper fire taking place all around them. Hickson believed that these individuals were spotting for the Germans and were getting information on their positions to the German snipers. To clear the street, Hickson opened up with Bren gun fire, which scattered the civilians and stopped the flow of information to the snipers. After killing a German sniper firing from an upper window and heavy hand-to-hand fighting in the streets, Hickson withdrew his small force back to the casino, his ammunition exhausted.

At 1010hrs C-in-C West HQ received a report from 571 Infantry Division that the breach at the beach had been finally sealed off. At the same time 3 Battalion's Reserve Company had been moved from the east side of the port to the west side, thus giving 571 Infantry Regiment Reserve Companies on both banks of the port. Since the tanks had come ashore and landed on the beaches all the troops of 3 Battery 302 Artillery Regiment had been firing despite the smokescreen.

The Germans found that their telephone communications between Regimental HQ and 571 Infantry Regiment functioned sporadically but they were able to keep wireless operations open. However, between the Regiment and its 3rd Battalion situation on the eastern heights communications were proving to be difficult. Smoke made visual signals impossible, telephone communications were constantly interrupted, they could not establish

---

5   See Report No. 108, Part II, The Attack on the Main Beaches, Section 54.

wireless communications at all and the only really effective means they had at that time to communicate was by runner.

As long as the regiment had the support of naval artillery guns situated in strongpoints along the coast and able to fire on the beaches in front of Dieppe the Germans felt that they could hold out against the enemy landings. However, to ease things a bit, Division moved a reserve company up to 571 Infantry Regiment in order to release an engineer company that was engaged with the Allies at the southern front of Dieppe. This would now enable the regiment to launch an immediate counterattack on the beach.[6]

---

6   See Report of 302 German Infantry Division, Operations Section -1a, on the Dieppe Raid.

Chapter 12

The Essex Scottish on Red Beach

Red Beach was also overlooked by the lofty buildings along the BOULEVARD DE VERDUN and by pillboxes on the Esplanade wall: while snipers in the upper part of the Casino were able to harass the Essex on the beach with fire at longer ranges.[1]

Red Beach was considerably different to White Beach, most notably in that it did not have a building such as the casino that enabled some infiltration by the Canadians into the town itself as we have seen. This beach was wide open and had its main feature in the east headline, which was lined with caves in which the Germans had placed weapons and gun installations. In addition to the headland, the large high buildings situated along the Boulevard de Verdun overlooked Red Beach as well.

In terms of obstructions, the Germans had placed two wire obstacles on the beach in front of the sea wall, with wire running around the entire wall itself. As the troops rushed out of the landing craft up the beach towards the first wire obstacle a squadron of cannon-firing Hurricanes[2] arrived and began shooting up the German defensive positions on Red Beach with their 20mm cannon shells. Only one man was lost in the dash up the beach to the first obstacle.[3] However, once the air attack was over the Germans began raining fire down on the Canadians as they breached the first obstacle and crossed to the second.

---

1   Report No. 108, Part II, The Attack on the Main Beaches, Section 58.

2   It is highly likely that these were indeed Hurricane IIc fighters armed with four 20mm cannon.

3   This information comes from Lieutenant Colonel D.F. McCrae, War Diary, Essex Scot, August 1942, Appx VI.

There was at this time a great deal of light MG fire on the wire obstacles which caused several casualties amongst the troops while crossing said wire. Somewhere between 30 and 40 per cent of the Essex Scottish personnel were either killed or wounded.[4]

The Germans were now pouring mortar fire and artillery fire onto Red Beach as the remaining Essex Scottish managed to get to the sea wall. Several attempts were made to cross the wall and move into the buildings along the sea front on the Boulevard de Verdun but they failed and the Canadians suffered more heavy casualties. To understand the strength of the German defensive fire and its effect on the Allied troops on the beach we turn to Lieutenant Colonel D.F. McCrae, commanding the Essex Scottish, who was on the receiving end of this murderous fire.

The 3-inch mortars were set up but almost instantly were destroyed by bomb or shell fire. Smoke cover was put over by the 2-inch mortars and the crossing of the sea wall was attempted. This crossing was met with intensive gun and mortar fire as well as LMG fire and almost all of the assaulting troops were killed or badly wounded. The Companies were reformed and, despite the loss of some officers, started a second assault under cover of smoke. By this time some of the 2-inch mortars had been destroyed by enemy fire and the second attack suffered similar fate to the first. By this time the wireless sets were largely destroyed; there being only the 18 set in C Company still functioning. The enemy continued to shell the beach with heavy mortar fire and MG fire on the flanks, causing many casualties. A third attempt on a reduced scale was made to cross the wall and was met by a hail of fire, causing most of the personnel to become casualties.[5]

At approximately 0610hrs, 12 men from the Essex Scottish managed to cross the esplanade and penetrate German lines, where they shot up several German vehicles including a lorry filled with newly arriving German troops,[6]

---

4   Ibid., McCrae War Diary, Essex Scot.

5   Ibid., McCrae.

6   This information comes from Major C.E. Page, who had heard of the destruction of a truck filled with German troops while he was in a prisoner-of-war camp, which may be the same truck that Sergeant Stapleton and his men shot up.

entered the buildings and dealt with several snipers.[7] This small group of men was led by Acting CSM C. Stapleton and for some time were thought to have been the only party of Essex Scottish that managed to get into the town.

Another smaller group of men managed to cross the wall and rush forward. Of the nine men that did this, seven were cut down during the crossing but both Private J.T. Flemming and Corporal C.H. Grondin managed to get to the buildings that lined the Boulevard de Verdun. Moving through the buildings or houses one by one, they met up with Sergeant Stapleton and his group and joined forces. At this point they began clearing the houses along the boulevard, killing several German snipers. Coming out behind the houses, they advanced down the Rue Théophile Gelée towards the harbour, where several trawlers were anchored. Their objective was to clear the houses that overlooked the harbour. All the while they were under fire from German snipers and machine guns. This small party led by Stapleton managed to kill several of the snipers and get to their objective, when Private Flemming was wounded. Stapleton ordered him back to the beach.[8]

It must be remembered that the information here comes from reports that were written shortly after the war. They are from personal accounts of the men who took part in the actions and may or may not be accurate as they are based upon memory. However, the key here is not whether the Canadians did or did not get into the town, it is how the Germans managed to stop the Allied assault.

Most of the remaining Essex Scottish who had not been killed or wounded were now pinned down on the beach or along the sea wall, unable to take the fight to the Germans.

By about 0630hrs the Essex Scottish had suffered at least 75 per cent casualties, a large number of officers being killed or very severely wounded. Offensive action however was continued from behind the sea wall by firing at slits in pillboxes, windows and any-where the enemy showed themselves . . . Offensive efforts by the

---

7   This information comes from a letter written by Lieutenant Colonel Jasperson to his banker in London from a prisoner-of-war camp in France, 23 August 1942, copy on CMHQ file 10/Jasperson F.K/1.

8   The information in this paragraph is from Private Flemming's account and as he was sent back to the beach to be evacuated with the rest of the unit he did not know what happened to CSM Stapleton and his party, War Diary, Essex Scot, August 1942.

remnants of the Essex Scottish were continued for some hours by getting ammunition from the casualties until finally about 1030hrs there was practically no ammunition left. Ammunition was taken from the wrecked tanks and used as far as it would go.[9]

Throughout this time, continuous German mortar fire came down on the hapless Canadians stuck in the shelter of the sea wall. One of the buildings on the sea front was a tobacco factory and several men of the Essex Scottish found themselves just west of this building in a depression in the beach. This depression ran along the front of the sea wall and acted as a trench, enabling many of the men to take shelter. It was clear that attacking across the sea wall would have meant certain death for the attackers. Using the depression as a fire trench, the men of the Essex Scottish took turns every five minutes or so in firing at the German defensive positions. Private J. Mair was in this party of men and had with him an anti-tank rifle, which he used to good effect in killing several snipers in the tower of the casino and other high buildings.

In order to illustrate the situation on the ground and the intensity of the German fire, we can look to the account by Lieutenant Colonel F.K. Jasperson.

Mortar and shell splinters were whistling all around me, some as close as 8 feet but none got me. The most I suffered was periodic showers of stone etc. on my tin hat and body which did me no harm. The experience was quite harrowing and how I was missed God only knows. The scene of it all will be imprinted on my mind forever. There are many things I would like to say but obviously can't. But I do want it known that the personal acts of bravery in this show are beyond words. I saw no one jittery and all fought splendidly in the best tradition. And that goes for all ranks. Major Willis was undoubtedly outstanding. Badly wounded in the chest, arms and head he carried on directing his company when it seemed humanly impossible to do so; and I am sure when he received his last wound it was due to his effort in trying to draw a man back to safety. Lieutenant Green with a foot shot off had it bound up and

9   Report from Lieutenant Colonel D.F. McCrae, War Diary, Essex Scot, August 1942, Appx VI.

continued to hobble on leading his platoon when a second bomb finished him. Personal bravery was so outstanding by all that it is most difficult to distinguish between cases.[10]

The German Sea Commandant of Seine-Somme Sector sent a message to GHQ West via the Naval Commander Channel Coast that stated:

English still landing (at Dieppe). 17–20 tanks on the beach firing at the town. English destroyers laying smoke-screen. One troop transport has been sunk east of Dieppe. MG and cannon attack: of enemy fighters (time not given.).

Another message from the same source followed immediately: '0735 English are landing units. Destroyers laying smoke. About 20 tanks on the beach. Four destroyers cruising 3 sea miles off the port entrance. English fighters guard the landings.'[11]

---

10   This information comes from a letter written by Lieutenant Colonel Jasperson to his banker in London from a prisoner-of-war camp in France, 23 August 1942, copy on CMHQ file 10/Jasperson F.K/1.

11   See Report of 302 German Infantry Division, Operations Section -1a, on the Dieppe Raid, Appendix B, Report on the British Attack on Both Sides of Dieppe on 19 August 1942.

Chapter 13

Allied Tanks

For the assault on the main beaches of Dieppe the infantry, Essex Scottish Regiment and the Royal Hamilton Light Infantry were to be supported by tanks of the 14th Canadian Tank Battalion, known also as the Calgary Regiment.[1]

The landing craft carrying the tanks were organised into five groups, Nos 8, 9, 10, 11 and 12. They were to land in four waves right after the infantry had touched down.[2] However, only two waves of tanks were ordered into action. The third and fourth waves remained offshore waiting for orders that never came. They returned to England.

The fate of the tanks and the landing craft on the main beaches of Dieppe illustrate how effective, intense and deadly the German defensive fire was. The first wave of tanks arrived five minutes later than planned and met with very heavy fire. Their first objective was to destroy the pillboxes immediately after landing in order to pave the way for the engineers and working parties to come ashore.

However, because of the heavy fire encountered on the beach, the landings of the tanks from the first wave was less than successful. While many tanks did manage to land, many of the LCTs they came in were either heavily damaged or sunk. For example, after LCT145 beached successfully and landed its three tanks, it was hit and 'drifted broadside-on some 60yards from the beach and after an unsuccessful attempt to tow her back, was sunk'.[3] LCT127 also managed to get its tanks ashore even though it was heavily damaged. Shell fire cut the chains of its ramp, which then folded under

---

1   Report No. 108, Part II, The Attack on the Main Beaches, Section 39.

2   This information is from Op Jubilee Combined Report, The Dieppe Raid, Canadian Military Headquarters, The Execution and Air Battle, Section 199.

3   Ibid., Op Jubilee Combined Report, The Dieppe Raid.

the hull. This craft received a direct hit in the engine room also, killing and wounding most of the crew and setting the ammunition and magazines on fire. Two of the craft's AA gunners remained at their posts firing away at the German positions until they were hit or they ran out of ammunition.

LCT159 also had its ramp chains cut by gunfire and came in with the ramp half down. Taking on water, it remained on the beach. The fourth LCT in the first wave was also hit but this was before it was able to touch down and embark its tanks. The hail of shells set the craft on fire and it sank in deep water. Another direct hit from German fire hammered into LCT163, setting the engine room on fire as it was coming in to land. Unfortunately, the helmsman was overcome by the fumes and the vessel swung sharply to port. Another attempt was made to land it when another rating took the wheel but he was killed and was unable to bring the craft into shore. A third man took the wheel in order to make another attempt at landing but he too was killed by German gunfire. On its fourth and final attempt LCT163, now with another man at the wheel and using the cover of the damaged and sinking LCT145, it managed to make it to the beach and unload the tanks and infantry. From there, LCT163 'then returned to the Boat Pool after making an unsuccessful attempt to tow away LCT145'.[4]

The first wave of landing craft carried 18 tanks in total and 14 of them landed successfully on the beach. The remainder were either heavily damaged or sunk.

Of these, five managed to move over the beach and cross the esplanade wall.[5] Three other tanks had stalled on the ramp of LCT127 due to cold engines, while another tank had managed to climb the steps 'up the wall near the casino'.[6] Of the fourteen tanks, six were over the esplanade within twenty minutes of landing. Three turned west, advancing along the Boulevard Marshal Foch. 'In all probability it was these which entered the town for tanks were subsequently seen in the Rue Grande having passed through an opening in the Quai du Hoble [Hâble] or possibly through a house that was knocked down by the tank commanded by Lieutenant W.C. Patterson.'[7]

---

4   Ibid.

5   Two of these tanks had been fitted with a track-laying device that had been tested successfully five days before the raid on 14 August 1942, Op Jubilee Combined Report, The Dieppe Raid.

6   See Op Jubilee Combined Report, The Dieppe Raid.

7   Ibid.

East of the casino, two of the six tanks had engaged the German defences, pillboxes and fortified positions, destroying many of them. The last of the six tanks got caught up in a tank trap on the esplanade. As to the fate of these tanks, it is most likely they tried to return to the beaches.

> There is evidence which suggests that some of the tanks penetrated into the town and, having expended all their ammunition subsequently returned to the beaches. Their exact movements, however, are obscure.[8]

The rest of the tanks landed in the first wave did not get off the beach. One had its turret blown off, while another suffered severe damage to the turret and two more lost their tracks, making them completely immobile. The commander from one of the tanks that had lost its tracks managed to climb out and get into the tank behind it that was in better shape. This tank swung its 6pdr gun around and engaged the German anti-tank gun that had knocked out the first tanks and completely destroyed it.

By now 0600hrs, the Germans were fully aware that the Allies were attempting to land tanks and so the fate of the second wave was far worse than the first. The Germans now intensified their fire, from mortars, anti-tank weapons and machine guns.

LCT Nos 124, 125, 165 and 168 made up the second wave, or flight, of tanks coming into land on the main beaches. They arrived on time at 0605hrs. The first casualty was LCT124, which came into the beach, embarked its tanks and was hit so many times and suffered such severe damage that it sank in deep water off the beach. LCT125 managed to make two landings, the first where it unloaded only one tank and on the second it was hit so many times that its officers and crew were either killed or wounded. On board was the commander of the 4th Canadian Infantry Brigade, Brigadier Lett, and the commander of Combined Operations Headquarters, Lieutenant Colonel E.G. Parks-Smith, Royal Marines, who was in charge of the Beach Provost Party. Both men were badly hit, with Parks-Smith mortally wounded. Despite all the damage, LCT125 managed to offload its tanks and was towed back to England.

---

8   Ibid.

Also on board LCT125 was Lieutenant Commander Andrews, who had transferred over to the landing craft just before touchdown. He was in charge of the tanks in this wave. Upon landing, Andrews' tank rolled off into 8ft of water despite only being waterproofed to wade in 6ft. Andrews and his crew baled out of the tank and managed to get to the beach, where Andrews climbed into another vehicle that was subsequently hit and exploded.

Eleven tanks of the second wave were successfully landed on the main beaches, although one was drowned immediately. It must be remembered that throughout these landings the tanks and landing craft were under murderous German fire, which was only intensifying as time went on. LCT165, for example, lost control when its steering gear and ramp were pounded by German shells. This craft had to be towed off by another raft. LCT166 managed to get its three tanks off within two minutes of touching down on the beach and they got as far as the esplanade wall. The tanks from LCT165 were landed successfully on the beach but only one got to the wall, while the other two suffered direct hits and went no further.

In all, 28 tanks were landed by the 24 LCTs that had sailed from England. Of these, only seven managed to cross the esplanade, while the rest became casualties. Strangely, there was no attempt by the tanks to destroy or penetrate the esplanade wall or concrete road blocks set up by the Germans with their 6pdr guns from the tanks. Despite the fact that some tanks reached the esplanade and crossed it they were unable to achieve their objectives and so the tanks failed. One of the reasons for this could be that the Royal Canadian Engineers' Beach Assault and Demolition Parties took very heavy casualties at the moment of touchdown as they rushed or drove off the landing craft. 'Of eleven officers and 314 Other Ranks they lost nine Officers and 180 Other Ranks, killed, wounded, missing or prisoners of war.'[9]

> Most of these casualties occurred at the moment of touchdown or shortly afterwards between the water's edge and the Esplanade Wall which was, in consequence, not demolished except at one place near the Casino. The wall itself was nowhere more than three feet in height and did not, therefore, constitute an insurmountable obstacle. The nature of the shingle at its base, however, and

---

9   Ibid.

the angle at which it sloped were such that track-laying devices were indispensable.[10]

Other reasons for the failure of the tanks was due to the tracks spinning and sinking into the shingle on the beach. The anti-tank fire from the road blocks on the Boulevard de Verdun and from the eastern headland was particularly vicious and intense. However, key to the failure was the high casualty rate of the sappers; only nine returning to England from the 71 that landed in four LCTs and two LCAs. This meant that all the obstacles that had to be destroyed in order to make way for the tanks could not be tackled.

The German Army High Command decided to launch an air reconnaissance of the Dieppe defence line in order to get a better picture of the events taking place up and down it. The aircraft sent to carry out the task arrived back at its base at 1000hrs. The subsequent report from the flight arrived at Army High Command from 3rd Air Fleet via the Air Liaison Officer at 1100hrs:

a) In Dieppe two large fires, riding at anchor 5–6 destroyers which are taking cover in smoke; identified 50–80 landing craft.

b) 40km Northwest of Dieppe 6 large transports, apparently tank transports fully loaded.

c) 60km Northwest of Dieppe 3 medium-sized freighters, 1 S-Boat.

d) Area Selsey B111 (England) 26 large transports each of 6,000 tons, 3 destroyers in convoy. Decks closely crowded with troops.

e) South-east of Eastbourne small boats, moving East, apparently are protecting forces.

f) Other sea area: nothing observed.

g) English fighter commitment over Dieppe very strong, in action with weaker own forces. Reports b, c, and d, were food for thought. The question immediately asked by C-in-C West about the direction of movement of the 26 large transports could not be cleared up, at least not up to this point.[11]

---

10   Ibid.

11   See Report of 302 German Infantry Division, Operations Section -1a, on the Dieppe Raid, Appendix B, Report on the British Attack on Both Sides of Dieppe on 19 August 1942.

Based on this reconnaissance report, von Rundstedt released another situation analysis that stated:

> The ships outlined under reports b and c according to the English landing plan probably belong to the 'floating reserve'. If one brings this reserve into operational connection with the fleet of transports in the rear mentioned under report, the enemy undertaking may be the beginning of an attempt to establish the Second Front.
>
> It is also possible that the enemy is carrying out the attack on Dieppe for reasons of deception, in order to attract the motorized reserves of GHQ West thither and then carry out a major operation at another point. C.-in-C West must keep Brittany in mind.
>
> Whichever way this may be, it remains our task to batter and wipe out the enemy at Dieppe with all our means in the shortest possible time. The situation there has been so far clarified that the reserves already committed or moving up will suffice for this task.
>
> If the enemy cannot establish a beachhead at Dieppe, neither the floating reserve nor the fleet of transports as an operation reserve will be of any use to him.
>
> He may, however, have prepared the 26 transports as a second wave for a main effort, probably against Normandy.[12]

British tanks were still cruising up and down the beach being hit by heavy German defensive artillery and anti-tank fire. The town itself had been cleared of Allied soldiers and the Germans held the high ground on both sides of Dieppe, able to continue to attack what was left of the Allied tanks and infantry on the beaches. Improvising various forms of motor transport, 2 Battalion, 570 Infantry Regiment, were positioned in d'Arques Woods, south of Dieppe, in the divisional reserve role.[13]

By 0600hrs, on HMS *Calpe*, the Allied headquarters ship, the realisation was beginning to sink in that the operation was not going as planned. The situation on Red and White beaches as we have seen was not entirely

---

12   Battle Report of the German Commander-in-Chief West (GHQ Army Group D) on the English Landing Attempt at, and on Both Flanks of Dieppe, 19 August 1942.

13   See Report of 302 German Infantry Division, Operations Section -1a, on the Dieppe Raid, Appendix B, Report on the British Attack on Both Sides of Dieppe on 19 August 1942.

unfavourable. Green Beach, however, as far as anyone knew on HMS *Calpe* was not turning out well. They were not aware if any landing had taken place on Yellow Beach and had not heard from the Royal Regiment of Canada at Blue Beach. The third and fourth waves of tanks were waiting offshore in their LCTs waiting to head for the beaches and embark their troops and tanks. However, no orders had been given for them to do so and in the event they returned to England, losing LCT307 along the way due to it being bombed.[14]

A decision was then taken by Major General J.H. Roberts to reinforce Red Beach. He was particularly worried about securing the eastern headland in order to make operations on the beach safer. He knew that some tanks had already gone ashore and so he felt that sending in more infantry would help to secure this eastern headland. As a result he sent in the floating reserve of the Fusiliers Mont-Royal. This reserve was split into two groups. The first went in under cover of smoke to Red Beach at 0704hrs and landed success-fully. However, Roberts' intelligence had been wrong when it told him the German fire on Red Beach had decreased. It was as murderous as ever and was increasing in its intensity, to the point that the Fusiliers, once touched down, could do nothing in terms of their objectives. Many tried to find cover behind stranded or destroyed tanks.

The second group of approximately 300 officers and men landed to the west of White Beach and took cover under a cliff. Visibility was poor due to the smokescreen. Several times they tried to move to the flanks, first to the right to support the South Saskatchewan Regiment, but were repulsed by heavy German fire. With this route closed to them they moved to the left towards the casino, where they came up against the concrete wall with pillboxes housing heavy machine guns. 'It proved impossible successfully to assault on the narrow front between the cliff and the sea, which was their only line of advance.'[15]

At 1200hrs 288 men of this group surrendered, with more than 100 being wounded.

However, one small group of Fusiliers did manage to get off the beach and into the town despite the desperate fire from the Germans. Sergeant P. Dubuc and his men, sheltering along the concreate wall, managed to destroy two of the closest pillboxes. They then moved back to a stranded tank that had been

14   Ibid., Op Jubilee Combined Report, The Dieppe Raid.
15   Ibid.

left dry as the tide went out. Using the tank's 6pdr gun they opened fire on a wide number of German defences on the western headland until the ammunition ran out. From there, Dubuc collected his men and advanced along the Rue Alexandre Dumas into the town west of the casino. As they advanced they briefly met up with another party of Fusiliers attacking German positions from houses along the Boulevard de Verdun. Dubuc pushed on, taking his men towards the harbour, destroying a machine gun post along the way. Eventually, they reached the Bassin du Canada, where they attacked several Germans on two barges in the Bassin. Dubuc shifted his advance and began moving along the railway tracks on the western side of the Bassin until they came across a large German patrol. With their ammunition gone they had no choice but to surrender. After rounding up the Fusiliers, the Germans left the men in the charge of just one soldier. The Canadians quickly overcame this individual and ran, scattering through the town trying to get back to White Beach. Sergeant Dubuc was lucky enough to get to the beach and board a landing craft, which took him back to England.

Chapter 14

Withdrawal From Red and White Beaches

By 0900 it had become clear to me that the troops ashore were in difficulties and were unlikely to gain possession of the East and West cliffs, which dominated the main beaches . . . It was obvious therefore that the military situation was serious and it was becoming steadily more difficult for ships and craft to close the beaches. Accordingly, I advised the General that the withdrawal should take place with as little further delay as possible, and should be confined to personnel. I considered that 1030 would be the earliest practicable time, as it was necessary to warn the Air Officer Commanding 11 Group and to pass instructions to the landing craft. The General agreed . . .[1]

At 0900hrs the decision was made to withdraw Allied troops from Red and White beaches largely due to the increasing intensity of German fire and the realisation that because of that intensity, the Eastern and Western headlands on either side of the town of Dieppe could not be taken. The beaches were still under heavy and continuous German fire from mortars, machine guns, artillery, anti-tank guns and the Luftwaffe when it was possible for them to attack. In short, the situation was getting worse. All the Canadian mortar attachments had been destroyed. HMS *Garth*, which had been offshore supporting the landings with its naval guns, was now low on ammunition. An LCT was being towed away from White Beach by HMS *Alresford*, so both these ships were unable to stay in the fight. The third and fourth waves of tanks that had not been ordered into battle and remained on their LCTs were now escorted home by these two ships.

---

1   See Naval Forces Commander as cited in Report No. 108, Part II, The Attack on the Main Beaches, Section 226.

On board HMS *Calpe* was controlled pandemonium as there were always several landing craft alongside unloading wounded, seeking new orders or bringing in reports from the beaches since most of the radio sets had been destroyed on landing. All the while, the ship was under continuous fire from the Germans but its commanding officer, Lieutenant Commander J.H. Wallace, managed to prevent it being heavily damaged.[2]

Once the landing craft had embarked its troops, those that were able to returned to a boat pool that had been set up off Red and White beaches and been kept under an almost complete smokescreen throughout the operation.

The time set for the general withdrawal for all forces was 1100hrs. However, at 0950hrs the Boat Pool officer left HMS *Calpe* 'with instructions to initiate the withdrawal at about 1030hrs, using LCAs to ferry troops to such available LCTs as could be anchored offshore. He proceeded accordingly to round up the various groups of landing craft, instructing them to lie about one and a half to two miles off their respective beaches and be ready to go in when ordered.'[3] As we know, the time later changed to 1100hrs.

As far as General Roberts was concerned, any of the tanks that had been landed would have to be abandoned in order to ensure as many personnel as possible were re-embarked and returned to England. Regarding the third and fourth wave of tanks still sitting offshore, the Naval Force Commander stated that 'in view of the volume of enemy fire it was out of the question to send tank landing craft inshore.'[4]

With the time of withdrawal set for 1100hrs, orders were given to increase the air cover over the beaches to six fighter squadrons from three at 0930hrs. A smokescreen was ordered to be laid between 1100hrs and 1130hrs over the beaches in order to cover the withdrawal. The Naval Force Commander ordered his destroyers to support the landing craft as they went into the beaches to pick up the troops.

> At about 1022, the destroyers were ordered to form on a line to bear 070 degrees to 250 degrees and to follow the landing craft in. All vessels suitably placed were instructed to make smoke. The wind

---

2   This information comes from Op Jubilee Combined Report, The Dieppe Raid, Section 236.

3   See Report No. 108, Part II, The Attack on the Main Beaches, Section 231.

4   See Appendix 16 to Enclosure No. 13, Report of Naval Force Commander.

was onshore and slightly from the West, and an effective screen of smoke prevented the landing craft from being fired upon until they were close inshore. Unfortunately, the smoke also hid the beaches from the destroyers and it was very difficult to see what was going on, or to offer effective support by gunfire. Nevertheless, without the smoke it is doubtful whether any withdrawal would have been possible.[5]

The German Headquarters of 571 Infantry Regiment received a report from its 2 Battalion HQ that enemy landing craft were turning away from the beach back towards the sea.

Naval Signal Section reported that 5 Allied ships were heading away from the beaches some 5kms from shore. However, on the beach in front of Dieppe Allied tanks were still trying to get up to the town while being pounded by heavy fire from German 3rd Battery 302 Artillery Regiment, Anti-tank guns of the Anti-Tank Company as well as from 571 Infantry Regiment and along with whatever AA guns were available and within range. Under such heavy concentrated fire the tanks had no chance and were soon still and burning. At 1200hrs 571 Infantry Regiment HQ ordered the beach mop up operations to begin and troops of 2 Company 302 Engineer Battalion began the process moving amongst the burning hulks of Churchill tanks and the dead, dying and wounded Allied soldiers.[6]

In area Fecamp–Dieppe 3–6km off the coast 7 English large naval units, heavy and light cruisers, with 10–15 escort vessels, 1 light cruiser and another naval unit sighted moving in the direction of the English coast.

This rearward movement too may be connected with that above mentioned. Everything points to the enemy's having recognized

---

5   C.B. 04244, Para 939, Enclosure No. 13, Report of Naval Force Commander.
6   See Report of 302 German Infantry Division, Operations Section -1a, on the Dieppe Raid, Appendix B, Report on the British Attack on Both Sides of Dieppe on 19 August 1942.

the failure at Dieppe and cancelled the operation. This may mean annihilation for the parts of his force which landed.

GHQ West doubts whether the size and class of the reported warships is correct. Experience shows that large destroyers are easily confused with cruisers.[7]

No more ships in front of Dieppe, destroyers have left. Burning landing craft on the beach. Several tanks still driving up and down, they are being fired at by Army guns which have been run up to the beach. Beach appears to be sealed off.[8]

On the western beach of Dieppe, one German defence gun manned by elements of 302 Artillery Regiment was still firing at the hapless Allies caught in the open on the beach. The German anti-tank gun on the west mole had been knocked out by a direct hit. At the very tip of the mole one officer and two men were still holding out but their prospects were bleak indeed.[9]

From the air Allied positions at the casino on the Dieppe beach and Allied boats on the beach itself were pounded relentlessly by German fighter-bombers and bombers.

Fighter commitment until 1130hrs 288 aircraft, of those 18 fighter bombers. Successes: 24 aircraft shot down for certain, 4 probables. 1 destroyer damaged, 3 own losses. Bombers so far committed: 54. No success reports are yet available.[10]

One German unit that was still waiting to be called into action was 2nd Battalion, 570 Infantry Regiment, still in its divisional reserve role and stationed on the western edge of d'Arques Woods waiting for its call to attack.

---

7   This message came through at 1200hrs from (F) Staffel 122 believed to have been Long Distance Reconnaissance Squadron 122. The actual report was sent between 0930 and 0953hrs but did not arrive at GHQ West until 1200hrs.

8   This report was from Naval Commander Channel Coast who sent it via Naval Group West to G.H.Q. at 1230hrs.

9   See Report of 302 German Infantry Division, Operations Section -1a, on the Dieppe Raid, Appendix B, Report on the British Attack on Both Sides of Dieppe on 19 August 1942.

10   This is a message from 3rd Air Fleet to GHQ West that provided a brief overview of the air battle.

No. 572 Infantry Regiment HQ received several reports that indicated a large convoy of roughly 30 ships had been spotted well out to sea in front of Dieppe and was being mercilessly attacked by the Luftwaffe.

As far as the Fusiliers are concerned, those that were still alive and able to move or be moved were re-embarked under considerable intense fire from the Germans. While the accounts from the Fusiliers are thin on the ground, we can look to Private G. Provencal for an indication of what it was like for them and how difficult the Germans were making it for the Canadians to get off the beaches:

> He and his comrades re-embarked under an intense fire, he himself being wounded by a piece of shrapnel in doing so. He got aboard an LCA which he left ten minutes later because it was sinking, and the men were bailing with their steel helmets. He reports three enemy air attacks on the boats.[11]

Further evidence of the German determination to wipe out as many of the Canadians as they could as they withdrew can be seen from Sergeant W. Gagne of the Fusiliers who, while boarding an LCT, saw Lieutenant Menard get hit in the head by shrapnel, pieces of which were flying all around them.

Up at the casino the RHLI had organised an all-round defence as the men who had been in the town retreated back to the building. Sergeant Stewart had almost given up hope of getting back to England when the orders came through from Captain A.C. Hill to get the wounded down to the beach. Thus began the withdrawal of the troops from the casino, which took place in stages, the first to go being the riflemen.[12] However, as the Bren gunners were covering the withdrawal, Stewart stayed with them until Hill ordered them to withdraw as well. Sergeant Stewart managed to get onto a destroyer and back to England, while Captain Hill was captured by the Germans.

---

11   War Diary, Les Fusiliers Mont-Royal as sited in Report No. 108, Part II, The Attack on the Main Beaches, Section 231.

12   See Report No. 108, Part II, The Attack on the Main Beaches, Section 238.

There was no organised beach party at work, and men simply got aboard the boats which came in any way they could. In these circumstances, some craft inevitably became overloaded.[13]

Stewart managed to get aboard an overcrowded LCA, which subsequently sank and he ended up swimming around for more than two hours before he was rescued by another LCA.

Sergeant Hickson had a similar experience. He managed to get aboard an overcrowded LCA and quickly got the men to start bailing out the water with their helmets. They limped out to sea and transferred to a destroyer, which took the wounded first. Hickson was one of the men who transferred to the destroyer, likely HMS *Calpe*, and returned to England.

Of all of the units evacuated on that fateful day, the Essex Scottish had the fewest number that managed to get to the beaches and be re-embarked.

Somewhere about 1100hrs aircraft laid smoke on the water front and LCAs came in to attempt to evacuate the troops. An effort was made to get those not wounded and the wounded who could be moved into the LCAs but enemy fire destroyed so many of the LCAs that very few of the troops got off. I got away myself with a small party of wounded in a small wooden row boat and we were eventually picked up by a smoke laying ship and later transferred to a beach protection ship where there was a surgeon.[14]

On the beach a large number of Essex Scottish took cover behind a stranded LCT. The account below provides a brief glimpse of the situation the men had to endure, primarily suffering heavy German cross fire. Let us also not forget that the Luftwaffe was still active and still able to attack the men on the beach and the ships despite the air battle overhead.

When we withdrew we had to go back through a hole in the wire and then about 100yds down the beach, all of which was under very heavy cross fire and with no protection till we reached a beached

---

13   Account of CSM Steward, RHLI, Report No. 108, Part II, The Attack on the Main Beaches, Section 239.

14   Report of Lieutenant Colonel McRae, War Diary, Essex Scot, August 1942, Appx VI.

LCT where, with a large number of other soldiers, we took cover until we were able to board an LCA. We had to leave this LCA later as it was hit and transferred to a LTC always under fire.[15]

On all the beaches smoke was used to cover as much of the withdrawal as possible. As far as the men of the 14th Army Tank Regiment (The Calgary Regiment (Tank)) are concerned, virtually none of the men who landed returned to England. One of the reasons for this is that these men decided to remain in what tanks were still serviceable and working in order to cover the withdrawal of the troops. The guns of the tanks remained in action until the end. 'CSM Stewart was convinced that the continued fire of the tank on the beach in front of the Casino contributed materially to the safe withdrawal of many of the infantry.'[16]

At 1250hrs HMS *Calpe* came out of the smoke cover and steered towards the eastern end of Red Beach looking for survivors and to get a clear idea of the situation on the beach. As it closed, the German machine gun post on the breakwater opened up and the destroyer came under heavy fire. Those on the destroyer could see only the wrecked and destroyed tanks on the beach, stranded or burning landing craft and the bodies of the dead. No troops or landing craft were waiting to be taken off so the destroyer turned back into the cover of the smoke. Around this time a signal was received that the troops on the beach had surrendered. This was probably why there were no more waiting for evacuation.

The troops included Brigadier Southam in command of the 6th Canadian Infantry Brigade, who was compelled to surrender at 1308hrs. He had directed the battle first from the beach and then from the Casino and had remained in touch throughout with the Essex Scottish Regiment, one of whose wireless operators belonging to C Company continued to transmit up to the last moment, the very heavy fire to which he was subjected being clearly heard in the earphones of the telegraphists on board the Headquarters Ship.

15   Account from Private E.R. Cousineau, Report No. 108, Part II, The Attack on the Main Beaches, Section 244.

16   See Report No. 108, Part II, The Attack on the Main Beaches, Section 247.

The surrender at White Beach took place a few minutes after the arrival of German reinforcements at the Dieppe railway station.[17]

As far as the Germans were concerned, reports came into the Intelligence Section at GHQ West enabling them to issue a statement at 1310hrs regarding the situation that revealed 'the English are retreating, a second simultaneous operation seems to have been cancelled'.[18] Around the same time, von Rundstedt issued another analysis of the Dieppe operations:

> The enemy is withdrawing. He has been repelled completely east of and at Dieppe; to the West of Dieppe near Pourville, and in the woods and gullies to the West of it, mopping up is in progress and it is merely a question of time. Now it is up to us to destroy what can be destroyed. For that purpose every weapon and every barrel must employed. C–in–C West therefore orders the following: It is up to us now – and I am pressing this point – to wipe out just as many of the enemy as is in any way possible. Therefore, battleworthy units of the 10 Pz Div, armour and artillery, drive forward at once! Every available weapon must now contribute to the complete destruction of the enemy. The whole front on which the enemy has landed must be cleared up in the shortest of time![19]

At 1430hrs von Rundstedt's HQ received a report from 571 Infantry Regiment HQ that Dieppe was clear of the enemy and that more than 600 prisoners of war had been taken. To all intents and purposes the operation was over.[20]

At 1545hrs HQ 81 Corps advised GHQ West of the following:

> Dieppe and Pourville in our hands! In the woods of Varengeville only single stragglers. In the last hour three destroyers, two

---

17   This information comes from Op Jubilee Combined Report, The Dieppe Raid, Section 246.

18   Battle Report of the German Commander-in-Chief West (GHQ Army Group D) on the English Landing Attempt at, and on Both Flanks of Dieppe, 19 August 1942.

19   Ibid., Battle Report of the German Commander-in-Chief West (GHQ Army Group D).

20   Ibid.

torpedo boats, and several landing craft were sunk by artillery fire. Operation as good as ended; about 1100 prisoners is our estimate. 10 Pz Div is moving up. Advanced guard should be arriving at Dieppe now. 302 Inf Div has cleared the situation up by itself, assisted only by flak and the Luftwaffe.

Thus, the enemy's Dieppe operation was smashed in just over 9 hours! The extent of the English defeat began to appear as early as midday and increased until 1700hrs as detailed reports came in. Not only did the enemy lose heavily on land, but also, he must have suffered very heavy losses at sea which can merely be estimated.

Our own losses seem moderate and compared to the losses of the English they appear trifling.[21]

No. 571 Infantry Regiment HQ at Dieppe reported to Division at 1445hrs that the beaches were clear of Allied units.[22]

An interim report from HQ 15th Army was sent through to GHQ West at 1710hrs that confirmed the previous situation report they had received at 1545hrs.

From this and other reports it is evident that the English Army used for the attack two brigades, probably more, and in addition 'Commandos'. Tanks landed only at Dieppe and they were destroyed without exception. The number of landing craft which the enemy put to sea from transports is estimated at 300–400, which beached in waves of 40–60 craft. In the early morning hours strong English fighter forces appeared, about 16 squadrons, partly with fighter bombers as fighter escort for the convoys. These squadrons were continuously relieved by new units! At 1100hrs a strong fighter force (about 15 squadrons) with 12 twin-engined bombers went into the Abbeville area and dropped bombs from a height of 4,000 metres.

---

21   See Report of 302 German Infantry Division, Operations Section -1a, on the Dieppe Raid, Appendix B, Report on the British Attack on Both Sides of Dieppe on 19 August 1942.

22   Ibid.

English fighter escort regularly relieved remained above the Dieppe area until 1500hrs and after 1400hrs it was even reinforced. Thereafter gradual decrease in enemy fighter activity.[23]

Thirty minutes after this report was received at GHQ West, von Rundstedt issued new orders that the destroyed and smashed Churchill tanks on the beaches in front of Dieppe be examined immediately. As such a senior staff officer was sent from the HQ to carry out this task.

Final reports were coming into GHQ West regularly from all sections, providing the HQ with a situation update. For example, at 1750hrs Commanding Admiral France advised von Rundstedt's HQ that the port barrier net at Dieppe 'and the port remain intact (though, of course, some damage has been caused by shelling and bombing)'.[24]

Von Rundstedt then sent a report to the High Command Armed Forces/Armed Forces Operations Staff at 1815hrs. This report advised that: 'No armed Englishman remains on this Continent!' It went on to state that:

The 302 Div Arty succeeded at the last moment in sinking three enemy destroyers and two torpedo boats which had come close inshore and several landing craft.

Prisoners 1500, of these 60 Canadian officers. 28 tanks destroyed, some of them American. Precise figures follow. High and bloody losses by the enemy. Initial interrogation of prisoners is being carried out. They were re-loaded at sea onto M-boats. There were Canadian, English, American and Free French. Operations appear as follows: Landing group of 300–400 landing craft, protected by 13–15 cruisers and destroyers and several groups of fighters. Behind that a floating reserve of 6 transports and 3 freighters. Between the continent and England an operational reserve of 26 transports. According to present findings, about 3 brigades and about 30 tanks landed. Our own losses not yet established but within moderate limits.

---

23 This report was sent immediately on to the Army High Command as detailed in the Battle Report of the German Commander-in-Chief West (GHQ Army Group D) on the English Landing Attempt at, and on Both Flanks of Dieppe, 19 August 1942.

24 See the Battle Report of the German Commander-in-Chief West (GHQ Army Group D) on the English Landing Attempt at, and on Both Flanks of Dieppe, 19 August 1942.

813 Arty Troops near Pourville held their strongpoint in close-quarter battle but the guns were blown. Troops had high bloody losses. Harbour of Dieppe intact, ports barrier intact, in front of port entrance one destroyer ('Hunt' class) sunk by fighter bomber. Air Force equipment at Berneval is fit for immediate use. Crew together with Army Coastal Troop 2/770 defended strong point in close-quarter battle.[25]

Finally, at 1945hrs, von Rundstedt's office sent a teletype message out to HQ 81 Corps, HQ 15th Army, Naval Group Command West, 302 Infantry Division, 3rd Air Fleet and Commanding Admiral France that summed up the operations of the entire day:

English, Canadian and American troops undertook in the morning of 19 August 1942 a large planned landing attempt in the area of 81 Army Corps near Dieppe. It was smashed by the brave 302 Div in co-operation with the Air Force, local Reserves, Corps Reserves, part of 10 Pz Div and the coastal artillery committed in that sector.

The enemy has suffered very high bloody losses. He has lost many landing craft, several cruisers, destroyers, torpedo boats and many aircraft. Over 1500 prisoners have been taken.

I wish to express to all commanders and troops who took part my appreciation and thanks. I was able to report today, 'The troops have fought very well.' My thanks also go to the Air Fleet which helped the Division in continuous combat and again and again attacked the enemy at sea, and the members of the Navy who had a battle on the open sea before the landing and those who were committed on land.

Signed Commander in Chief West, von Rundstedt, Field Marshal[26]

---

25   This report was signed personally by Commander in Chief West, Field Marshal von Rundstedt according to the Battle Report of the German Commander-in-Chief West (GHQ Army Group D) on the English Landing Attempt at, and on Both Flanks of Dieppe, 19 August 1942. He ended his report by saying 'Herewith the battle action on land has come to an end.'

26   As noted in von Rundstedt's report on the Dieppe Landings in report of the German Commander-in-Chief West (GHQ Army Group D) on the English Landing Attempt at, and on Both Flanks of Dieppe, 19 August 1942.

Chapter 15

Casualties: Red and White Beaches

In spite of heavy casualties to both personnel and craft, the Navy went in again and again to every beach until it was heard that our men on White and Red Beaches were either killed or overwhelmed, when any further attempts would have been of no avail.[1]

The RHLI originally left England with a complement of 31 officers and 551 other ranks. They lost seven officers and 120 other ranks during the operation, while of the wounded one officer and five other ranks died of their wounds. One officer and nine other ranks, while prisoners of the Germans, died of their wounds. Eight officers and 90 other ranks were prisoners of war. The number of wounded that returned to England included five officers and 103 other ranks. The numbers of wounded who were prisoners of war amounted to seven officers and 69 other ranks, while 49 in total were listed as missing. Total casualties for the RHLI amounted to 30 officers and 449 other ranks, leaving only one officer and 102 other ranks who were not casualties. 'A total of 7 officers and 210 other ranks, or considerably less than half the unit, returned to England after the operation. This unit, it will be noted, had a higher total of its personnel killed than any other except the Royal Regiment of Canada; and it had more officers killed than any other unit.'[2]

Casualties of the Essex Scottish were higher than any other unit. The full complement was 32 officers and 521 other ranks that left England for the operation. Four officers and 75 other ranks were killed, while two other ranks who were wounded died. For those who were prisoners of war (PoWs), one officer and seven other ranks died of their wounds. The total number of

---

1   General Roberts as quoted in Report No. 108, Part II, The Attack on the Main Beaches, Section 280.

2   CMHQ file 18/DIEPPE/2 cited in Report No. 108, Part II, The Attack on the Main Beaches, Section 284.

Essex Scottish who were PoWs included ten officers and 248 other ranks; of those, three officers and 115 other ranks were wounded when captured. The regiment had 17 of all ranks listed as missing. The total number of casualties for the regiment was 30 officers and 501 other ranks. Only two of the officers from the full complement of officers remained on the landing ships.[3]

Not one officer from the Essex Scottish returned to England unwounded. In fact, the only officer who managed to get back to England was Captain D.F. MacRae. His regiment was the Stormont, Dundas and Glengarry Highlanders and he had been attached to the Essex Scottish for the operation. Aside from him, 47 other ranks returned to England, with 27 of them having been wounded.[4]

The number of troops embarked from England from the Canadian Les Fusiliers Mont-Royal included 31 officers and 552 other ranks. Of these, six officers and 83 other ranks died, while five others were listed as missing presumed killed, '5 other ranks died of wounds, and one officer and 3 other ranks died of wounds while prisoners of war'.[5]

The wounded of the regiment included two officers and 51 other ranks, while 229 other ranks and 13 officers were PoWs. Of the prisoners of war, 97 other ranks and five officers were wounded. The regiment's total number of casualties were 487 other ranks and 28 officers, which means that only five officers and 121 other ranks returned from the operation.[6]

Very few of the men of the 14th Canadian Army Tank Battalion managed to return to England. However, this unit also had few casualties. The total number embarked was 385 men and 31 officers. Of these, eight other ranks and one officer were killed and one man died of his wounds while a prisoner, while four other ranks were listed as wounded. As prisoners of war, there were 13 officers and 127 men, with 20 of them wounded. One officer and two other ranks were listed as missing.[7]

---

3   See the War Diary of Essex Scottish, August 1942.

4   CMHQ file 18/DIEPPE/2 cited in Report No. 108, Part II, The Attack on the Main Beaches, Section 285.

5   Report No. 108, Part II, The Attack on the Main Beaches, Section 285.

6   CMHQ file 18/DIEPPE/2 cited in Report No. 108, Part II, The Attack on the Main Beaches, Section 285.

7   The information is from CMHQ as of October 1943 as cited in Report No. 108, Part II, The Attack on the Main Beaches, Section 286.

As we have seen, the third and fourth waves of tanks were never deployed ashore. This added to the total number of men and officers who returned to England from the 14th – 231 other ranks and 14 officers in total.

The Royal Canadian Engineers suffered badly on the beaches. Eleven officers and 306 other ranks were embarked from England. The total number of casualties for the engineers was nine officers and 184 men killed, wounded, missing and in captivity.

Chapter 16

Landing at Blue Beach

The naval statement of the time, then, is probably accurate; but whatever the exact time, the unit was certainly placed upon the beach so late as to make its task far more difficult than it would have been earlier.[1]

On Blue Beach the plan was for the Royal Regiment of Canada (Royals) to land and capture the headland immediately east of Dieppe. For the operation the unit had been code-named 'Doug' and was to land at 0450hrs (Zero hour). However, Blue Beach was flanked on either side by high cliffs and was only 200 yards long. Beyond the beach in a rising gully lay the village of Puys.

Several tasks had been planned for the regiment to carry out. One company was to take out the light anti-aircraft guns situated on the eastern side of the gulley and then advance on the barracks that the Allies believed had once been Les Glycines holiday camp. In this area there were several German machine gun posts and these were to be destroyed. The Germans had placed a heavy anti-aircraft battery near the edge of the cliff west of Puys, which was to be dealt with by a company from the Royals, including a series of light anti-aircraft guns in the same area. The same company was to attack the German marines coast guard house west of Puys and then form up with the Essex Scottish, who should have crossed the harbour from the west. South of the village of Puys was a German four-gun coastal battery that the main body of the battalion was to attack and destroy. They were also to attack machine gun posts and light anti-aircraft positions that were part of the same defensive system in the Puys region. In this area was a gasworks that was also part of the regiment's tasking, which they were supposed to blow up. After that they were then to go into brigade reserve.

---

1   This comes from Report No. 101, The Raid on Dieppe, August 1942, Section 69.

Included with the Royals was one detachment of 4th Field Regiment, Royal Canadian Artillery (part of the 2nd Canadian Infantry Division) and one of 3 Light Anti-Aircraft Regiment, Royal Canadian Artillery. The Royals also included an AA detachment to assist in the capture of German anti-aircraft emplacements and guns on the eastern headland so they could be turned on German ground and air targets for the duration of the operation.

The plan also called for the Field Artillery detachment to be involved in the capture of the four-gun entrenched battery that was, if taken intact, to be used against another German battery south of Dieppe. C Company of the Black Watch of Canada had been seconded to the Royal Regiment for the raid on Dieppe and were under the command of Captain R.C. Hicks. According to the war diary of the Royal Regiment of Canada, the role of the Black Watch was to 'land a little to the east of Puys beach, and perform a left flank protecting role'.[2]

While the Detailed Military Plan does not go into detail regarding this part of the force, it is likely, according to later reports, that they were to head for the Les Glycines area. The two artillery detachments, the Royal Regiment of Canada and the Black Watch detachment, were code-named Edward Force.[3]

HMS *Queen Emma*,[4] a Norwegian liner that had been converted by the British to a troop ship for carrying mostly Commandos, for the Dieppe raid carried the Royal Regiment of Canada and the two artillery detachments. This ship sailed from Portsmouth, as did HMS *Princess Astrid*, a cross-Channel ferry that had been converted into a troop ship. Elements of the Royals were also carried in this ship.

Why go into all of this detail about the role and plan of the Royals? The previous paragraphs outlined what the Royals were supposed to achieve once they had landed on Blue Beach. However, 'In the event, the Royal Regiment and attached troops were quite unable to carry out the tasks assigned to

---

2   From the War Diary of Royal Regiment of Canada dated 19 August 1942, cited in Report No. 101, The Raid on Dieppe, August 1942.

3   From interview with Captain G.A. Browne and the War Diary of the Royal Regiment of Canada, August 1942.

4   See Wikipedia, HMS *Queen Emma*, entry https://en.wikipedia.org/wiki/HMS_Queen_Emma

them; the regiment was shot to pieces on the beach, and no elements of any strength managed to penetrate beyond it.'[5]

This disaster had ramifications for the rest of the operation and was largely because the Royals were late in landing on Blue Beach. Part of that is due to the naval engagement by Group 5 against the German convoy and their subsequent dispersal but, according to the reports, the main reason is the slowness of the flotillas in forming up after they had left the landing ships.

> The boats were lowered promptly and smoothly and according to plan. There was, however, some delay in them forming up owing to an unknown MGB (Motor Gun Boat), almost certainly No. 315, taking station ahead of them in almost the position which our leading MGB 316 had arranged to take. As a result the Flotilla formed up astern of her and it was a little while before they realised that they were in fact astern of the wrong MGB and took station behind their leader MGB 316.[6]

The comments from the Flotilla Officer of HMS *Princess Astrid* are echoed by the comments of his counterpart on the *Queen Emma*. He stated that the craft were lowered into the sea at 0300hrs but that the flotilla did not move off until twenty-five minutes later, which meant that it now had to proceed faster than had been planned. This resulted in the two mechanised landing craft from the *Queen Emma* being unable to keep up with the remainder of the flotilla as they were both loaded up with 100 men and their equipment. These two LCMs, in company with four LCAs astern of them, constituted a second wave, landing later than the rest of the flotilla.

The following is an account of the experiences of the LCMs from Captain J.C.H. Anderson, on the port side of *Queen Emma* in one of the two LCMs.

> Difficulty in forming up never fully overcome, and as the flotilla moved off in line astern, our LCM gradually lost contact until, at shortly after 0400hrs, we were entirely alone.

---

5   See Report No. 101, The Raid on Dieppe, 19 August 1942, Section 61.

6   Report from the Flotilla Officer of HMS *Princess Astrid*, Appendix 3 B to Enclosure No. 13 Report of Naval Force Commander, as cited in Report No. 101, The Raid on Dieppe, August 1942, Section 62.

A short time after this, the LCM developed engine trouble and stopped. As the engine room hatch is in the floor of the craft, it necessitated moving men, 3" mortars and their dollies to allow the stoker to enter the engine room. Within a few minutes the craft again proceeded toward the shore. At the first sight of land it was at once apparent that we were heading directly into the harbour mouth, for a church spire appeared on high ground which could be none other than the east headland. Turning left, we proceeded close in shore to the beach at Puys. From the time that contact with the flotilla was lost until after touchdown, no other craft was sighted to my knowledge. Intense fire was not brought down on us until the landing ramp was dropped. I estimate touchdown at 0530hrs.[7]

The entry in the war diary of the R. Regt. C., dated 19 August 1942, states that the plan was for 'the Battalion to land in two waves, the first wave consisting of "A" ad 'B" Companies and Bn H.Q. Group'.[8] As we have seen previously, the Flotilla Officer of the *Queen Emma* believed that the second wave was made up of two LCMs and four LCAs, which were behind the main flotilla and landed late onto Blue Beach. However, the war diary account may not be accurate as according to the Detailed Plan, *Queen Emma* had five LCAs and carried both C and D Companies of the R. Regt. C.[9] However, to find the most reliable source as to the unit's plan of attack we can turn to Major J.C.H. Anderson:

> The BN was to land in three waves, 1st wave to consist of A, B, and C Coys, C Coy right, A Coy centre and B Coy left. BN HQ Advance Group under the Bn 2 i/c Major G.P. Scholfield, was with this wave, as also were the AMLO's party and the HM's party,

---

7   Report by Major J.C.H. Anderson, comments on draft report 29 May 1943, cited in Report No. 101, The Raid on Dieppe, August 1942, Section 63.

8   See Report No. 101, The Raid on Dieppe, August 1942, Section 64.

9   It appears that Lieutenant Colonel Catto, the Army officer in charge of both companies, was also aboard *Queen Emma*. The war diary account of this part of the operation seems to come from a report from Major P.E.R. Wright that is based on interviews conducted with men in hospital after the raid. These statements are attached to the diary as an Appendix. Thus, it would appear that the war diary entry may be inaccurate.

and were to land between C & A Coys. Second wave to consist of D Coy and Bn HQ under command of Lieutenant Colonel D.T. Catto, and were to land ten minutes after the first wave. A third wave composed of Edward Force, to supply reserve Bren teams and left flank protection after the original assault, were to land ten minutes after the second wave.[10]

Perhaps the most conspicuous object for the approaching fleet of landing craft towards Blue Beach was the mile-wide gap in the cliffs at Dieppe. Acting on this fact, the senior officer of the Blue Beach landings, Lieutenant Commander H.W. Goulding, DSO, RNR, stated that they 'steered for the centre of Red and White beaches as intended until I could recognise the town'.[11] As they approached the men on the landing craft could see the red and green lights on the piers of Dieppe. Reaching a point where they were 2 miles from the town of Dieppe. Goulding steered 'the flotilla towards the beach steering a course to pass 7 cables from the East Pier'.[12] The landing craft were challenged by flash lamp as they passed the pier but no firing broke out and the craft continued on.

The report from the *Princess Astrid* Flotilla Officer stated that they were 17 minutes late and touched down on Blue Beach at 0507hrs. Yet a report from Captain G.A. Browne, who was attached to the R. Regt. C. as the Forward Observation Officer, stated:

> Royals touched down at 0535 hours, as I remember my first message to HMS Garth, 'DOUG TOUCHED DOWN 0535.'[13]

While Captain Browne believed he was 45 minutes late in touching down on Blue Beach he was with the second wave and could only really speak with first-hand knowledge of 'C' and 'D' Companies. Looking at the timings, it

---

10   Report by Major J.C.H. Anderson, 29 May 1943, cited in Report No. 101, The Raid on Dieppe, August 1942.

11   Report No. 101, The Raid on Dieppe, August 1942; at this point, having recognised Red and White beaches they would have then changed course and headed for their touchdown points on Blue Beach.

12   Report of Lieutenant Commander Goulding, Appx 6 to Enclosure No. 13, Report of Naval Force Commander.

13   See Report No. 101, The Raid on Dieppe, August 1942, paragraph 67.

is clear that the time he states in his quote above was the same time as the second wave touched down. Evidently, he had not realised that there was a long period of time between the first and second wave and he later stated that he had no idea that his group was not one of the first to touch down on Blue Beach.

The actual time of the first-wave touchdown of the Royals on Blue Beach was approximately 0530hrs, according to the war diary. This estimate may have been based on one of the statements taken later in England by Major Wright of a man in hospital who estimated the touchdown as around that time. However, the estimates from reports and other sources do vary. Whatever the exact time, the Royals were on Blue Beach much later than the planned 0450hrs, where they would have been under the cover of darkness. As a result, when they did land they were, to all intents and purposes, landing in the early morning light where defensive obstacles that littered the shore at Puys could be clearly seen as they approached.[14] Because they were late, they lost the element of surprise and were spotted by German observers and under fire before they landed.

The Germans opened fire when the landing craft were about 100 yards from the beach. They were using small automatic weapons firing 6mm calibre armour-piercing bullets. Major Scholfield of R. Regt. C. was slightly wounded before landing, as was a naval officer.[15]

The moment the assault landing craft touched down and lowered their ramps onto the beaches, the German heavy machine guns opened up. Almost immediately the Allies suffered heavy casualties as the troops tried to disembark onto the beaches. 'In several cases officers and men were wounded or killed on the ramp as they made to leave the boats.'[16]

A message was received at German GHQ West stating that:

> Observation posts of divisional artillery observed enemy ships in the front of Puys. Third battery 302nd Artillery Regiment laid down defensive fire in front of Puys.

---

14 This is borne out by Corporal Ellis of A Coy, who stated that objects could be clearly seen a half a mile out from the beach, cited in Report No. 101, The Raid on Dieppe, August 1942.

15 Report from the Flotilla Officer of the *Princess Astrid*.

16 Report No. 101, The Raid on Dieppe, August 1942, Report from the *Princess Astrid* Flotilla Officer, Section 71.

Third battery 302 Artillery Regiment observes large number of enemy ships heading for Pourville. Heavy defensive fire by two artillery troops directed to that area, situation report transmitted by wireless to GHQ West as telephone communications disrupted as the lines destroyed.[17]

At Puys there was a large sea wall approximately 12ft high at the head of the beach. It was covered with heavy wire and on the landward side there was a deep and thick tangle of wire that would be difficult to cross. The Germans had built several pillboxes along the wall as part of their defensive strategy. However, not all of them were manned. According to Corporal Ellis of the Royals, the only man to cross the sea wall and return to England, the pillbox on the western section of the wall he found to be empty. 'The evidence of this NCO indicated that the enemy was not in strength on the western side of the gully, for he found several minor prepared positions here empty. He believed, however, that at least one house on the western side overlooking the beach was held by the enemy.'[18]

According to the reports, the Allies believed the main German defences were concentrated on the eastern side of the gulley that ran down to the beach. In particular, the Germans had fortified a large house that sat on the cliffs. This house was clearly seen in air photographs and in pre-war photos.[19] Eyewitness accounts from Allied soldiers suggest that this house must have had several automatic weapons stations and 'other houses may have been similarly equipped'.[20]

There was a big house just back from the wall, and there seemed to be a machine gun firing from every window.[21]

---

17   See 302 Infantry Division Report.

18   Report No. 101, The Raid on Dieppe, August 1942, Para 72 based on the interview of Corporal Ellis, Report No 89, Canadian Military History Section 72.

19   See 'G' War Diary, H.Q. 2 Canadian Division, August 1942, Appx 59. The pre-war photos can be seen in Combined Operations Report C.B.04244 (held at the National Archives in Kew).

20   See Report No. 101, The Raid on Dieppe, August 1942, Section 72.

21   Private J.E. Creer, B068191, 'A' Coy, the Royals, cited in Report No. 101, The Raid on Dieppe, August 1942, Section 72.

In one of the LCMs that beached with the second wave, Private J. Murphy stated that:

> I first fired into the house on the right when Corporal Ruggles 'B' Coy shouted to look at the house on the left. I saw fire from this one and fired into each of the windows of the first floor. I think each floor had six windows. By the time I would get to the sixth window the first one would open up again.[22]

Approximately 50 yards back from the sea wall and parallel to it was 'the house on the right', which is believed to be the large light-coloured building that was prominent on many of the aerial photographs. This may be the house referred to by Private Creer. If it was, it had three rows of nine windows that faced the beach. 'It may however have been less strongly held than the house on the left, which was well placed to enfilade the beach.'[23]

The Germans had a large supply of mortars of varying sizes that were well concealed and these units opened up on the troops as they came ashore. The Canadians on Blue Beach found themselves under heavy mortar fire and very soon after that the Germans began firing their light artillery guns in support of the mortars. These were in addition to the fire from the heavier coastal guns in higher positions not far from the beaches that had also opened up on the Royals.

> The DF fire of the German artillery (as I was later told by a German soldier, 75-mm Infantry guns) was apparently extremely well surveyed, for the shells burst precisely at the water-line at impeccably correct intervals and timing. I saw two ALCs sunk by hits or splinters from this fire. From a Gunner's point of view, it was admirable shooting.[24]

---

22   Private J Murphy, B–67330, Report No. 101, The Raid on Dieppe, August 1942, Section 72.

23   See Report No. 101, The Raid on Dieppe, August 1942, Section 72.

24   This quote is from Captain Browne as cited in Report No. 101, The Raid on Dieppe, August 1942, Section 73.

Apart from the houses, the Germans had concealed their defensive positions very well. According to the report by Corporal Ellis, who spent more than an hour on the shore and engaged a German machine gun post next to an empty pillbox, he did not see a single German soldier on the beach.

> The beach was plainly visible to the Germans, whose own fire positions were extraordinarily well concealed from our view. The ROYALS were shot down in heaps on the beach without knowing where the fire was coming from.[25]

The men who escaped the killing zone of the ramps on the landing craft as they came ashore managed to move up the beach and shelter at the lee side of the sea wall. While they were protected from the machine gun fire coming from the houses, they were not protected against the mortar fire. Indeed, in his report, Corporal Ellis maintained that the sea wall where the men had taken shelter was enfiladed by machine gun fire situated on high ground east of their position. The result was very heavy casualties among the men sheltering along the sea wall.

Those sheltering men tried to cut or blow passages through the wire obstacles on the sea wall. By doing so, they would be able to reach the German defensive positions and stop the deadly fire raining down on them and on the landing craft. Remember that this was still the first wave and the second wave had yet to arrive.

Several Bangalore torpedoes were fired at the top of the wall to try to break through the obstacles. From Corporal Ellis's account we know that he assisted the commander of A Coy, Captain G.G. Sinclair, in 'laying and firing' a Bangalore torpedo at a recess at the western end of the sea wall that had two flights of stairs and provided some cover from the ferocious German defensive fire. Once the gap had been made, Corporal Ellis pushed through and 'went up the hill to the right'. Captain Sinclair was killed when he tried to lead an attack through this passage. At the top of the hill, Corporal Ellis came across a soldier who had been with him when the Bangalore torpedo had been blown.[26]

---

25   Ibid., Section 74.

26   Report No. 101, The Raid on Dieppe, August 1942, Section 76; Note the other soldier might have been Captain Sinclair's Batman.

When Major Wright conducted his interviews and collected statements from the men in hospital who had survived the Dieppe Raid and managed to get back to England he found two versions of the actions of Lieutenant W.G.R. Wedd from different individuals. This lieutenant acted with considerable gallantry. The men in the hospital told Major Wright that after a Bangalore had blown a gap in the eastern end of the sea wall, Wedd led the remains of his platoon, only ten men, through this gap and was never seen again. However, a different account was told to Captain Browne by officers who had survived the operation and ended up as PoWs and was later told to Major Wright after the war:

> Leaving the ALC at touchdown with his platoon, Lt Wedd reached the wall with little more than a section, and there found he was still being fired upon by one of the wall posts, a pillbox. There being apparently another way of attacking the weapon, he left his corner of relative shelter and sprinted the short distance directly toward the pill-box with a M36 grenade. With complete disregard for his own safety, and displaying great skill, he flung the grenade through the fire slit of the pill-box, killing all its occupants and putting the gun out of action. His body, riddled with bullets, was later picked up in front of the pillbox. I could not myself witness this act from my position farther WEST on the beach, but it was verified later at VERNEUIL by Officers of the Battalion who had seen it and spoke of it.[27]

27　Quote From Captain Browne, Report No. 89, the Operation at Dieppe, 19 August 1942, Personal Stories of Participants, cited in Report No. 101, The Raid on Dieppe, August 1942, Section 77.

Chapter 17

Blue Beach Second and Third Waves

The second wave landed on Blue Beach later than intended, as reported by *Queen Emma*'s Flotilla Officer:

> The landing was not affected until 0525hrs owing to the fact that the craft had travelled a mile or so to the westwards of Dieppe and had to retrace their path.[1]

Indeed, the actual time when the second wave touched down could be said to be somewhere between 0525hrs and 0535hrs.[2]

Two Support Landing Craft, LCS 25 and LCS 8, supported the second wave's approach using their light weapons that delivered 'close and spirited fire in reply to the beach defences from almost point blank range'.[3] At the same time, Allied aircraft bombed and strafed the German positions on the cliffs above the beaches as well as laying down a smokescreen.[4] By the time of the second wave run in the smoke 'laid by the RAF had almost entirely disappeared, traces only remaining in the treetops above the beach'.

Morale among the men of the Royals in the landing craft was cool and steady, as Captain Browne reports:

---

1   See Report No. 101, The Raid on Dieppe, August 1942, Section 78.

2   The Flotilla Officer from *Princess Astrid* states that the second wave was seen approaching the beach around 0530hrs, while Lieutenant Commander Goulding states it was 0528hrs and Captain Browne 0535hrs.

3   This quote is from a report by Lieutenant Commander Goulding, as cited in Report No. 101, The Raid on Dieppe, August 1942, Section 79.

4   The smokescreen as laid down by allied aircraft was seen by Lieutenant Commander Goulding and the *Princess Beatrix* Flotilla Officer. Both reports indicate that the first wave was withdrawing as this air attack took place and both state that the bombs appeared to fall on the beach, which supports the notion that this was the smoke-laying attack originally planned for 0510hrs.

It was their first experience under fire, and although I watched them closely, they gave no sign of alarm, although first light was broadening into dawn, and the interior of the LCA was illuminated by the many flares from the beach and the flash of the Bostons' bombs. The quiet steady voice of Captain Thompson, seated just behind me, held the troops up to a confident and offensive spirit, although shells were whizzing over the craft and (they) could hear the steady whisper and crackle of SA fire over the top of the LCA At the instant of touchdown, small arms fire was striking the LCA, and here there was a not unnatural split-second hesitation in the bow in leaping out onto the beach. But only a split-second. The troops go out onto the beach as fast as (in) any of the SIMMER exercises, and go across the beach to the wall and under the cliff.[5]

Canadian Press correspondent Ross Munro was in the same landing craft as Captain J.C.H. Anderson and as the second wave ran into shore they could see the beach was 'dotted with the fallen forms of men in battle-dress'.[6] On the far right of the beach, C and D companies of The Royals were, by this time, landed. The Commanding Officer's party from D Company found themselves 'in a sort of re-entrant on the western side of a spur of the cliff just beyond the west end of the sea-wall, and C Coy being on D Company's left and opposite the west end of the wall'.[7]

Murderous German fire greeted the occupants of the landing craft as they touched down on the beach. Munro's article in the *Glasgow Herald* stated that 'vicious bursts of yellow tracers from German machine guns made veritable curtain about the craft, and bullets clanged against its armour'.[8]

As soon as the ramp at the bow of our boat fell fifteen Royals rushed the beach and sprinted up the slope, taking cover along the Cliffside. Machine-gun fire held back the rest.[9]

---

5   Report No. 101, The Raid on Dieppe, August 1942, Section 80.

6   The first of Munro's articles that appeared in the *Glasgow Herald*, 21 August 1942.

7   Quote From Captain Browne, Report No. 89, the Operation at Dieppe, 19 August 1942, Personal Stories of Participants, cited in Report No. 101, The Raid on Dieppe, August 1942, Section 81.

8   Munro's first article that appeared in the *Glasgow Herald* dated 21 August 1942.

9   This quote is from the article by Munro that was published in the *Globe and Mail*, Toronto, 22 August 1942.

Under the heavy fire the Canadians suffered many casualties. In the LCM carrying Munro the German fire was replied to by Captain Anderson, Corporal Ruggles and many others. Over many of the wounded and dead men, Corporal Ruggles slowly worked his way forward to the bow of the craft, stopping to fire at the German positions within his range. When he finally reached the ramp, to his surprise he realised that the craft was beginning to withdraw from the beach. 'As we were backing out, I had a brief glimpse of the men crouched against the cliff, or wall, and many others lying on the beach and some in the water.'[10]

A later study of personal accounts, unit files and diaries and reports indicated that a large proportion of the Royals that returned to England were passengers in this single LCM. 'Among them was Captain Anderson, one of the two officers to return, who was wounded while firing at the enemy from the boat and collapsed across Mr. Munro's legs.'[11]

As an aside to the arrival of the second wave, several of the wounded from the first wave were taken off the beach by the landing craft from the second wave. This is backed up by some of the statements made to Major Wright, who interviewed wounded soldiers in hospital in England after the raid. For example, Private Creer stated 'some officer shouted to us on the beach that it was hopeless. He said if you can get back in the boats do so.'[12]

Behind the second wave assaulting Blue Beach came the Black Watch component of Edward Force, or what could be called the third wave. This was commanded by Captain Hicks of the Duke of Wellington Regiment. Personnel from the Royal Canadian Naval Reserve almost exclusively manned the landing craft of this flotilla, which was made up of six LCAs. One of these, however, was empty because of the casualties suffered by the Black Watch in the grenade accident and another one, which had been fitted with a mortar and was intended to land at Blue Beach, was redirected to Red Beach, where it landed.[13]

---

10 This quote is from the personal account by Corporal Ruggles as cited in Report No. 101, The Raid on Dieppe, August 1942, Section 82.

11 This quote is from Report No. 101, The Raid on Dieppe, 19 August 1942, but the information contained in the report was originally from the article by Munro that was subsequently published in the *Globe and Mail*, Toronto, 22 August 1942.

12 Report No. 101, The Raid on Dieppe, August 1942, Section 83.

13 This information comes from a report by Captain Hicks in collaboration with the surviving boat officers of his LCA as cited in Report No. 101, The Raid on Dieppe, 19 August 1942, Section 84.

According to the original plan, this third wave was supposed to be called in to land by those already on the beach if needed. However, no such signal came from the already landed troops. By 0525hrs this third wave, Edward Force, was sailing a mile from Blue Beach and parallel to it. So a decision had to be made to land the troops or not and 'this was made jointly by the Flotilla Officer and Officer Commanding Troops'.[14] The Black Watch were then landed in the same place where the main body of survivors from the first two waves were gathered, under the cliff to the west of the sea wall. The survivors of the previous two waves had set up Bren guns among the rocks on the gullies and beaches and were firing up to the German positions in the house on the eastern cliff. German troops could be seen by naval craft on the west cliff as well and were engaged by these craft.

> In the centre part of the Beach it was observed that about thirty of the troops from the first landing were apparently casualties. To the westward side of the Beach up against the base of the cliffs, the main body of the First landing of troops were heavily engaged firing up to the enemy on the cliff-top also against enemy positions in houses half way up the cliffs to the East.[15]
>
> At 0545 our four Craft touched down at the Westward end of the Beach and close to the Main Body of Troops; all troops borne were successfully landed.[16]

In his personal account Captain Browne confirms the above accounts, writing that: 'Edward Force and the Prize Troop RCA, the detachment of 4 Canadian Field Regiment, were landed a hundred yards or more farther WEST down the beach than D Coy and the CO's party.'[17]

---

14 This quote is from the report by Lieutenant J.E. Koyle, RCNVR senior Boat Officer, as cited in Report No. 101, The Raid on Dieppe, 19 August 1942, Section 85.

15 This quote is from the Commanding Officer, Duke of Wellington, as cited in Report No. 101, The Raid on Dieppe, 19 August 1942, Section 85

16 Also, from the Commanding Officer Duke of Wellington's Report.

17 See Report No. 101, The Raid on Dieppe, 19 August 1942, Section 86. Captain Browne refers to the Prize Troop, whose role was to capture enemy guns and either destroy them or use them to support the landings. The term was an analogy of a naval 'prize crew'.

The only men of the Black Watch unit that returned to England on the day of the operation were the casualties from the grenade accident, disembarked before the expedition sailed; as well as two men who went ashore in charge of these casualties and one private who wrenched his ankle landing on Blue Beach and was taken back on board the landing craft.[18]

The rest were taken prisoners of war with the exception of Lieutenant Jack Colson, who was killed on the beach.

> I was right beside Jack Colson when he got his – a burst of machine gun fire right through the eyes and head . . . Except for poor Jack, the BW didn't lose a man! – but we had a few wounded. As you know by now, they were certainly waiting for us – and they really gave us the works.[19]

According to the reports there appears to have been one LCA running in that was carrying stores and may have come in on its own. The craft became mixed with the Essex Scottish at Red Beach and instead of landing there sailed along the coast to Puys.

> Other boats of the RRC could not be seen but they had evidently landed. Beach was strewn with bodies in and out of water and up to the wall. Men arriving at wall were trapped as beyond wall and also the beach side was swept by the MG and sniper fire. Those near the wall were being treated to grenades dropped from the cliff above or mortar fire.[20]

This craft managed to land a single load of ammunition and took on some wounded men before pulling away with four gunners still on board.

---

18   This was Private O'Toole, D-82705, War Diary, RHC, 20 August 1942, Private O'Toole's statement Appx 12 August 1942.

19   This quote is from a letter from a PoW camp in France dated 24 August 1942 signed by someone named 'Mark' who is believed to be Lieutenant M.G. Mather, RHC and is held at the National Archives.

20   This quote is from the four men of the store-carrying LCA that observed the situation at Blue Beach near Puys as cited in Report No. 101, The Raid on Dieppe, 19 August 1942, Section 88. This is also referenced in 3 Canadian LAA Regiment's War Diary, Appx 6, August 1942.

At this point it is worth looking at the actions of the 3in mortars of the Royal Regiment because some of the reports indicate there is a connection to this single LCA. Referring to Captain Browne's personal account, he states that 'the Battalion's 3-in mortars were never fired, and scarcely set up, two crews in quick succession being shot down at them, until I think, there were no more mortar personnel left'.[21]

The men who returned in this single LCA (also referred to as an LCM) indicated that there were two detachments of mortar crews carried by the craft but that they were both lost in deep water while they were trying to land under heavy German fire.

However, it does appear that the Royals managed to get a mortar set up at the edge of the beach a little while after the second wave had touched down. It also appears that some bombs were fired:

> It was then that Sgt Peaks of B Coy went after the 3" mortars. The mortar section had been wiped out.
>
> An SLC that was laying off shore had just laid a heavy smoke-screen so Sgt. Peaks took advantage of it and got the mortar set up. I couldn't make out who helped him on account of the smoke but here were three others. They didn't get many more than three bombs away when Jerry found them with his machine-gun and they were cut to pieces.[22]

This incident is confirmed in a statement from Corporal Jackson of B Company during the interviews carried out by Major Wright. Jackson told Wright that after the second wave came in, he saw an NCO set up a 3in mortar at the water's edge under heavy German fire. It fired around fifteen bombs 'before the enemy machine guns got the range and killed the whole mortar crew'.[23]

---

21 Browne referred to the information in this quote as being from what he'd been told by the Royal Regiment of Canada's mortar officer.

22 From an account by Private M. Hamilton, C Coy, who presumably saw this from the single LCA as cited in Report No. 101, The Raid on Dieppe, 19 August 1942, Section 86.

23 It is likely that this is the same incident as mentioned by Private Hamilton and we are assuming that the NCO identified is Sergeant Peaks, who was killed in this action.

The landings on Blue Beach were supported by HMS *Garth*, a destroyer, which began its initial offshore bombardment at 0512 to 0519hrs on German positions overlooking the main beaches at Dieppe itself. It then shifted its fire to the eastern part of the harbour, at the harbour's head and stopped this initial bombardment at 0535hrs. From there, it steamed towards the cliff west of Blue Beach, where it began pounding German batteries on top of the cliffs. Its targets shifted again at 0610hrs to the German defensive positions on the east side of the harbour entrance at Dieppe. Thirty-five minutes later it began pounding the batteries on the east cliff again as often as it could, the opportunity permitting. At this point HMS *Garth* became engaged in a duel with the German gun batteries west of Puys:

> I found throughout that their fire was extremely accurate and it was impossible to go in and carry out a steady bombardment.
>
> It was a matter of going in through the smoke till close, squaring off and then retiring, then circling round and repeating the manoeuvre. On each occasion we were straddled and it seems extraordinary that more ships were not hit.
>
> I was in touch with the FOO 2 from 0541 to 0747, during which time he was held up at the foot of the cliff and most messages received concerned wounded and the fact that they were held up, which were passed to HMS Calpe. He called for fire at a white house on the cliff top, which we answered, but I regret did not hit. He was not in a position to spot and all we could see were the shorts on the cliff face.[24]

Also adding to the offshore bombardment was SGB8 (Support Gun Boat 8) but its support was nowhere near as good as HMS *Garth*'s was. A signal had been sent from the shore to SGB8 asking for support shortly after the landing on Blue Beach but the reply that came back from the craft was that it had to cover its primary task, which was the 'warning and cover against surface attack from the westward of Dieppe'.[25] While this information comes

---

24   This quote is from HMS *Garth*'s Commanding Officer, Appendix 23 to Enclosure No. 13, Report of Naval Force Commander, as cited in Report No. 101, The Raid on Dieppe, 19 August 1942, Section 86.

25   This quote is from Lieutenant Commander Goulding's report as cited in Report No. 101, The Raid on Dieppe, 19 August 1942, Section 93.

from Lieutenant Commander Goulding, the After Action Report from SGB8 claimed that it had 'led the landing craft at the rear of Group 3, which had become separated from MGB 316 towards Blue Beach until she saw they were headed in the right direction'.[26] From there, according to the report, it remained about 1,000 yards off Blue Beach until 0540hrs.

> Owing to the extremely confused situation on shore I was unable to give fire support without the risk of hitting our own troops. At 0540 I left the vicinity of Blue Beach to carry out Task I, at that time being under fairly heavy fire from small calibre guns.[27]

However, after completing Task 1, SGB8 returned to Blue Beach and ran about 700 yards into the shore, where it 'opened up on a field gun emplacement, radio aerials and snipers on the cliffs, some hits being scored'.[28] It kept up this bombardment until 1210hrs, by which time all the Canadian troops on the beach had been killed, wounded or taken prisoner.

Captain Browne managed to get off the beach not long after 0610hrs and moved inland with Lieutenant Colonel Catto's group of officers and men. They did this by cutting a path through the barbed wire defences erected by the Germans at the western end of the sea wall. At this point no Bangalore torpedoes were available to them so they used wired cutters to get through.[29] The reports indicate that the path through the barbed wire was cut by the colonel, Sergeant Coles and two other men.[30]

Also, at 0610hrs German C-in-C West received a message from the Puys theatre that stated:

---

26 Ibid.

27 From the War Diary of SGB8 as cited in Report No. 101, The Raid on Dieppe, 19 August 1942, Section 93

28 Ibid.

29 The Bangalores assigned to D Coy had been lost over the side of the landing craft and the men of C Coy who looked after the Bangalores had been shot to pieces when they touched down on the beach.

30 Browne wrote in his report that the party was made up of 'Lt Col Catto, Captain J.G. Housser, Lieutenant Y.S. Ryerson and Lieutenant T.L. Taylor of the Royals along with Sergeant E.F. Coles and eleven other men of this unit; and Captain Browne himself with Lieutenant J.D. McFetridge, RCA and three of his men of 3 Cdn Lt AA Regt.'

British landing craft on the beaches near Puys. One of the landing craft was destroyed by anti-tank guns and the attack has failed.[31]

Shortly after the men got through the gap they had cut the Germans set up a machine gun post trained on the gap itself to stop further incursions and no other Allied soldier was able to follow Lieutenant Colonel Catto's party. 'The Colonel and his small party were now cut off from the remainder of C and D Company's (Coys) on the beach. It was now nearly 0700hrs British time.'[32]

Above the west end of the sea wall, at the top of the hill, the party came across two houses, which they quickly cleared after German fire came from the first house.

> Sounds of firing on the left flank had now died completely away. From the centre and the right flank we could hear intermittent bursts of German automatic fire and the steady detonations of their mortar bombs. From this we inferred that A and B Coys had been knocked out, and that the survivors of C and D Coys were still pinned down in the angle of the cliff, being cut up by mortars. We discovered that we could not get back to the beach, nor could we get back to the cliff edge because of LMG fire from the left flank, up on the hill-side.[33]

The men moved slowly westward along the clifftop, trying to avoid a strong German patrol advancing from the fortified house. Their aim was to meet up with the Essex Scottish. They decided to move west and then south to the main road between Puys and Notre-Dame-de-Bon-Secours. As they moved, they stayed hidden as much as they could and in the cover of the woods they could see from their location that they were just east of the six-gun 88mm battery that had been one of the objectives of the Royals.

---

31   See Report of 302 German Infantry Division, Operations Section -1a, on the Dieppe Raid, Appendix B.

32   See Captain Browne's report as cited in Report No. 101, The Raid on Dieppe, 19 August 1942, Section 96.

33   Ibid., section 96.

The 88mm Battery of 6 guns on the cliff top between ND de Bon Secours and Puys served its guns magnificently. It was low-level-bombed at least four times and machine gunned oftener by our fighters after 1000hrs, that is, between 1000hrs and 1600hrs, with us as witnesses, and mean time the guns were back in action within a matter of a few seconds, firing up the departing aircraft. Once, after a low-level attack, only two guns were instantly back in action, the other times always at least four.[34]

At this time Colonel Catto decided a reconnaissance of their situation was in order. They discovered that the beaches could not be seen from the clifftops near their location. Using the roads as well was out of the question as the Germans had those in the area covered by machine guns. The final straw was that they could see no sign of any ships so they realised they were trapped and decided to surrender.

The situation suggested that we were trapped. After long consideration the decision was taken to surrender. We surrendered at 1620hrs.[35]

After the failure of the Royals to achieve their objectives, at roughly 1000hrs, von Rundstedt's HQ C–in–C West had received a report via telephone that Puys was once again in German hands.

More than 500 Allied soldiers had been killed or taken prisoner. There was no longer any danger of Allied incursions or attacks in the area even if there were more enemy landings. The Regiment (571 Infantry Regiment) had suffered no stoppages or losses of heavy weapons.[36]

Immediately afterwards, von Rundstedt issued another situation analysis:

---

34   Ibid., section 97.

35   Ibid., section 98.

36   See Report of 302 German Infantry Division, Operations Section -1a, on the Dieppe Raid, Appendix B.

The enemy picture clears up. Although enemy landing attempts still continue, 302 Inf Div has already started to counterattack with reserves. While the heights on both sides of Dieppe remain firmly in our hands, little can as yet be said about the situation in Dieppe proper. Further to the West, near Pourville, landings still seem to continue. At any rate, ships are moving to and from the beach at that point. Situation at Quiberville unclear, it has not yet been established whether Quiberville itself has been attacked at all. Enemy landing attempt at St. Aubin still possible.

On the basis of the above appreciation of the situation, which indicates that the enemy is landing in considerable strength having committed at least two brigades, and possibly a whole division; and because further developments are still uncertain, C-in-C decides to commit 10 Pz Division. That order stated that: 10 Pz Div will be placed under command of General Kuntzen (HQ 81 Corps) to clean up the situation at Dieppe immediately. 10 Pz Div can move vanguard at 1000hrs, main force at 1100hrs.[37]

Situation at Puys Northeast of Dieppe also cleared up. 302 Div reports approximately 500 enemy casualties or prisoners. High ground on either side of Dieppe in our hands as well as East height at Pourville; the English are on the West height. 813 Troop near St. Marguerite was taken and is now recaptured. They are again firing with two guns.[38]

On the beach the remaining Allied troops who had been bombarded by mortar bombs, 75mm infantry guns on top of the cliffs, stick grenades thrown down on to them from the clifftops and machine guns from positions they could not reach, surrendered. Over half the men on the beach had been killed and the rest were wounded. It is doubtful if there were many men on that beach that day who did not suffer some sort of wound. Captain Browne wrote in his report that from their hiding point in the woods they heard the

---

37   This order to 10 Panzer Division came in by telephone from HQ 15th Army at 0947hrs, by 10 Pz Div at 0951hrs and by HQ 91 Corps at 0954hrs.

38   This situation report was sent by CGS 81 Corps to GHQ West at 1003hrs outlining the events that had taken place up to that point.

survivors of Blue Beach landings being marched past as prisoners of war shortly after 1000hrs.

Throughout the bombardment Gunner H.J. Rowe had been clinging to a capsized landing craft not far from the beach. 'Once the firing had died down the Germans came down with stretchers and started clearing the beaches,' he wrote.[39]

> He was with a corporal who organised a small party to attempt to get up the cliff. As soon as they came into the open three were killed and Gnr. Rowe was wounded . . . He saw a captain and a party try to scale the cliff. All of the party were knocked out and the captain alone got half way up the cliff and then his body came rolling down.[40]

By 1130hrs all the Allied attacks that had taken place at Puys had been beaten back by the German defensive forces.[41]

---

39 Report from Gunner Rowe in his statement to Major Wright as cited in Report No. 101, The Raid on Dieppe, 19 August 1942, Section 100.

40 Report No. 101, The Raid on Dieppe, August 1942, Section 101; this is from Major Wright's interviews. In this case, he is referring to Gunner Rowe.

41 See Report of 302 German Infantry Division, Operations Section -1a, on the Dieppe Raid, Appendix B.

Chapter 18

Withdrawal From Blue Beach

The withdrawal attempts from Blue Beach were a mess. Conflicting reports from different sources tell a sad and confused story. This begins with LCA209 from *Queen Emma*'s flotilla, which tried to evacuate the remaining soldiers on the beach at around 0600hrs. The differing witness statements make it difficult to pinpoint an accurate time. The *Queen Emma*'s Flotilla Officer states that they received a signal from Blue Beach asking for the evacuation of the beach party at 0700hrs.

> LCS8, which was still patrolling off the beach, and LCA 209 were the only craft to pick up this message and the LCA went in under cover of the LCS. Upon reaching the beach the boat was swamped with soldiers and forced to retire. Very heavy fire was encountered and many of the soldiers were killed or wounded. Owing to the jam and excess of personnel in the boat it was impossible for the doors to be closed up, and a fair amount of water was shipped. When the craft was about fifty yards from the beach, she was hit with some heavy guns and capsized. The enemy still continued firing and as far as is known only two of the crew and one soldier were saved from the boat.[1]

The Flotilla Officer from the *Princess Astrid* describes the same incident but states that it was after the craft from the second wave had disembarked their troops and withdrawn back to *Astrid*'s flotilla.

> Lieutenant Ramsey, RNVR, who had been the last to disembark troops on Blue Beach, returned to the beach and was seen to touch down. His boat 'broached to' and was subsequently pushed off

---

1   See Report No. 101, The Raid on Dieppe, 19 August 1942, Section 115.

from the shore only to be overturned by 'a burst of gunfire.' Men in the water were seen to be picked off by snipers.[2]

Lieutenant Goulding states that he received the request for evacuation at 0545hrs and of the incident with LCA209 states that it was 'heavily shelled, cannon-fired, swamped and overturned'.

Other reports come from wounded soldiers in hospital interviewed by Major Wright, including Gunner Rowe, Corporal Ellis and Captain Browne, all of whom provided differing details of the same incident. Private E.J. Simpson, HQ Coy Royal Regiment of Canada, stated:

> Later an AL craft landed on the beach and orders were given to board her. There was a terrible scramble and nearly everyone (still alive) made for the small ramp doors. The slaughter was awful. The boat had to be pushed off the beach. It was so full of holes it began to sink. At that time, I would venture to say at least fifty men were aboard. Bullets were still pouring in and a bomb landed alongside. It turned over on its keel and stayed afloat. A few men swam away, while others and myself clung to the still floating craft. We were only about a hundred yards from the shore and were still being blasted by enemy fire. From what I saw, there was no life on the beach.[3]

Gunner Rowe's account adds to the detail. He stated in the war diary regarding the men clinging to the boat that:

> If anybody on shore or was 100yards off shore moved the slightest bit, the move was rewarded with a sniper's bullet. The chap clinging next to him was hit three times immediately after moving from the pain of his wounds.[4]

---

2   Report by Lieutenant Commander Goulding, Report No. 101, The Raid on Dieppe, 19 August 1942, Section 115.

3   See Report No. 101, The Raid on Dieppe, 19 August 1942, Section 117.

4   This passage comes from the War Diary of 3 Canadian LAA Regiment, August 1942, Appx 6.

At the top of the cliff Corporal Ellis saw this LCA and managed to get back down to the beach, where he was able to help push it off. When it capsized he began to swim out towards it, which is when his watch stopped at 0630hrs. Captain Browne had witnessed the same incident before he left the beach around 0700hrs. This puts the time in the statement by the *Queen Emma*'s Flotilla Officer as being an hour or so late. Of the rush to get aboard the LCA, Captain Browne said 'it was the only instance suggestive of panic that I saw or heard on Blue Beach'.[5]

Once the LCA capsized some of the men swam away from it, such as Sergeant J.E. Legate, while the rest clung to it to await rescue, which happened four hours later.

Commander D.B. Wyburd's report stated that LCP(L)s were ordered to move from Green beach to Yellow beach around 0950hrs to evacuate the troops trapped there. These craft closed on what they thought was Yellow 1 Beach around 1005hrs but actually turned out to be Blue Beach. Sub Lieutenant J.E. Boak, RCNVR, who was commanding LCP (L) 19, stated that as the unarmoured landing craft approached the shore they were hit with a storm of artillery fire, mortars and machine guns from the German defenders. Boak stated that along with sub-lieutenants J.E. O'Rourke and W.R. Sinclair, they could see the men clinging to the capsized LCA (which they referred to as a raft).

> As LCP(L) 19 passed close to the LCA, her crew shouted to the soldiers to jump, and four of them caught hold of ropes trailing from the boat. Three of these men were pulled into the LCP(L); but the fourth dropped off and was presumably drowned. Another boat believed to have been LCP(L) 80, commanded by Sub-Lieutenant B Franklin RNVR, picked up the rest of the men on the LCA but this act of gallantry cost the lives of two of his crew and Mr Franklin himself was wounded.[6]

According to Mr Boak's statement made after the operation, the men saved by him and his crew were Private L.W. Roberts and Private J.N. Wallace

---

5   Ibid.

6   Report of Naval Force Commander, Appendix 7 to Enclosure No. 13, as cited in Report No. 101, The Raid on Dieppe, 19 August 1942, Section 120.

and Private Simpson. The fourth man who fell off the ropes into the sea was Private Armstrong. All three were from the Royals.[7]

The Naval Force Commander ordered an attempt at evacuating Blue Beach but this produced no results. Timings are difficult here as they had not been recorded accurately. Lieutenant Commander Goulding stated that once the evacuation order had been received he relayed those orders to ML291. With this craft, several LCAs and an LCS that had a jammed turret they headed towards Blue Beach. Goulding wrote that 'the beach itself was not visible, but the silhouette of the valley above the fog was quite plain'. Once this little flotilla was abeam of the beach Goulding asked the commander of MB291 to fire on the White House with his 2pdr gun, which was done as the opportunity arose:

> With the exception of 2 LCAs, I ordered Landing craft to stay where they were, and led the two LCAs in towards the beach. After proceeding about 100 yards, fire opened up from the shore on a very heavy scale of all types of weapons, and it was quite impossible to proceed further without some fire support. The ML did not exchange (return?) the shots.[8]

There is a differing account of the above incident by Lieutenant Commander C.W. McMullen RN, who was in ML291. Earlier, he had been in the landing craft going into White Beach and had supported them there when the order to help Lieutenant Commander Goulding evacuate the troops on Blue Beach came in. McMullen stated that ML291 proceeded towards Blue Beach followed by an LCM and four LCAs.

> When in a position I reckoned to be east of Blue Beach I closed the land until I could just see the cliffs above me at about 500 yards distance. I recognised the Water Tower and shape of the cliff as being that of the East Cliff above Blue Beach and I then asked Lieutenant Commander Goulding to come alongside his LCS

---

7   There were two men named Armstrong of the rank of Private in the Royals that were reported missing after the operation.

8   Lieutenant Commander Goulding's report, Naval Commander's Report, as cited in Report No. 101, The Raid on Dieppe, 19 August 1942, Section 123.

suggesting that he went inshore with two boats well to the East and then work west towards Blue Beach to see if he could see anything.

He replied that he considered it hopeless to approach Blue Beach without the support of a bombarding destroyer.

This discussion was terminated by the smoke haze lifting from the cliffs and a heavy fire being opened on us from a variety of machine guns along the cliff tops.

The boats withdrew under the cover of a smokescreen laid by ML 291, in the course of which her First Lieutenant was seriously wounded, and the attempt was abandoned. Two immediate signals were soon afterwards received but as ML 291 had the incorrect signal cards I had to go alongside another ship to get the signals ordering evacuation.[9]

The *Queen Emma*'s Flotilla Officer also wrote about this incident after receiving the evacuation orders around 1000hrs:

Lt Cdr. Goulding took charge of the craft off Blue Beach and tried to effect a landing. The enemy fire was far too strong for this to be attempted and the craft were forced to retire. An endeavour was made to obtain the help of some heavier support but eventually the landing craft were ordered to return to England.[10]

More attempts were made to evacuate the beach later in the morning, as can be seen by the report from Lieutenant Hewitt, *Princess Astrid*'s Flotilla Officer:

Three LCAs and one LCS proceeded to Blue Beach by orders received from an ML to attempt an evacuation. When in close proximity to the beach one LCA (Lieutenant Mace, RNVR, 10th Flotilla) was sunk, probably by bombing, and the remaining craft made several attempts to approach the beach under heavy gunfire. One of the last attempts to reach Blue Beach was made shortly

---

9   Report No. 101, The Raid on Dieppe, 19 August 1942, Section 124.
10   Ibid., Section 125.

after 1100. Fire from the beach was still terrific and there was no sign of life on the beach.[11]

As such, from the evidence it would appear that Lieutenant Ramsay's LCA was the only craft that touched down on Blue Beach for the purpose of re-embarking troops and taking them back to England.

---

11   Lieutenant Hewitt's report, Naval Commander's Report, Report No. 101, The Raid on Dieppe, 19 August 1942, Section 129.

Chapter 19

Blue Beach Casualties

The Royals suffered very heavy casualties. Their full strength when they left England was 554 all ranks, 26 of which were officers.[1] However, only 2 officers and 54 other ranks returned. From these numbers 1 officer and 29 men were hospitalised because of their wounds and six of the men died. In March 1943 the Canadian Overseas Records Office gave the total number of casualties for the Royals on Blue Beach as 26 officers and 498 other ranks.[2] Neither of the two surviving officers who returned came back unwounded. Captain Catto lost an eye and was wounded while Captain Anderson suffered a head wound.[3]

In March 1943 the Canadian Overseas Records Office received information that 14 officers and 252 other ranks from the Royals were prisoners of war. They had also heard that two other officers and eight other ranks had died of their wounds after being captured. Six officers and 135 other ranks were listed as killed and two officers and 64 other ranks as missing. It is likely that all of the missing had died.

There can be few if any cases in the history of the Canadian Army of units suffering a larger proportion of fatal casualties in half a day's fighting.[4]

---

1   These figures are from Canadian Section, GHQ, 2nd Echelon, Overseas Records Office, 31 December 1942, C.M.H.Q., file 18/Dieppe/1/2.

2   Ibid.

3   Casualty Return, War Diary, R. Regt. C.

4   See Report No. 101, The Raid on Dieppe, 19 August 1942, Section 132.

Churchill tank landing: A Churchill tank, 'Talisman' of 3rd Troop, 'A' Squadron, 48th Battalion, Royal Tank Regiment, leaves a tank landing craft (TLC316) during a combined operations exercise at Thorness Bay on the Isle of Wight, 27 May 1942. (© IWM (H 20194) Released, Wikimedia)

German soldier and Churchill tank: German soldiers guarding a destroyed Allied tank. (Tomkins, R., Creative Commons Attribution-Share Alike 4.0 International Licence, Wikimedia)

Churchill tank with destroyed track: The Dieppe raid used amphibious tanks, this one is smoking and a track is destroyed. (Tomkins, R., Creative Commons Attribution-Share Alike 4.0 International Licence, Wikimedia)

Canadian bodies on the beach: A burning LCT (Landing Craft, Tank) TLC5 No. 121 near the beach after the raid by Allied (mostly Canadian) air, naval and land forces on German defences. Churchill tanks and bodies of Allied servicemen are seen on the beach. The tank at left is one from 9 Troop, 14th Army Tank Battalion (The Calgary Regiment (Tank)), which was transported by TLC5. (Library and Archives Canada, reproduction reference number C-014160, Released, Wikimedia)

Carnage on the beach: Destroyed Allied tanks and landing craft littering the Dieppe beach. Photo: Tomkins, R., Creative Commons Attribution-Share Alike 4.0 International Licence, Wikimedia.

Churchill tank: German soldiers examining a Calgary Regiment Churchill tank abandoned during the raid on Dieppe. (Library and Archives Canada, Released, Wikimedia)

Jock Anderson: Captain Jock Anderson of the Royal Regiment of Canada, cup of tea in hand, recounts his experiences to Brigadier Tees after disembarking at Portsmouth. (IWM Copyright, Released, Wikimedia)

Canadian PoWs: Canadian prisoners of war being led through Dieppe by German soldiers. (Library and Archives Canada/C-014171, Released, Wikimedia)

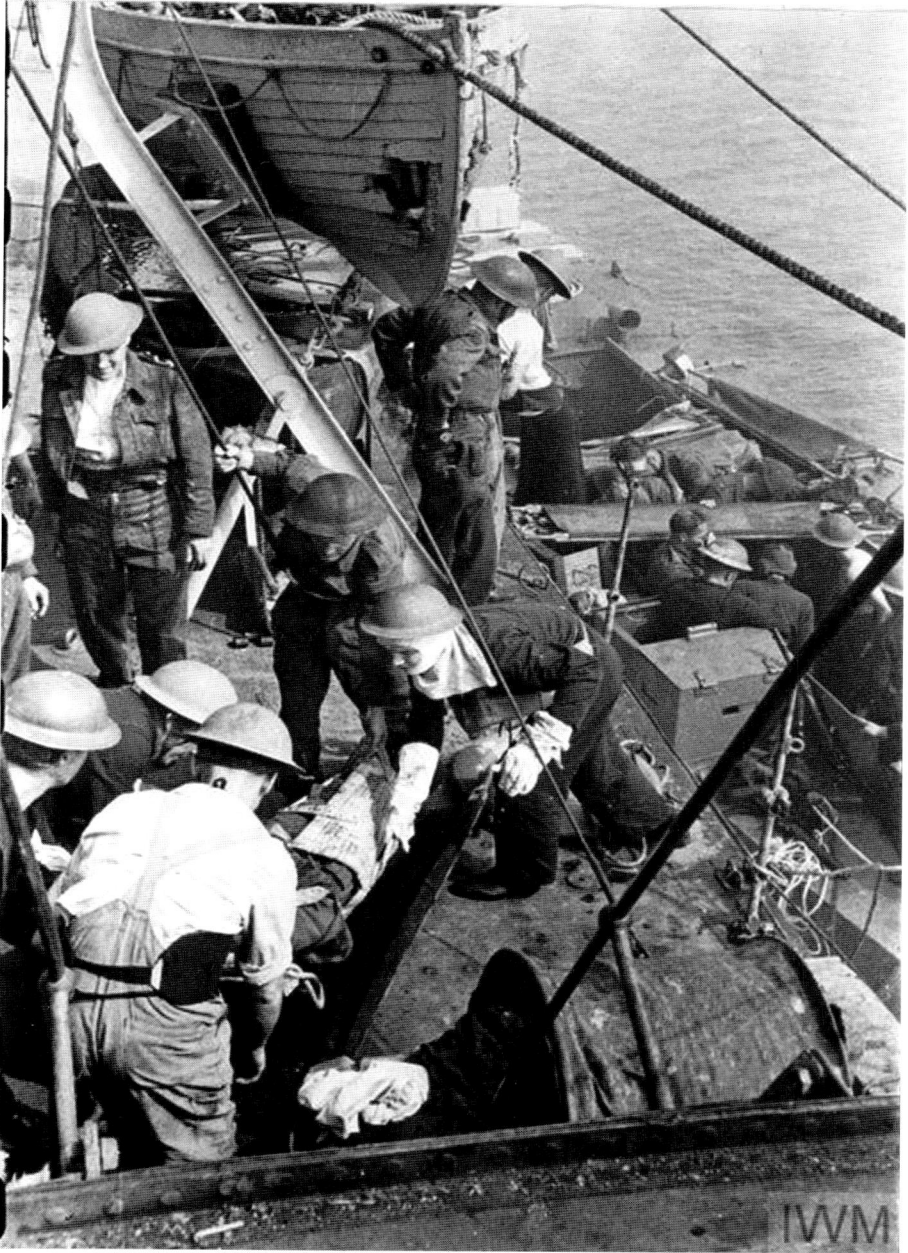

Wounded soldiers coming aboard: Wounded soldiers being brought on board a destroyer after the Combined Operations daylight raid on Dieppe. (© IWM (A 11236) Released, Wikimedia)

Ship smoking: An Allied naval vessel putting down a smokescreen off the French coast. Behind the smokescreen some of the landing craft are visible. In the foreground are infantry and naval personnel. (© IWM (H 22608) Released, Wikimedia)

Landing craft: Two of the landing craft, one containing a Bren carrier, alongside a destroyer after returning from the beaches during the Combined Operations daylight raid on Dieppe. The landing craft mechanised are (left to right) LCM (1) 169 and LCM (1) 2. (© IWM (A 11228) Wikimedia)

German and Allied injured soldiers: German officer and soldiers with injured Allied soldiers and destroyed tank. (Tomkins, R., Creative Commons Attribution–Share Alike 4.0 International Licence, Wikimedia)

Germans on a Churchill: Destroyed British tanks are recovered on the beach at Dieppe. Here German soldiers are sitting on a wrecked Churchill. (Released, Wikimedia)

Royal Navy and the Dieppe raid: Light naval craft covering the landing during the Combined Operations daylight raid on Dieppe. MGB321 is nearest the camera (partly obscured by some sailors in the foreground), while submarine chaser QO14 can be seen in the middle distance. This is photograph A 11234 from the collections of the Imperial War Museums. (Released, Wikimedia)

Churchill on the beach: Wounded British and Canadian soldiers on the beach, and behind them a destroyed Churchill, PK 698. (German Federal Archives, Creative Commons Attribution-Share Alike 3.0 Germany licence, Wikimedia)

A low-level aerial reconnaissance photograph of the Dieppe waterfront taken by the Army Co-operation Command a few days before the raid. (RAF official photographer, Released, Wikimedia)

German PoW in Newhaven: A German prisoner, Unteroffizier Leo Marsiniak being escorted at Newhaven. He was captured at the gun battery at Varengeville by No. 4 Commando. (4700-37 IWM, Released, Wikimedia)

A wounded Canadian soldier being disembarked from the Polish Navy destroyer ORP *Ślązak* at Portsmouth on return from Dieppe. (Sergeant A.W.P. Wooldridge, War Office Official Photographer, H 22637 IWM, Released, Wikimedia)

Boston: A Douglas Boston III of No. 88 Squadron, RAF, flying from Ford, Sussex, heads inland over France after bombing the German gun batteries defending Dieppe (seen at upper left). (RAF official photographer, CH 6541 IWM, Released, Wikimedia)

Propaganda: The waterfront at Dieppe following the raid. A knocked out Churchill tank is visible in the centre. (German propaganda photograph Dieppe Raid, Released, Wikimedia)

Spitfire Mk VB, R6923, QJ-S, of 92 Squadron, RAF, based at Biggin Hill, Kent, banking towards the photographing aircraft. R6923 was originally a Mark I, converted to a Mark V after serving with No. 19 Squadron and No. 7 Operational Training Unit in 1940. It was shot down over the sea by a Bf 109 on 22 June 1941. (CH2929 IWM, Air Ministry Official Second World War Collection, Released, Wikimedia)

Spitfire Mk VB AD233, ZD-F. On 25 May 1942, AD233 was shot down by Fw 190s over Gravelines while being flown by Squadron Leader Jankiewicz. This particular Spitfire was paid for from fundraising in the Dutch East Indies. (COL 188 IWM, Released, Wikimedia)

Spitfire Mk VB BM590 AV-R 'Olga', of 121 Squadron, RAF, based at Debden, Essex. (CH 7337 IWM, Released, Wikimedia)

A Spitfire Mk IX does a flypast at Hood Aerodrome, Masterson, New Zealand. It has been rebuilt in the markings of Alan Deere, New Zealand's most famous fighter pilot of the Second World War. This was the latest mark of Spitfire at the time of the Dieppe raid and there were only a handful of these available at the time. (Public Domain, Wikimedia)

The Essex Scottish were the only other unit at Dieppe that had higher casualties than the Royals. As of March 1943, the number was 532 all ranks. However, this unit had a higher number of men taken prisoner than the Royals did, which meant their fatal casualties were four officers and 64 other ranks listed as killed, while of those listed as missing, there was one officer and 35 other ranks.

As far as the Royal Highland Regiment of Canada (the Black Watch) is concerned, their casualties were much lighter. Their original embarkation strength was four officers and 107 other ranks. Their casualties were reported as being three officers and 71 other ranks, of which two officers and 64 other ranks were captured and one officer was missing. These figures do not include the casualties from the grenade accident.[5]

Casualties for 4 Field Regiment, RCA, were light yet none of those embarked for the operation, three officers and 20 other ranks, returned. Two other ranks were listed as killed while the rest were captured and became prisoners of war for the duration of the war. Captain Browne, however, managed to escape from the Germans and was held in unoccupied France until the Germans marched in on 11 November 1942. However, he managed to escape and returned to England.[6]

The embarkation strength of 3 LAA Regiment, RCA, was nine officers and 236 other ranks. The vast majority of these men, however, did not land as they were intended for an AA role on the main beaches. Instead, the small detachment of two officers and 24 other ranks landed on Blue Beach. Of these, one officer and one other rank were killed and one officer and nine other ranks were taken prisoner. Seven other ranks were listed as missing. Seven other ranks from this detachment returned to England and of those three were wounded.[7]

5   Canadian Section, GHQ, 2nd Echelon, Overseas Records Office, 31 December 1942, CMHQ, file 18/Dieppe/1/2.

6   Ibid.

7   War Diary, 3 Cdn LAA Reg, August 1942, Appx 6.

Chapter 20

Green Beach Landings

The South Saskatchewan were to land at Zero (0450hrs) and establish a bridgehead through which the Camerons, landing half an hour later, would advance to attack the aerodrome and, if time permitted, the Divisional Headquarters.[1]

Green Beach was an area of intense activity. Here, the South Saskatchewan Regiment (S. Sask.) under the command of Lieutenant Colonel C.C.I. Merritt (code-named Cecil) was to land first at 0450hrs (zero hour) near Pourville. Half an hour later they were to be followed by the Queen's Own Cameron Highlanders of Canada, under the command of Lieutenant Colonel A.C. Gostling (code-named Goose).

The principles for their attack were:

> S Sask Must secure Green beach with the minimum delay to enable Camerons of C to pass through without opposition. Green beach station will only close down when it is assured that White and Red beaches are in our hands and therefore that a route for withdrawal is open to S Sask R and Camerons of C.[2]

The plan called for one company of the S. Sask. R. to attack the high ground east of Pourville, where they were to capture two light AA guns near Saint Nicolas, an RDF station on the nearby cliff and other light AA guns in the area. Once they had achieved this they were to move on to join up with the Royal Hamilton Light Infantry (RHLI) coming from Dieppe and then take part in the attack and capture of Four Winds Farm. Also heading east, a

---

1   See Report No. 101, Operation Jubilee, The Raid on Dieppe, Section 137.
2   Report No. 101, Operation Jubilee, The Raid on Dieppe, Part 2, Section 138.

second company from the regiment was to capture AA guns on the high ground near the farm and then support the RHLI[3] in its capture of the farm itself. Once that was achieved they were to consolidate and mark out an emergency landing strip for British aircraft in the area.

West of Pourville, another company from the regiment were to attack the machine gun post on the cliff and put it out of action. Once done, they were to hold the area until the Camerons (the Queen's Own Cameron Highlanders of Canada) had landed 'and the beach was clear of craft'.[4] The rest of the unit, consisting of one other company and the Battalion HQ, were to attack and occupy La Maison Blanche in the town of Pourville. Then the plan called for them to secure Green Beach and join up with the RHLI, who by then should have captured Four Winds Farm. Finally, after consolidating, they were to cover the Dieppe west flank, which was a group of buildings south-east of the farm.

The infantry landing ships, *Princess Beatrice* and *Invicta* took the South Saskatchewans across the Channel. Each ship carried ten LCAs and two LCMs. The landings were entirely successful as they arrived on the beach only a few minutes later than had been planned. Both Flotilla Officers of the two landing craft put the landing time at 0452hrs.[5]

That time is corroborated by individual reports and personal accounts. 'All Companies landed approximately the same time 0455hrs.'[6]

The regiment landed with little resistance from the German gunners and almost the entire unit landed at the same time. 'Actually, we were on the beach before fire was opened and we got over very quickly.'[7] This idea of little German resistance to the South Saskatchewan landings was also mentioned by the *Invicta*'s Flotilla Officer, who stated that the landing was 'unopposed except that LCA315 which touched down 2 minutes later on the extreme right flank was fired upon by a light machine-gun post. Military personnel in this craft suffered several casualties as they disembarked.'[8] However, the

---

3   The RHLI were supposed to have one troop of tanks co-operating in the attack on Four Winds Farm.

4   Report No. 101, Operation Jubilee, The Raid on Dieppe, Part 2, Section 139.

5   Report of Naval Force Commander, Appendices 3 D and 3E to Enclosure No. 13.

6   Report No. 101, Operation Jubilee, The Raid on Dieppe, Part 2, Section 300.

7   Major J.E. McRae, Report No. 107.

8   Report of Naval Force Commander, Appendix 3E to Enclosure No. 13.

Germans did lay down some fire on the LCAs as they moved away from the shore after having discharged their troops and materiel. Interestingly, many of the survivors in their personal reports believed that the Germans purposely held back their fire until the landings had taken place on Green Beach.

According to Major McRae, the whole unit landed in a single wave comprised of, west to east, C Company, B Company, Bn HQ, D Company, A Company and Special Platoon. The task for the last sub-unit was to capture the wired strongpoint under the east cliff. The area to the south and east of Pourville was to be dealt with by C Company, while the town of Pourville itself was to be cleared by B Company, who were also to deal with a wired position a short distance inland on the west bank of the Scie. The German defensive positions at Four Winds Farm were to be captured by D Company, while the RDF station, the searchlight position on the cliff edge, the nearby battery and light AA guns were to be dealt with by A Company.

Some accounts have suggested that all the regiment landed west of the Scie instead of on both sides as per the plan. However, many of the personal accounts from the Special Platoon in particular do not support this idea. In order for this to be the case there should have been accounts of soldiers having to cross the bridge in the village of Pourville and no such reports exist within the platoon. There is, however, no doubt that both A and D Companies were landed west of the Scie and did have to cross the river by the bridge.[9]

> Some Allied elements were moving along the western slope of the flooded area of the Scie towards Petit Appeville where they ran into resistance from patrols of the Regimental Engineer Platoon.
>
> Adding to the German resistances were 4.7 inch anti-tank guns and other forward sections. According to the German reports Quiberville-East had been put 'out of action'. At the same time 2 more Allied platoons advanced along the eastern bank of the flooded area in a southerly direction towards Hill Ferms aux

---

9   See Report No. 107, Operation At Dieppe, 10 August 42, Further Personal Stories of Participants, Major McRae.

Quatre-Vents. This hill was firmly in German hands and would prove to be a difficulty for the Allies.[10]

At this point it is worth looking at a brief description of Pourville as it was at the time of the operation. It lay on what was a narrow dyke between the Channel and the marsh flats of the Scie. An 8ft-high sea wall separated the village from the beach. This wall was heavily covered with wire. In order for the Canadians to get through, the wire was cut in different places, enabling them to move into the town. Around 100 yards from the beach, just inside the town, the Battalion HQ was set up in a garage.[11]

According to Major McRae's account, one of the first objectives for C Company was clearing a large white hotel that overlooked the beach[12] along with nearby machine gun posts on the clifftops. It turns out that this building was filled with foreigners who had been brought in by the Germans for forced labour. The Germans suffered some casualties to their guards as C Company slowly cleared out the building. It was here that the Canadians were told that the Germans had positioned themselves on the hill behind the hotel.[13]

Sergeant H.E. Long took No. 13 Platoon and charged up the hill to attack the Germans, who were in a slit trench in front of the large white house. According to reports, there were about 50 to 60 German defenders here with four heavy machine guns. During the attack Sergeant Long was wounded along with several others. With the attack now stopped in its track for lack of leadership, Private W.A. Haggard and Private G. B. Berthelot decided to take charge and began organising an attack on the German positions. With two sections of the platoon being pinned down directly in front of the German defences, Private Haggard moved a third section to a position where it could attack the German rear. He then instructed the other section leaders to open fire when they heard the third section open up on the Germans. Haggard led this third section in attacking the defenders. However, in this action, Private

---

10 Report of the German Commander-in-Chief West (GHQ Army Group D) On The English Landing Attempt At, and On Both Flanks of Dieppe, 19 August 1942.

11 This information comes from Major McRae's personal account as in Report No. 107.

12 This is according to Major McRae and the building could be the long white building just behind the sea wall that appears in the aerial photographs.

13 Local French inhabitants gave C Company this information.

Berthelot was wounded as he raced across open ground, firing his Bren gun from the hip. The Germans, realising that they were now getting fire from three sides and suffering severe casualties, gave in relatively quickly. Private Haggard took twelve prisoners as the rest of the German defenders had been killed in this attack. He marched them back to Pourville and another five were taken prisoner along the way.[14]

Of the other platoons, No. 13 had quickly occupied the motor transport garage and cleared it of German troops. At the same time, No. 15 platoon had attacked into the centre of the village, where they destroyed a German defensive position and moved on to the right towards their objective – the machine gun post on the cliff edge. The platoon was commanded by Lieutenant L.R. McIlveen, who found that the post was unoccupied and appeared not to have been used for some time. He moved the platoon to the Maison Blanche, 'where some enemy soldiers, still in the vicinity, were killed or captured'.[15]

Throughout this time, the Germans had not been idle. The following order was issued by C-in-C West HQ Division to the German 1st Battalion 571 Infantry Regiment at Ouville at 0814hrs: 'Should 813 Artillery Troop be endangered, proceed immediately thereto with a reinforced infantry company for immediate counterattack.'[16] At the same time, the German 3 Battalion 570 Infantry Regiment had been ordered to the Ouville area and was expected to arrive shortly.[17] This would then free up 1st Battalion 571 Infantry Regiment from being Regimental Reserve to be ready for immediate counterattack towards the Scie, Saâne or Dun valleys. Around this time Division also ordered Command 1st Battalion, 571 Infantry Regiment to link up with 3rd Battalion 570 Infantry Regiment for the latest information on what was happening with 813 Artillery Troop.

North and West of Ouville, companies from German 1st Battalion 571 Infantry Regiment had been in their forming up positions since 0619hrs when they were ordered to get to the assembly area

---

14   Lieutenant Buchanan, S. Sask R., states that many prisoners were taken in and around Pourville and by 0800hrs they had between 50 and 60 German prisoners.

15   From the account by Lieutenant L.R. McIlveen cited in Report No. 101, Operation Jubilee, The Raid on Dieppe, Part 2, The Execution of the Operation, Section 139.

16   Report of 302 German Infantry Division, Operations Section -1a, on the Dieppe Raid, Appendix B, Report on the British Attack on Both Sides of Dieppe on 19 August 1942.

17   It had been in Corps Reserve and was released by Corps Hqs at 0726hrs.

by 0719hrs to launch an immediate counterattack against a strong Allied presence near Pourville. However, Division was not aware of the Battalion's regrouping actions as the conversation over the telephone had been broken off once the order had been given.

It was generally agreed at Division that the Allied penetration at Pourville was the most vulnerable and dangerous point in the divisional sector. 1st Battalion carried out their task as quickly as they could assembling in the southern sector near Hautot and waited for the arrival of 3rd Battalion 570 Infantry Regiment that had been ordered to Offranville instead of Ouville and had lost considerable time while waiting to be moved by transport to mount a counterattack.[18]

C Company, South Saskatchewan Regiment, had managed to capture most of their objectives and the situation for them was well in hand. Smaller degrees of success were achieved in other sectors by the Canadians in and around Pourville. On the high ground east of the town lay the objectives for A and D Companies, who had been landed west of the River Scie. They now needed to enter the village and cross the bridge to get to their objectives. The bridge, however, lay firmly in German hands and was overlooked by well-prepared positions on the high ground east of the structure. Surprise was impossible as the Germans were in a high state of readiness. The Special Platoon (Allied), commanded by Lieutenant L.L. England, had landed on the far eastern side of the battalion and did not have to cross the bridge as they were already on the eastern side of Pourville. The Platoon did not come under fire when they landed but as they worked their way inland towards a strongpoint on the left they came under heavy fire from a road block roughly 100 yards from where they landed.[19] Lieutenant England was wounded and the platoon suffered several other casualties. With Lieutenant England now unable to continue the advance, Sergeant R.R. Neil took charge and set up a reconnaissance of the strongpoint. This indicated that there was no way the platoon could have cleared or destroyed the strongpoint with the weapons

---

18   Report of 302 German Infantry Division, Operations Section -1a, on the Dieppe Raid, Appendix B, Report on the British Attack on Both Sides of Dieppe on 19 August 1942.

19   According to Major McRae this road block was near the curve in the road, Report No. 107.

they had so they asked for mortar support via wireless. That mortar support, however, never materialised. Realising that they could not clear the German defences in this sector, they moved off to the right, further inland, and joined up with elements of A Company who had managed to cross the bridge.

A Company's objective was to capture and clear the RDF station and as such they had been landed on the battalion's left flank, which meant they would have to cross the bridge in the town of Pourville to get to their objective. Once landed, they crossed the sea wall west of the river and moved along the main road into the town to the dreaded bridge. The road had been heavily wired on both sides, making it very difficult for the attackers to use the countryside to attack. By wiring the road in such a way, the Germans had created a funnel effect that forced the Canadians down a specific point directly into the fire of their machine guns firing on fixed lines from higher ground. The company was to meet up at the curve in the road but it lay beyond the bridge. Sergeant B.H. Smith reported:

> I went over the bridge followed by one section and came under very heavy LMG fire, the remainder of the Pl then crossed under the bridge.
>
> As we advanced from the bridge the fire was very heavy from two pill boxes situated one above the other, well up on the forward slope of the hill. There were snipers and riflemen from the slope of the hill and back along the road.
>
> The MGs seemed to be firing on fixed arcs and were very accurate and all were mutually supporting, covering nearly all dead ground.[20]

Immediately, Sergeant Smith and his men took cover near the road block and began returning fire at the pillboxes and individual German snipers on the hillside. Before they could move forward, the pillbox at the bend in the road needed to be cleared and this was done through an individual act of bravery and courage by Private C.E. Sawden.

---

20   Sergeant B.H. Smith, A Company, S. Sask R., as cited in Report No. 101, Operation Jubilee, The Raid on Dieppe, Part 2, Section 150.

Past the road block, running along the base of a hill I saw Pte. C. Sawden take out an MG post. Pte Haselhan threw smoke and Pte. Sawden went forward under covering fire and threw grenades into the post.[21]

Sadly, Private Sawden was listed as killed in action by the time the reports were written.

More and more elements of A Company arrived and, together, with the survivors of the Special Platoon, tried to move towards the RDF station. This small force was now under the command of Captain T.W. Osten. They moved along the road that ran inland along the base of the hill, then turned uphill towards some small woods and a little valley that ran in the direction of the RDF station. The hope was that the trees would give them cover as they advanced towards the station. Unfortunately, every route they tried to get to the station was covered by heavy German fire.

As we came up behind a hedge row we were met with very heavy MG fire from two hills and were forced to ground. We tried to beat down his fire and advance but this was impossible. Four truck-loads of reinforcements were seen coming up to these positions.

We then moved back about 50 yds and to the right, planning a right flanking movement. Here again we came under very heavy MG fire, the enemy guns always supporting one another. Here we were joined by more of our own men and some of the Camerons of Canada. Lieutenant Dickin joined us at this point and displayed great heroism.

The Germans then brought mortar fire to bear on us, which was very accurate. We could do nothing here so tried a left flank-ing movement. Here we met the same results. We were in a small orchard with a few houses scattered around, some containing a few Germans, and a few in the trees. We cleared these, but came under heavy mortar fire, MG and incendiary fire. This gun seemed to be

---

21   Private P. Wanner witnessed the actions of Private Sawden, as cited in Report No. 101, Operation Jubilee, The Raid on Dieppe, Part 2, Section 151.

the same size as a two pounder, could be fired as in AA or at troops at a very rapid rate.

Here a French family assisted us by dressing our wounded.[22]

Both flank attacks on the German positions failed.

While these attacks were unsuccessful, some elements of A Company did manage to get within a short distance of the RDF station and they found it to be very heavily defended and heavily wired. Lance Corporal A.F. Bales later stated that 'when we reached the RDF station we found the enemy too strong for the weapons we had. Arty was badly needed.'[23] As a result, A Company requested fire support to deal with the heavy defences in and around the RDF station but the fire support that did come was ineffective.

D Company's objective was to attack the German positions at the Four Winds Farm but first they had to cross the bridge in Pourville. The company managed to scale the sea wall after landing and moved rapidly onto the main road, where they turned left towards the bridge. Here they ran into heavy fire. According to the reports written shortly after the operation, 'the Company Commander, Major J.C. McTavish, and two runners were the first to cross, and then portions of Nos. 16, 17, and 18 Platoons followed, the men either rushing across the bridge or swimming or rafting across the river'.[24]

We got over the wall and well into town before we were fired on, which was at the concrete bridge at the river. The bridge was covered with fire from the hill to the left and made it very hard for us to get across. Some of our boys got over the bridge, some swam the river. I for one had a tough time swimming the river as my equipment dragged me down. As we crossed the river I heard mg fire for the first time.[25]

The attempt at rushing the bridge was not without casualties. Private J. Krohn saw Lance Corporal Carswell wounded along with two others. He states:

---

22 This quote is from Sergeant Smith as cited in Report No. 101, Operation Jubilee, The Raid on Dieppe, Part 2, Section 152.

23 See Report No. 101, Operation Jubilee, The Raid on Dieppe, Part 2, Section 153.

24 This is according to Lieutenant J.S. Edmondson who witnessed the action.

25 From an account by Lance Corporal H. McKenzie see Report No. 101, Section 154.

Lance Corporal Chilton, Evenden, Carswell, Picford and myself were fired upon when we reached half way across. Chilton, Evenden and Pickford made a mad dash for the other side, Carswell was wounded together with two other boys beside me. It was too late for us to be able to make the dash. One more boy fell right beside me, so I flattened out, rolled myself over the side, into the Canal at the same time dragging one of the boys with me. The bridge was under heavy fire by this time. The rest of the company had to wade the Canal.[26]

Directly ahead of these men was a pillbox that had a commanding view of the bridge. According to Private Krohn's account, it was silenced by AA fire but this could be the same position that was cleared by Private Sawden. Those positions cleared of the Germans immediately east of Pourville were quickly reoccupied by them.

The Commanding Officer, Lieutenant Colonel Merritt, then decided to intervene personally in the situation the battalion had become involved in east of the village of Pourville. Up until this point Merritt had remained at his HQ but when it became clear that A and D Companies were having difficulty he went forward to check out the situation himself.[27] At the bridge No. 17 Platoon was pinned down by heavy machine gun fire. Its commander, Lieutenant J.R. Nesbitt, described what happened when Merritt came forward. A decision was taken that 'we should dash over the bridge. He [Merritt] led the way and we crossed OK and I do not think we had any casualties.'[28]

By force of his will, Merritt also ensured that other companies managed to get across the bridge under heavy fire.

Lt-Col Merritt led several parties across the bridge in Pourville which was swept by machine gun, mortar and fd gun fire continually. He was constantly exposing himself. On many occasions he crossed over the bridge, urging his men forward and calling

---

26 This account is from Private J. Krohn, Report No. 101, Operation Jubilee, The Raid On Dieppe, Part 2, Section 154.

27 This comes from the evidence of Lieutenant L.L. Dickin, who was at the time acting as Intelligence Officer.

28 From the report by Lieutenant Nesbitt cited in Report No. 101, Operation Jubilee, The Raid on Dieppe, Part 2, Section 155.

'see, there is no danger here'. The men followed him splendidly but were shot down time after time.[29]

More than half of our Company were across the bridge when I arrived. The Colonel, when he saw we were being held up, crossed the bridge several times urging the men forward, and the men followed. The dead were piled 2 deep for about 50 ft along the bridge.[30]

For his brave actions Lieutenant Colonel Merritt received the Victoria Cross. The award citation stated that 'this gallant officer personally led the survivors of at least four parties in turn across the bridge'.[31]

Merritt then organised further advances across the bridge under withering German fire. 'He led an attack right up to a pillbox and threw grenades inside.'[32] A report by Sergeant B.P. McBride tells of Merritt's inspiring example:

The first time I met the Colonel we were over the bridge. There was heavy fire coming down on the road as I joined a group of men who were held up. I heard the Colonel speak and he said 'We must get ahead lads, we need more men up front as quick as possible, who's coming with me.' I replied, 'We are all going with you.' He said, 'Good lads, let's go.' We ran up the road with Colonel Merritt leading, disregarding all danger, he led us straight up the road and after about 40 yards he stopped. Soon the Colonel said, 'Are you ready again?', we answered, 'OK, Sir', and away we went again right up to the road block. There we left Colonel Merritt and went to re-join A Company.[33]

---

29   Evidence from Captain Carswell's report cited in Report No. 101, Operation Jubilee, The Raid on Dieppe, section 156.

30   From Lieutenant Edmondson's report, cited in Report No. 101, Operation Jubilee, The Raid on Dieppe, Section 156.

31   Ibid.

32   Ibid.

33   From a report by B.P. McBride cited in Report No. 101, Operation Jubilee, The Raid on Dieppe, Section 157.

Despite all of this gallantry, the Canadians were unable to capture the Four Winds position, which the Germans had heavily fortified. Although D Company advanced towards it alongside elements of the recently landed Camerons, their attack was stopped by German mortar and machine-gun fire.

> At this point we captured two prisoners and also suffered a few casualties. Private Fenner was wounded very badly being shot in both legs while engaging the enemy in Bren Gun fire, which he was doing very effectively. We dragged him down the hill on his back where we dressed his wounds.[34]

While this book is primarily about the German experience of the Dieppe landings, it is worth noting the Allied attempts to take their objectives and as such there is another account of Private Fenner's actions that states he 'crawled up on the hill and walked straight into enemy positions firing a Bren gun from his hip and reached the top of hill killing a considerable amount of Germans'.[35]

However, one section attacked the Four Winds position by advancing straight up the hill from the Scie valley and managed to reach the edge of the position before being pushed back by covering German fire. This route had been considered by planners as impracticable. Once they had reached the edge of the Four Winds defensive position German fire came from all directions, including positions dug in up the valley inland. The Canadians managed to withdraw safely.

> After we crossed the bridge we turned right and followed road for 500 yards. Consolidated with some of C and A Company. We then made our way over the road, up the hill and reached our objective. Here we killed several Germans and were later forced to withdraw and fought a rear-guard action suffering light casualties. We withdrew to the road and took up a firing position there.[36]

---

34 Evidence from Lance Sergeant Coldwell cited in Report No. 101, Operation Jubilee, The Raid on Dieppe, Section 158.

35 This is from an unknown source cited in Report No. 101. The report also states that Private O.C. Fenner was awarded the Military Medal for these actions.

36 From a report by Sergeant K.A. Williams, cited in Report No. 101, Operation Jubilee, The Raid on Dieppe, Section 159.

Once Merritt realised that D Company were unable to take the German position at Four Winds Farm he ordered them to move left and join up with A Company with their attack on the RDF station. This order from Merritt was received before the whole of D Company had been able to reach its rendezvous point. 'The combined efforts of all the men available, however, were inadequate to the task in the face of the enemy's skilfully sited machine-guns and mortars.'[37] At that time the Canadians required support from artillery, air and mortars but none was available.

> Request by both A and D Companies for arty support were passed to the FOO who immediately went forward. Fire brought down was not effective and was of no assistance in helping these Companies forward, they called for mortar fire at this point and we were unable to give this as our detachments had been knocked out by this time. Small parties of these Companies worked forward but aside from taking out some enemy posts were unable to assist their Companies forward.[38]

The Forward Observation Officer (FOO) for the South Saskatchewan was Captain H.B. Carswell, who tried to bring naval fire from HMS *Albrighton* onto the German positions. However, he was unable to accurately observe the exact positions of the Canadian troops in the area. The only point he could see was a group of two houses situated just west of the cliffs where he thought most of the German fire was coming from.

The Commanding Officer of HMS *Albrighton* stated:

> Three indirect shoots were reported but he [Carswell] was unable to spot. He also indicated targets on the cliff between Dieppe and Green Beach for direct bombardment and I think the ship silenced the fire of one light gun position. The ship could not remain stationary long as enemy gunners soon started getting close.[39]

---

37   See Report No. 101, Operation Jubilee, The Raid on Dieppe, Section 160.
38   See Major J.E. McRae, Report No. 107.
39   Report from the Naval Forces Commander, Appx 26 to Enclosed No. 13.

While the fire support from the ships offshore was the only artillery available to support the troops it was not always effective. However, much of the light machine gun fire was used effectively in support.

> The initial advance inland of A, D and B Companies was supported by LMG fire onto the heights east of Pourville. In particular a German heavy Mortar was engaged by Private Godrey of D Company. This mortar was causing many casualties. Other entrenched Germans on the same height were also engaged. This fire fight continued until approx. 1000hrs when the fire fight was continued by six men under Corporal Jackson.[40]

The 3in mortars of the S. Sask. R. also provided support for the troops trying to advance east of Pourville. However, the fire from the mortars was not as effective as it could have been. They were situated on the west side of the bridge and were out of range of the German defensive positions to the east. These weapons quickly fell silent as they ran out of ammunition. Three shots were fired against the eastern hill before the bombs from Corporal J.B. McAlpine's mortars were spent. 'All my detachment were disappointed because of our not having enough Mortar bombs.'[41]

In order to deal with the Allied units that had broken into the Scie valley near Pourville, the German Reserve Corps HQ ordered the Reserve[42] to be moved to Pourville and be placed under Division's command. At this time there were no plans for any units of Corps Reserve to be committed to the fight at Dieppe as Pourville became more of a concern.

At the western edge of the woods near D'Arques Woods was the German 3 Battalion, 570 Infantry Regiment, which had sufficient motor transport to move all its companies including the machine gun company. At the same time, this battalion was also a reserve unit should the Allies begin airborne landings.

---

40 Account from Lieutenant Edmondson, Report No. 101, Operation Jubilee, The Raid on Dieppe, Section 163.

41 Account by Corporal McAlpine, Report No. 101, Operation Jubilee, The Raid on Dieppe, Section 164.

42 This unit was made up of the Reinforced Klemm Regiment less one battalion, 81 Anti-tank Company and 1 Battery, 332 Artillery Regiment.

At 1036hrs the German C–in–C West HQ decided to commit the Corps Reserve Regiment to the counterattack on Allied units fighting at Pourville.

> At Pourville, Division was aware that several Allied landings had taken place there despite the heavy fire from 3rd Battery 302 Artillery Regiment and AA Artillery. The Allies had managed to push into the town itself and Pourville was now a key danger area for us. Also, Division was unaware that on the eastern side of the Scie Valley the Allies had advanced over the high ground of Hill Ferme aux Quatre-vents as well as on the western side of the valley heading towards Hautot.[43]

German fighter bombers, known as 'strafers', were to attack Allied landing craft at Pourville and Dieppe. In particular they were to be committed to the western section of Pourville as well as west of the flooded areas of the Scie valley against buildings on the hillsides, where the Allies might find cover and set up defendable positions.

The Corps Reserves Regiment was tasked with launching a prepared counterattack against Allied positions at Pourville, which was the sector considered by Division to be the most dangerous. At this time, 3 Battalion, 570 Infantry Regiment, had not yet arrived at Offranville.[44]

German HQ now took the decision that Pourville was the main area that required an all-out counterattack. The Germans, by this time, had managed to subdue the fighting at Dieppe, as we have seen in earlier chapters, so Pourville and the attack by the commandos at Varengeville were the critical areas. The problems at 813 Army Coastal Artillery Troop would have to wait.[45]

> At 1047hrs GHQ West requested from Naval Group West a commitment of U-boats for reconnaissance purposes in the Channel near Dieppe but this request was refused by Commander Naval

---

43   See the Battle Report of the German Commander-in-Chief West (GHQ Army Group D) on the English Landing Attempt at Dieppe, and on Both Flanks of Dieppe, 19 August 1942.

44   Ibid., Battle Report of the German Commander-in-Chief West.

45   This was the British Commando attack on the gun battery at Varengeville against German 813 Army Coastal Artillery Troop.

Group West 'because U-Boats are ill-qualified for reconnaissance and because their commitment East of Cherbourg is impossible due to danger from mines and enemy air superiority. Commitment of same at the western exit of the Channel towards the Bristol Channel and in the Bay of Biscay has not yet been considered necessary.'[46]

It was now obvious to Allies, the remaining troops of A and D Companies along with elements of the Camerons and other troops, that the capture of their objectives east of Pourville was impossible. The only thing they could do was to take up defensive positions on the ground they had already gained and wait either for reinforcements or for the order to withdraw. 'At about 0945 hours orders were received to hold a perimeter until 1100hrs. This was done by using a small scattered force in front, heavy with Bren Guns, and the main body about 100yrds back ready to counterattack.'[47] At 1100hrs the withdrawal began as the covering troops began to move back towards the beaches. From the reports it seems the Germans were prepared to let them go.

> It would seem that the enemy had been content to limit himself to holding his positions; admirably disposed in posts chosen long before, and highly skilful in the fire-fight, he had no desire to initiate counterattacks which would bring him to closer quarters with the men who had come from the sea.[48]

During the operation B Company had become widely scattered. They had landed with 10 Platoon on the left, 11 on the right and 12 in the middle. No. 10 Platoon was ordered to the bridge, where they suffered several casualties yet some of the members of the platoon were able to cross the bridge and move up the hill. Elements of 10 and 12 Platoons were sent to support other

---

46   See the Battle Report of the German Commander-in-Chief West (GHQ Army Group D) on the English Landing Attempt at, and on Both Flanks of Dieppe, 19 August 1942.

47   Account by Lieutenant Dickin who had come forward from Bn Hq, Report No. 101, Operation Jubilee, The Raid on Dieppe.

48   This quote is directly from Report No. 101, Operation Jubilee, The Raid on Dieppe, Section 165.

companies bogged down in Pourville but they were ineffective. On the right of the river a wired position was attacked by 11 Platoon 1,500 yards south of Pourville. At 0915hrs this platoon ran into trouble and called for help. Much of this information comes from Major F. Mathers, who at this point took command of the elements of B Company still left in Pourville and ordered 12 Platoon to advance and assist 11 Platoon. While he states that this platoon took the wired position, the actual men on the spot stated that they had managed to silence the German fire with anti-tank rifles but they were unable to occupy the positions.

> At the time of the order to withdraw, No. 11 was holding the position it had reached, and the bulk of Nos. 10 and 12 was apparently in position on the high ground east of Pourville, with part of No. 10 Platoon at the bridge.[49]

In Pourville itself, Major McRae remained in charge at Battalion Headquarters, which he repeatedly moved for safety purposes. Some of his men reported that he appeared to be gifted with some kind of sixth sense for every time he moved the HQ mortar fire would come down on the spot they had just moved from, although on the second move, which was a clearing in the village, they were hit by German mortar fire and suffered several casualties. After this they moved three more times without any problems, finally to a position on the southern edge of the village.

Lieutenant Colonel Merritt was constantly on the move in the forward areas encouraging and directing the troops under his command, a considerable number of which were Camerons. Moving with Merritt was a signaller with a No. 18 radio set who was unable to keep up with the colonel, which meant for long periods he was not in communications with his HQ.

> By this time, Division had not yet heard any reports regarding the Allied advance on the East bank of the flooded area of the Scie which had been over the dead ground of the Hill Ferme aux Quatre-Ventes.
>
> At Pourville West the fighting also continued as the Allies held the heights south and west of the Scie Valley. Their advance had

---

49   See Report No. 101, Operation Jubilee, The Raid on Dieppe, Section 166.

been halted by 1 Battalion 571 Infantry Regiment, who had them now under heavy fire. This same battalion of 571 Infantry Regiment had been under fire from the Allies at Hautot and also had elements fighting the British Commando withdrawal at Varengeville. Just after 1130hrs the Battalion had launched its counterattacks directly from its forming-up position.[50]

German Divisional HQ now ordered the Klemm Regiment to move as quickly as possible to Offranville along with 1 Battalion, 676 Infantry Regiment; 3 Battalion, 570 Infantry Regiment; and 81 Tank squadron in order to mount a counterattack on Pourville, seize the beach there and push the enemy back into the sea. Before the counterattack could take place the force had to arrive at Offranville and form up ready for its assault. Other units, such as 9 Troop, 302 Artillery Regiment, were placed under command of the Klemm Regiment. As of 1130hrs, 3 Battalion, 676 Infantry Regiment, was ordered to attack the British commandos towards Phare d'Ailly via Varengeville. However, some of the units under Colonel Klemm's command were still moving towards the forming up point at Offranville, and like, 1 Battery, 332 Artillery Regiment, would not arrive until later in the afternoon, too late to take part in the counterattack that was desperately needed.

Air Reconnaissance Group 123 then reported from 3rd Air Fleet that: 'Discussions with pilot reveals a convoy of 26 ships of 6,000 tons each, strongly manned with troops; left Selsey Bill (England) towards Northwest in direction of Portsmouth. Reconnaissance flights laid on for 1300hrs will report further position.[51]

As far as the Luftwaffe was concerned, fighter-bombers were due to carry out strafing runs on the Allied positions at Pourville-West at 1145hrs.

50   See the Battle Report of the German Commander-in-Chief West (GHQ Army Group D) on the English Landing Attempt at, and on Both Flanks of Dieppe, 19 August 1942.

51   This report, as cited in the Battle Report of the German Commander-in-Chief West (GHQ Army Group D) on the English Landing Attempt at, and on Both Flanks of Dieppe, 19 August 1942, was sent to GHQ West at 1150hrs.

Chapter 21

The Queen's Own Cameron Highlanders

At this point it is worth looking briefly at the fortunes of the Camerons during the operation. The Detailed Military Plan did not indicate any specific objectives for them but they were supposed to 'pass through Beach Head secured by S. Sask R., and move to aerodrome with best possible speed, bypassing all enemy opposition where possible. Contact with tanks vicinity North edge of Bois Des Vertus 2265.'[1]

From there, with support from destroyers bombarding German defensive positions from offshore and in co-operation with the 14th Canadian Army Tank Battalion, they were to capture the aerodrome and once that had been achieved they were to attack and capture the 110th German Infantry Division located at Arques, or possibly located in a nearby château, and then take out the nearby heavy AA gun installation. Once this was achieved they were to return to the beaches once the withdrawal order had been given.

None of this happened. Their passage to Green beach was uneventful and they landed a little later than the time laid down in the Detailed Military Plan. In charge of Group 6, Commander H.V. McClintock states:

> Had we trusted to our dead reckoning and continued at a steady course and speed from our turn on to the last leg of the track laid down we would have made the correct beach about 10 minutes late, which was the time we were aiming for. Unfortunately, when we sighted the coast we thought we seemed rather close and made a reduction in speed because the O/C Troops preferred to arrive late (rather) than early. Later when we could see a bit more we thought that we were rather too far to correct. The Camerons of Canada were, however, eventually landed on the right beach about half an hour late, 0550 instead of 0520hrs. The LCPs were

---

1   Ibid.

deployed about 2 miles from the beach and parted company with ML 190 Commanded by Lieutenant R.W. Ball, RNVR, as soon as the objective was quite clear.[2]

Group 6 comprised of three flotillas that deployed into two lines abreast half a mile out from the beach. As they approached the shore, the men in the landing craft could see that the S. Sask. R. had not been able to open up the bridgehead as they were supposed to. Shells hammered the beach and burst in the water. Despite this enemy fire all the boats landed safely, with only one sergeant of the Camerons being wounded while still on board the LCP.

One German defensive position on Green Beach, which the S. Sask. R. had not been able to silence, was a pillbox located east of the outlet of the River Scie. Ashore, Lieutenant Colonel Gostling directed and encouraged his men to push through the wire obstacles on the beach and it was while he was directing the wire-cutting operations he was killed by fire from the pillbox. 'Lt-Col A.C. Gostling was fatally wounded by the first burst from the MG in a pillbox built into the headland 100 yards on our left.'[3]

During the landing the battalion became separated, with elements landing on the beach west of the River Scie and the rest landing on the beach east of the river. The troops that had landed on the western side of the river crossed the sea wall without difficulty with few casualties, whereas those on the eastern side of the beach encountered German fire from positions that the S. Sask. R. had been unable to clear.[4]

Captain Runcie commanded D Company and Captain Campbell commanded C Company. Evidence from both men indicated that D Company, elements of B Company and two boatloads of C Company landed east of the river. This included Captain Campbell and C Company HQ. On the western side of the Scie the rest of the battalion – A Company, two platoons of B Company, most of C Company and parts of the Battalion HQ – touched down safely.

---

2   Report from the Naval Forces Commander, Appx 26 to Enclosure No. 13.

3   Account by Private W.J. Coll of the Camerons of Canada, which was also confirmed by Captain John Runcie, who was beside the CO (Lieutenant Colonel Gostling) when he was hit by machine gun fire from the left and died instantly.

4   This evidence is according to Captain Runcie and Major A.T. Law (second-in-command). Cited in Report No. 101, Section 174.

Those on the eastern side of the beach found themselves under heavy German fire. Captain Runcie mounted a quick reconnaissance towards the western side of the beach and discovered that the river could be crossed at its outlet, which was very shallow. He also discovered that the western side of the beach was clear of enemy fire. Taking 15 men of his company, along with the elements of C Company that had landed with him, Runcie, with a party of 30 men, crossed the river at the western side and advanced into Pourville. By the time he had done this, the rest of the men who had been stuck on the eastern side of the beach had managed to cross the sea wall and enter the town from the east.

The result of all this was that the Camerons were now divided into two main sections. After the death of Colonel Gostling, Major Law assumed command. The larger body of the battalion had landed west of the river (which Major Law now led). This section comprised all of A Company, 10 and 11 Platoons of B Company, most of all of the three platoons of C Company as well as the larger part of Battalion HQ. Major Law took the main body and struck inland from Pourville 'effecting the deepest penetration made by any portion of the force engaged that day'.[5]

However, the rest of the battalion remained in and around Pourville, considerably divided, and fought in varying numbers and strength mingled with the South Saskatchewan Regiment.

---

5   See Report No. 101, Section 177.

Chapter 22

The Camerons in Pourville

According to the reports there were two main groups of Camerons engaged in the fighting around Pourville and in the town itself. The first group, led by Captains Runcie and Campbell met up at the bridge with Lieutenant Colonel Merritt, who then brought this group of men under his command in order to reinforce S. Sask R. Runcie communicated with Major Law over the radio, who agreed with Merritt about taking command of this group. Throughout the balance of the action they were under the command of Lieutenant Colonel Merritt.

According to Captain Runcie, his main task was to clear the houses on the south side of Pourville's main street, west of the bridge, which he and his men did. Under heavy and accurate German mortar fire, Runcie's group cleared the vicinity of the bridge and as such, he stated that all the German defensive positions in this area had been completely cleared. However, as we have previously seen, the area around the bridge was continuously swept by enemy fire. Indeed, 'Captain Campbell confirms that some of the commanding positions on the high ground overlooking the bridge were never cleared.'[1] His belief was that the pillbox at the opposite end of the bridge on the high ground was never cleared, or if it was, it was quickly reoccupied by the Germans.

Captain Campbell's account is corroborated by CSM Mathers of the South Saskatchewan Regiment, who was at the bridge at the time. Once he had received the order to withdraw he sent two runners to 12 Platoon to inform them of the order but they were killed trying to cross the bridge. He subsequently sent two more men who both managed to cross the bridge under German fire and arrive at 12 Platoon, but one of the two was wounded.

Captain Young was the commander of B Company and he commanded the second group of Camerons. However, his company headquarters was all

---

1   See Report No. 101, Section 180.

he had of his own company, which was joined with No. 12 Platoon and part of D Company. This group of Canadians managed to penetrate inland from the town of Pourville.

> We worked our way under cover on the left of the river for about 500 yards. Then the Company Commander thought it was about time we called a halt & got organised before going further, on checking up I found we had only 12 pl. with us and a Pl of 'D' Company (under Lieutenant McKellar and Lieutenant McManus). It seems the Bn had got orders to proceed up the right bank of the river but somehow or other we never received it. The Company Com. had no way of communicating with anyone so decided we would carry on & do as much damage as possible.[2]

By this time Captain Young's group had moved along the east bank of the river some 500 yards from their original position. Indeed, according to reports, Captain Young led his group 'about a mile inland'.[3] This is supported by CSM Gouk, who stated that after they had moved inland they 'swung left from the river towards a small village where we knew the enemy were, snipers & MGs seemed to be in every house'.[4]

> We advanced up the side of a steep hill & made our way to a house, which was almost half a mile from the shore, all the time taking cover from MG fire and some snipers. I was kind of worried about all those bullets, but our company commander (Captain Young) told us they weren't very good shots during the last war and that he didn't think they had had much practice since, so I took his word for it and kept going.[5]

As Captain Young's party began the process of clearing the German defenders from the houses they were suddenly hit by accurate mortar fire.

---

2   Account by B Company, Company Sergeant Major, WO2 G. Gouk, cited in Report No. 101, Section 182.

3   Account by Private D.N. Davies.

4   Account by B Company, Company Sergeant Major, WO2 G. Gouk.

5   Account by Private C.W. Flemington, B Company, Report No. 101, Section 183.

Our casualties sure started mounting then, every corner you turned you seemed to run into mortar fire and they sure could place their shots. Well there was no stopping the boys then, they were seeing their pals for the first time being killed and wounded at their side and the only thought that seemed to be in everyone's mind was to have revenge.[6]

Beyond the houses was a series of slit trenches occupied by the German defenders. Captain Young decided that an attack against this position was called for. Whether or not this is where the mortar fire was coming from is not indicated in the initial reports but it seems likely it was. Private Davies provides some detail:

We reformed and saw the enemy about 40 yards ahead. Our 2 inch mortar fired 2 or 3 smoke bombs to cover our advance and Captain Young got up to advance and he was hit by MG fire and also by a mortar shell.[7]

This happened around 1030hrs and it left the party with 12 men, which included some from the Camerons and some from the S. Sask. R. The trench position, according to Private Flemington's account, had not been taken and they had lost their company commander. At the same time CSM Gouk had taken some men off to deal with enemy stragglers.

At this point Lieutenant Colonel Merritt arrived with a small party of men and began to reorganise the two groups into one unit, as Private Davies stated in his account.

Then the Colonel of the SSR came along and got more men which brought our total to about 25 men and wanted us to attack the strong point. We advanced and got under cover in a copse near the enemy under Major White (SSR [Saskatoons]). The enemy was too

---

6   Account by B Company, Company Sergeant Major, WO2 G. Gouk, Report No. 101, Section 185.

7   Ibid., Account by Private D.N. Davies, Report No. 101, Section 185.

strong so 7 of us were detailed under a Lance Corporal to hold our position until 1100hrs.[8]

With Merritt's arrival and reorganisation they were able to take out a German 4in mortar team.

These men were under heavy stress and strain as they fought their way through the houses trying desperately to clear them of the German soldiers. It is natural in the confusion of fighting with bullets and shells flying in all directions, smoke and so forth that some accounts written after the fact may not be as accurate as others. This appears to be the case concerning what happened after Captain Young's death. Corporal A. Brygider of No. 16 Platoon, the Camerons, 'an intelligent and courageous soldier who was subsequently awarded the DCM for his services in organising the evacuation of wounded under heavy fire',[9] states that a large group of men from D Company who had crossed the sea wall through a hole cut in the wire and managed to move along the east bank of the river found that:

> The platoon had been split up and that there were many men of the other two platoons among us. We formed sections of all the men there and advanced further up the bank. Here we met both the lieutenants (Lieutenant J.R.E. McManus and Lieutenant A.J. McKellar) and part of B Company. Here we again combined forces and advanced on some houses on the left of us. We went through these houses but found that the firing came from some houses further up the hill.[10]

At this point it was decided to undertake a left flanking attack on the houses mentioned above but before this could be mounted a mortar bomb exploded, causing several casualties. Corporal Brygider was then ordered to get the wounded men to a place of relative safety in the rear, which he did. He returned and met up with Major McTavish of the S. Sask. R. and again plans were made to attack the houses. Once again, they suffered casualties in

---

8   See Report No. 101, Section 187.

9   See Report No. 101, Operation Jubilee, The Raid on Dieppe, Section 188.

10   Account by Corporal Brygider, Report No. 101, Operation Jubilee, The Raid on Dieppe, Section 188.

the process of setting up the attack. The time was 1000hrs and Lieutenant McManus then ordered Brygider to take charge of the wounded and get them, including the ones he had just handled, back to the beach for evacuation back to England.

Lieutenant McKellar had managed to work his way forward and joined up with this party of men taking part in the uphill attack on the houses that proved to be unsuccessful.

Most of this action was taking place east of Pourville on the hillside where the Canadians were under heavy German fire throughout the operation. Men from both the Camerons and the S. Sask. R.s were involved here and throughout the morning they came together or separated depending on the circumstances of the operation as it ebbed and flowed. They did their best to get to grips with 'a largely invisible enemy on the higher ground whose mortar and machine gun fire was constantly inflicting casualties'.[11] It was not all one way for the Germans as the Canadians were able to capture three prisoners during this operation.

However, what was needed was artillery fire or tank fire that would have cleared out the German defenders and enabled the Canadians to penetrate deeper inland. They had neither, for the tanks did not get off the beaches and the fire from offshore was not effective enough to make a difference.

Throughout the morning the Germans mounted sustained, heavy and accurate mortar fire against the Canadians. Their observation of the Allied troops and their movement was also very effective to the point that, when the Canadians moved the German mortar fire followed them, thus keeping them under continuous fire. 'It was particularly remarked that wireless sets became a target as soon as they commenced to work, and sets had to be constantly moved in order to escape destruction.'[12]

> At Pourville, we [Germans] had retaken Pourville-East but in Pourville-West Allied soldiers remained hidden under the cover of a smokescreen. 2 Company 571 Infantry Regiment were ordered to attack Allied units still holding out in that area and moved quickly towards Pourville-West. At the same time Division received reports that the attack by 1 Battalion 571 Infantry Regiment on the

11   See Report No. 101, Operation Jubilee, The Raid on Dieppe, Section 190.

12   Ibid., Section 192.

western edges of the Scie Valley at Hill Ferme aux Quatre-Vents was progressing nicely.[13]

While the described actions were taking place in Pourville, Major Law, commanding the main body of the Camerons, took them up the west bank of the River Scie. Initially, the plan was for the Camerons to move out of Pourville and advance along the east bank of the river in order to rendezvous with the tanks at Bois des Vertus.

The Camerons came under heavy and accurate German mortar fire almost the moment they entered Pourville. Getting out from under this fire was an immediate task. Unfortunately, for the Camerons it was quickly realised that the S. Sask. R. had not been able to advance eastwards, which would have enabled the Camerons to advance along their original route inland.

> The Company immediately made for the assembly position on the East side of the river, some boat loads to the right and some to the left of the main road through Pourville which ran parallel to the shore. However, before long it was obvious that the SSRs were unable to cross the bridge and that the town was becoming congested with troops. A Company was then given permission to advance to the objective along the Western side of the river.[14]

These orders to advance on the western side of the river were issued over the wireless by Major Law. Using it, Law was able to keep up effective communications with the companies under his command but he was unable to keep HQ 6th Canadian Infantry Brigade up to date as their wireless set had been knocked out earlier on.

Having issued his orders, Major Law now took the Camerons on the main southern road out of Pourville towards Hautot. This brought them under heavy machine gun fire from Four Winds Farm and the German mortar teams observing their fire had followed the battalion as it moved, keeping them under constant bombardment. At the south end of Pourville,

---

13   See the Battle Report of the German Commander-in-Chief West (GHQ Army Group D).

14   Narrative from A Company The Camerons' war diary, cited in See Report No. 101, Operation Jubilee, The Raid on Dieppe, Section 194.

Law turned right, heading southwards, and moved into the cover of some woods advancing towards Bernouville. From the eastern side of the river they had been under heavy German fire but the move into the woods provided them with cover against this. However, it did not protect them against German sniper fire, which constantly harassed the Camerons. The snipers were extremely difficult to find and neutralise, yet Nos 7 and 9 platoons of A Company did manage to locate and destroy a German machine gun post.

Arriving at Bernouville, the Canadians took a left onto a trail, passing a nearby farm. Advancing along the trail, they emerged from the cover of the woods near the road and rail bridges across the Scie river at Bas de Hautot.

> In a wood around a farm two Germans suddenly appeared but were promptly dealt with by Cpt Morden of the I.Sec and most of the boys of 8 Platoon. Practically every man could claim a hit.[15]

A Company now moved over to the right, taking a post there to protect the flank while B Company, along with elements of C Company, continued down the trail towards the bridges at Bas de Hautot. There they stopped and took up positions. On the high ground that looked down on the bridges and the approaches to the village the HQ Group took up their positions. While east of the river, the Canadians could see considerable German activity but there was no sign of the tanks they were supposed to rendezvous with. They had no way of knowing that very few tanks, if any, had managed to get off the beach at Dieppe.

Knowing that time was getting short and that he had no idea of what was going on elsewhere, Major Law decided on a new course of action. At 0900hrs he issued new orders for his men to cross the Scie and secure the high ground beyond the bridges. From there, A and B Companies were to push north to take on the German position at Four Winds Farm.

German troops were seen moving south from Pourville just as B and C Companies began their advance towards the bridges. The Camerons opened fire on the German troops, who suffered heavy casualties. Snipers Private A. Huppe and Private E. Herbert killed 15 Germans between them.[16]

---

15   See Report No. 101, Operation Jubilee, The Raid on Dieppe, Section 197.

16   This is according to Major Law.

At the same time, a horse-drawn German mortar team was engaged as it moved up the western bank of the Scie River from the south. 'We came onto two Germans at a crossroads with a horse-drawn 4 inch mortar. We shot the two Jerries and wrecked the mortar. About 100 yards from there we shot three Germans behind a fence.'[17]

A slightly different account exists from Private W. Pinder, who stated that they encountered three Germans, two who were already dead when they arrived and the third one they took prisoner. Major Law's evidence states that this prisoner carried an anti-tank rifle during the subsequent Canadian withdrawal.

These, however, were not the only Germans they would encounter. More were arriving. Three German horse-drawn close support guns arrived, crossed the northernmost bridge and took up a position on the eastern side of the river. This position covered the rest of the bridges and the Camerons soon found themselves under fire from these guns. As their 3in mortars had been knocked out in Pourville, they had no ability to take out these recently arrived German guns. In addition to these anti-tank guns the Germans now swept the Canadians with heavy machine gun and sniper fire from the high ground near Le Plessis.

Realising that the position was untenable, Major Law decided that fighting their way across the river was out of the question. At 0930hrs he issued orders via the wireless for the unit to withdraw back the way they had come. He sent a message to the S. Sask. R. advising them of his action and began withdrawal proceedings.

With the withdrawal now under way, Major Law ordered C Company to act as rearguard and as a result they took heavy casualties. In this action, most of the company's platoons were separated as the withdrawal proceeded. The Germans, too, suffered casualties.

On the road south of Pourville the withdrawing Canadians again came under heavy German machine-gun and mortar fire while also being harassed by German snipers. At 0956hrs the Canadian force, now comprising a platoon of the S. Sask. R. that had been sent out to contact them, entered Pourville. By this time, the Camerons still had 80 per cent of their force intact.

---

17   From the account described by Private H.E. Barnes, Camerons of Canada. See Report
      No. 101, Operation Jubilee, The Raid on Dieppe, Section 200.

As the Camerons had advanced inland 9 Platoon 'met with part of a platoon from S.S.Rs. They had taken out a section of 3 snipers but were under machine gun fire from a brick building in the valley just across the river.'[18]

> Situation east of Dieppe cleared up. No more danger at Berneval. Dieppe, about 1 dozen tanks shot up. Mopping up on the beach proceeds satisfactorily. To the west of Dieppe enemy still in position at Pourville, counterattack with two battalions is under way and going well. Entered the western position of Pourville. Apparently, no more reinforcements from the sea. The general impression: withdrawal. This now confirms the C-in-C West's former appreciation made on the basis of reports of backward ship movements that the enemy attack on Dieppe has failed.[19]

Changes were now to take place as the Germans prepared for the final assault on the Allied units still holding out in the area of Pourville-West and the western edges of the Scie valley. The Corps Commander from Dieppe arrived at 1155hrs at Divisional Command Pourville and provided his observations. The boundary between 302 Infantry Division on the left and 10 Panzer Division on the right was to be the Scie river. But this was in the event that 10 Panzer Division was ordered to join the counterattack on the remaining Allied units.

At the same time, the Klemm Regiment was still moving towards its forming up point at Offranville, from which it was to launch a counterattack on Pourville. No. 3 Battalion, 676 Infantry Regiment, was also still on the move and was supposed to launch its attack on Varengeville.

---

18   From the Account of Lance Sergeant W.C. Maxwell, who also stated that his platoon fired at the building from 500 yards away with no effect. This group of men from S. Sask. R. could have been No. 11 Platoon.

19   HQ 81 Corps report to GHQ West at 1249hrs.

Chapter 23

Withdrawal From Green Beach

> Lt.-Col. Merritt had become convinced that there was no possi-
> bility of gaining control of his objectives on the high ground east
> of Pourville.[1]

Evacuation of the wounded from Green Beach had already begun by 0846hrs.
Lieutenant Colonel Merritt had realised by this time that he had no hope of
taking the high ground east of Pourville. Even though the S. Sask. R. were
already considering evacuation and withdrawal, it would be sometime before
the general order was given. During that time, the Germans reinforced their
positions and pushed forward into new ones that would see them effectively
harassing the evacuation every step of the way.

Captain Runcie was of the opinion that the withdrawal time was for
1000hrs rather than 1100hrs. The reason why this is mentioned is because
it might explain why, in some cases, the Canadians prematurely withdrew
from commanding ground, which the Germans quickly occupied. Major
McRae, on the other hand, knew the time was 1100hrs.

Where this discrepancy is most obvious is with C Company of the S. Sask.
R., who withdrew from the high ground they had taken and moved back
into Pourville, reaching the village by 1000hrs. This is borne out by Private
Haggard, who saw them move back to the beach before any of the LCAs
had arrived to pick them up. 'C Company had withdrawn back at 1000hrs to
Pourville in the face of counterattack by a battalion of the enemy.'[2]

C Company, S. Sask. R. was, by this time, under the command of Major
Orme, who instructed Lieutenant McIlveen to send No. 15 Platoon to
cover No. 14 Platoon as they were withdrawing from their position due the

---

1   See Report No. 101, Operation Jubilee, The Raid on Dieppe, Section 216.

2   From the account of Captain C.B. Buchanan, C Company Adjutant. See Report No.
    101, Operation Jubilee, The Raid on Dieppe, Section 217.

imminent arrival of a large German force. McIlveen and his men provided covering fire for No. 14 up to the point when they reached the village of Pourville, when they took up a new position at the main crossroads of the village. This would have been around 1000hrs. At this point the Camerons started coming through the positions held at the crossroads.

> A and B Companies of the Camerons took up covering positions, but these were in the vicinity of the crossroads, and the adjacent high ground was now in German hands. There is some evidence that before evacuation was complete the enemy had actually got into houses at the west end of Green Beach.[3]

As a battalion of German infantry advancing from the direction of Le Quesnot moved forward, C Company was forced back to a defensive position on the edge of Pourville supported by elements of the Camerons.[4] This is reinforced by the Intelligence Log of HMS *Calpe*.

As the withdrawal was taking place the Germans took positions along the cliffs to the right of Lieutenant McIlveen's platoon around 1100hrs. Fifteen minutes later Lieutenant Colonel Merritt arrived and 'organised an attack which successfully wiped out these posts, and then he returned to the beach'.[5]

Also at 1100hrs the Canadian troops holding the high ground east of Pourville on the same road by which they had advanced began their withdrawal to the beach. 'At 1100hrs we started retiring under cover of the LMG back towards the beach.'[6]

Several troops from the Camerons had taken up positions in the public house east of the bridge in Pourville. Both Captain Edmondson and Captain Runcie were included in this party of men. They received the withdrawal order 'Vanquish 1100hrs' by wireless. Edmondson then began organising his troops into two parties, one under Corporal Hart 'who took up a position

---

3   See Report No. 101, Operation Jubilee, The Raid on Dieppe, Section 217.

4   This information is from Major McRae, who directed C Company of S. Sask. R. to their fall-back defensive positions along with the elements of the Camerons to support them.

5   See Report No. 101, Operation Jubilee, The Raid on Dieppe, Section 219.

6   From the account of Private D.M. Davies, B Company the Camerons and from Lieutenant J.R. Nesbitt, D Company, S. Sask. R., See Report No. 101, Operation Jubilee, The Raid On Dieppe, Section 220.

near the bend in the road' while the other party of men remained in the pub under the command of Captain Edmondson and Corporal Jackson. This party of men provided covering fire from the upper storey of the pub for Corporal Hart's men.

> The bulk of the troops dropped over the cliff by 1100hrs. Between 1100hrs and 1125 we did not see anyone withdraw. We withdrew at 1125hrs.[7]

Despite all the Canadian efforts in fighting their rearguard action to support the withdrawal, the Germans were able to take up positions from which they could bring heavy and accurate fire onto the beach at Pourville. Indeed, this was true throughout the operation despite the best efforts of the Canadians to stop it.

The withdrawal at Green Beach was more successful than that at Blue Beach, which could be down to the early attempts by a handful of LCAs to pick up the troops.

> At 0930 LCA 521 went into Green Beach but was unable to contact anybody and was forced to retire under heavy fire from machine-gun posts and the battery on the East Cliff. At 1000 LCA 315 went into Green Beach. The Beach party could be seen taking cover under the wall, being held there by fire from light machine-gun posts on the West Cliff and by heavy calibre fire from the East Cliff which covered their line of retreat. One man was seen to attempt to reach the boat but was instantly killed. The boat was then forced to retire.[8]

At 1104hrs the first wave of LCAs came in to pick up the troops waiting for evacuation back to England. It was a harrowing time. The tide was now out, making the beach 200 yards wide so that every time the troops tried to move across it towards the boats they were caught in a crossfire of mortars,

---

7   From the account of Captain Edmondson, Report No. 101, Operation Jubilee, The Raid on Dieppe, Section 221.

8   This account comes from the Flotilla Officer of HMS *Invicta*, Report No. 101, Operation Jubilee, The Raid on Dieppe, Section 223.

machine guns, small arms and artillery. Lieutenant Commander Prior, Royal Navy, was on the beach preparing for the withdrawal. He had sent a message requesting the casualties be evacuated. One LCA did try to get in to bring off the wounded but as Prior was setting up a smokescreen, the landing craft came under heavy German fire and withdrew.

Prior had done an excellent job in ensuring that the wire obstacles had been cleared away and that the wounded had been placed under cover. Some of the prisoners taken by the Canadians were put to good use as stretcher bearers but the evidence indicates that few of the stretcher cases were evacuated safely. During this phase of the operation, the Camerons suffered far more casualties than they had done during the entire operation due to the heavy crossfire from the Germans on the cliffs overlooking the beach.

The Flotilla Officer of HMS *Invicta* describes the ferocity of the German fire:

> At 1100hrs LCAs 262, 317, 251 and 214 went into Green Beach. LCA317 was badly hit and had to be abandoned on the beach. LCA251 was filled with more troops than she could carry. All efforts to clear some of the men away were impossible and she sank under fire about 200 yards from the beach. LCA262 managed to reach L50 (Destroyer) alongside which it had to be abandoned and sunk. LCA214 left the beach fully loaded and was taken in tow by another LCA to a destroyer where she also had to be abandoned and sunk.[9]

At this point LCA250 and LCA315 began picking up survivors from the sinking landing craft and from those who managed to get back to the beach. These craft came in twice more to rescue as many as they could.

According to the account of the Commanding Officer of HMS *Prince Leopold*, the flotilla that this vessel was part of was destined to evacuate the men on Red Beach. Instead they ran into Green Beach.

> At the order to re-embark troops I proceeded to the beach, which lay behind a thick smokescreen; an ML warned me of men in the

9   Account of the Flotilla Officer of HMS *Invicta*, Report No. 101, Operation Jubilee, The Raid on Dieppe, Section 226.

water and coming through the smoke I found the men swimming out from the beaches to get away from the machine gunning at the flanks. There were some corpses in the water and those that were alive had little strength left. I picked about 20 men out of the water and proceeded towards the beach on the right flank of our flotilla. By this time, one engine was not working and the steering appeared defective. I stopped the boat before a group of men who had waded some 100 yards out, four were carrying a severely wounded man on a stretcher. We were now bow on to a machine gun position and it was impossible to manoeuvre the craft owing both to the mechanical defect and the weight of men clambering over the bow and stern; many were shot in the back as we pulled them over the bow. When every man in the vicinity was on board we had great difficulty in dragging the injured men from the lowered door. I gave orders to go astern on one engine which was a slow process, but by this time the steering had improved and we were able to put out to sea.[10]

In the accounts from the surviving officers and crewmen of various landing craft who witnessed the events on Green Beach some stated that LCA215 was bombed around 1100hrs and sank just off Green Beach. Some of the LCAs from the flotilla of *Prince Leopold* transferred the troops they had evacuated from Green Beach to larger ships and then moved off to assist in the evacuation from the Dieppe main beaches. More than twelve LCAs and other ships took part in the evacuation of troops from Green Beach, with the loss of at least four vessels.

The evacuation of Green Beach was not without offshore fire support from larger ships. HMS *Locust*, for example, from 1130hrs to 1145hrs bombarded German positions firing on the beach. The ship moved as close as it could to the shore, where it fired smoke bombs to provide cover for the evacuation.

Officers and crew of HMS *Locust* witnessed the beach come under intense German bombardment by artillery and aircraft around 1240hrs. For the next five minutes *Locust* turned its guns on the eastern cliff, firing on German positions that were giving the evacuation a difficult time. However, HMS

---

10   Account from Lieutenant D.R.V. Flery, RNVR, commanding LCA 197, Appx 2E to Enclosure No. 13, Report of Naval Force Commander.

Locust then came under German fire from 4in guns and from German dive-bombers, forcing it to retreat under the cover of smoke.[11]

Locust was assisted in its fire support by SGB9, which began making smoke until it could no longer do so. At 1234hrs it moved in closer to the shore toward the high ground at the end of the beach and began bombarding the German positions there from 600 yards out with 3in guns. The Germans returned the fire from SGB9 but it was ineffective. SGB9 then continued to fire on these German positions for another four minutes before it moved off at 1259hrs.

As far as the Germans were concerned, the first sightings of the boats returning to the beaches to evacuate the remaining troops occurred at 1253hrs from Pourville-East but, on first observation, they were not sure if the aim was for the British to land more troops or to take the remaining troops off the beaches and back to England. However, it soon became apparent they were withdrawing.

> By 1336hrs Division received reports that Pourville-East, Cau de Cote, was free of enemy soldiers and that fighting was over. An attack by one platoon from each 6 Company and 11 Company 571 Infantry Regiment had destroyed all Allied resistance there. Thick black smoke still covered Pourville-west. Finally, by 1358hrs Pourville fell silent, the fighting there was over.[12]
>
> Enemy who landed East of Dieppe annihilated! In Dieppe itself situation cleared up. A number of small points of resistance remain. Regiment in action estimates prisoners to number 1,000. High ground West of Dieppe to Pourville always remained in our hands. 1 Bn 571 Inf Regt committed against Pourville and have partly entered it. Enemy beachhead to the West of Pourville still 1km deep on a front of 6 km in area offering poor view (gullies and woods). Corps Reserve placed at disposal of 302 Div and attacking from Offranville against sector Pourville – Varengeville in support of attack by 1 BN 571 Inf Regt. One Bn has been moved ahead

---

11 This information on HMS *Locust* is from the HMS *Locust* Report, Appx 20 to Enclosure No. 13, Report of Naval Force Commander.

12 See the Battle Report of the German Commander-in-Chief West (GHQ Army Group D).

to St. Marguerite to prevent the English from escaping from the beachhead there.[13]

Offshore, Royal Navy destroyers were also involved in supporting the evacuation, primarily by embarking troops brought to them by the landing craft. One such destroyer was HMS *Bleasdale*, which from 1105hrs lay in close to Green Beach and came under 'unpleasantly accurate fire from shore batteries and machine-guns from the cliff'.[14] However, as the situation on Green Beach at the time was unknown, the ship was unable to provide any accurate fire support to help the men desperately trying to get off the beach and back home to safety.

Other destroyers such as HMS *Albrighton* and HMS *Brocklesby* were also able to provide support for the evacuation. *Albrighton* was able to bring 182 men back to England along with eight casualties.[15]

HMS *Brocklesby*, in addition to picking up men in the water near an overturned LCA, was able to bombard the German positions on the cliffs using her 4in guns. Reports from the commanding officer of this ship stated that they saw three German Ju 88 bombers fly in low, under the height of the cliffs, that used flame-throwing equipment against the Allied troops trying to get off the beach. This was immediately west of the beach.[16]

The Klemm Regiment was still in the process of forming up for its assault on Pourville and Varengeville but by 1400hrs this was no longer required. Instead, their job was changed to combing through the terrain between the Lighthouse and Pourville for prisoners, Allied and their own wounded, dead or missing. It became a clean-up operation only. Divisional Reserve was still stationed at d'Arques Woods awaiting orders to attack but, by mid-afternoon they were no longer needed for an attack.[17]

---

13   This report arrived at GHQ West from HQ 81 Corps at 1433hrs.

14   See Appendix 24 to Enclosure No. 13, Report of Naval Force Commander.

15   See Appendix 26 to Enclosure No. 13, Report of Naval Force Commander.

16   See Appendix 27 to Enclosure No. 13, Report of Naval Force Commander.

17   See the Battle Report of the German Commander-in-Chief West (GHQ Army Group D).

Several men were successfully evacuated from Green Beach but despite this several more were unable to be embarked on the ships as the German fire intensified. Those that remained formed a small bridgehead until they were forced to surrender and were captured. Reports from two key witnesses provide the details for the last few hours of the men on Green Beach. The two men in particular are Lieutenant Commander Prior and Captain John Runcie, who were both captured.

We will look at the accounts of these two men because they illustrate the depth of the German defences, the accuracy of their fire and their ability to repel the invaders.

According to the reports, Captain Runcie stated that:

> The evacuation was covered by a perimeter established in Pourville by those troops who had operated in the area throughout the morning. Through this the main body of the Camerons, who had gone inland with Major Law, withdrew to the beach. As evacuation proceeded, the perimeter was progressively narrowed and in the last stage the party remaining withdrew to the beach itself and took cover behind the sea-wall. Scaffolding which had been erected for the purpose of repairing the wall gave the troops the means of firing over it at the enemy. The party on the beach was commanded by Lieutenant Colonel Merritt and was composed of men of the S. Sask. R. and the Camerons, Captain Runcie being the senior officer of the latter unit. The party held on under fire in the hope that boats might arrive to take them off, but this did not take place and Captain Runcie is of the opinion that at this late stage it would have been suicidal for the craft to have attempted to return.[18]

Lieutenant Commander Prior believed that had there been a bombardment on the German positions on the hill east of Pourville they would have been able to get all the men off the beach. 'I requested the Army to fire all the houses on the fore shore to give us a smokescreen but the incendiary grenades were all defective.'[19]

---

18   See Report No. 101, Operation Jubilee, The Raid on Dieppe, Section 239.

19   Account from Lieutenant Commander Prior, Report No. 101, Operation Jubilee, The Raid on Dieppe, Section 240.

According to Captain Runcie's report, he saw Lieutenant Colonel Merritt run across the wide beach towards the water's edge under very heavy German fire in order to help a wounded soldier lying there. Merritt managed to pick up the soldier and carry him back to shelter under the sea wall without being hit.

At 1500hrs, according to Runcie's report, after he and Lieutenant Colonel Merritt had deliberated, realising that there was no more chance of the boats coming back for them, they surrendered to the Germans. Runcie goes on to state that in the prison camp that night he found, of the men of the Camerons, there were 120 other ranks. He believed that of the men that had been captured at the same time as he had been, those men of the 'rearguard' left on the beach, they were equally divided in numbers between the Camerons and the S. Sask. R.[20]

> Reports had come in from civilians that some British units had been spotted hiding in orchards, copses and gorges between Pourville and Quiberville so HQ 10 Panzer Division at 1600hrs ordered the 10th Motor-Cyclist Rifle Battalion to move through the area looking for these men who were supposedly hiding along with any other Allied stragglers. However, none were found during this operation.[21]

While the Canadians on Green Beach suffered heavy casualties, they were not as heavy as those on Blue Beach.

The Camerons left England with a total complement of 32 officers and 471 other ranks – 503 men all told.[22] Of this number, 24 officers and 322 other ranks were killed, wounded, missing or captured, and of this number six officers and 41 other ranks were killed. Five of the wounded later died of their injuries. The prisoners amounted to nine officers and 161 other ranks

---

20 Casualty reports from the Canadian Military HQ published March 1943 indicate there were nine officers and 60 other ranks of S. Sask. R., while the numbers of Camerons stood at nine officers and 161 other ranks as prisoners rather than casualties. So slightly different to Captain Runcie's count.

21 See the Battle Report of the German Commander-in-Chief West (GHQ Army Group D).

22 This information comes from the Overseas Records Office, 31 December 1942, CMHQ file 18/Dieppe/1/2.

with four other ranks dying while in captivity. Seventeen men were reported missing, while nine officers and 94 other ranks were wounded. In total, 265 all ranks of the Camerons returned to England; that included all of the wounded.[23]

As far as the South Saskatchewan Regiment is concerned, their strength on embarkation for the raid on Dieppe was 25 officers and 498 other ranks, a total of 523 men.[24] Casualties amounted to 19 officers and 320 other ranks, and of these two officers and 58 other ranks were killed, with five more men dying later of their wounds. Nine officers and 80 other ranks were captured during the raid, with two more dying of their wounds while prisoners of war. Seventeen of all ranks were listed as missing. The remaining troops that returned to England from the South Saskatchewan included seven officers and 159 other ranks wounded. This figure is nearly half of the total number that returned to England – 355 in all.[25]

---

23 See CMHQ file 18/Dieppe/2 from reports dated 1 March 1943.

24 See Overseas Records Office, 31 December 1942, CMHQ file 18/Dieppe/1/2.

25 Ibid.

Part 3
The Air Battle

Chapter 24

The Luftwaffe: A Deadly Foe

According to the Canadian official history of the Dieppe raid, the troops were originally embarked on 2 and 3 July and sealed on board their ships. High-ranking officers visited the various ships and all the troops were fully briefed. The operation was cancelled because of the weather and the troops were disembarked, but not before the Luftwaffe had attacked the ships lying in Yarmouth Roads near the west end of the Solent. The Canadian historian says: 'As the troops had been fully informed of the objective of the proposed raid, and once they left the ships it would no longer be possible to maintain complete secrecy, General Montgomery recommended the operation should now "be off for all time".'[1]

While we have concentrated exclusively on the land campaign and to some degree on the naval activities, we have not looked at what was really going on in the air. The air battle above the Dieppe landings was arguably the greatest air battle in the west up to that time. It was certainly one in which so many German fighter pilots in the west had not been involved with since the Battle of Britain days.

For the period of 1940–42 the Royal Air Force had been conducting daily raids into northern France, Holland and Belgium using mostly Spitfires and twin-engined medium daylight bombers. These raids were on a small scale and were designed to bring the Luftwaffe into battle. However, the number of German fighters that were actually able to get into positions where they could engage with the RAF was usually quite small.

Dieppe was different. For this operation there was a steady stream of aircraft, bombers, fighter-bombers and fighters crossing the Channel and remaining over the area to support the landings.

---

1   Johnson, (Johnnie), Air Vice Marshal, *Wing Leader*, Goodall paperback edition, sixth paperback edition, Crecy Publishing, 2019, Manchester, p.141.

The air effort would be controlled by Leigh-Mallory from his headquarters at 11 Group. The operation would begin with the bombing attacks against enemy strong-points and all ground attack leaders would report on their outgoing flight to a fighter controller in the headquarters ship. Flying fortresses of the Eighth Air Force would make their second daylight operation of the war when twenty-four of them attacked the airfield at Abbeville. Our own job was simple and straightforward. Spitfire wings of Fighter Command would maintain an air umbrella over Dieppe and although Lord Tedder later said that air umbrellas are apt to leak, we can claim that we held the Luftwaffe off the backs of the troops and naval forces below.[2]

Because the Luftwaffe, to all intents and purposes, was defending its territory, it could bring all of its might in the western sector to bear on the attacking Allies, thus creating a huge air battle that lasted for hours.

The enemy [Luftwaffe] reacted almost as had been foreseen, at first, he did not appear to appreciate the scale of our effort and he used only 25/30 fighters in each sortie. As the day went on the strength of his sorties increased to between 50/100 aircraft. At first fighter bombers, and later when the moves from Holland had been effected, night bombers in increasing numbers were used until all his resources on the Western Front were in action.[3]

In this sector there were two German fighter wings or Jagdgeschwader, JG 2 and JG 26. The area of operations for JG 2 covered the area west of the River Seine, while east of the Seine was the area covered by JG 26. Commanding JG 26 was Major Gerhard Schopfel, who by this point in the war had 40[4] kills to his credit and held the Knight's Cross. Most of his victories had been

2   Johnson, (Johnnie), Air Vice Marshal, *Wing Leader*, Goodall paperback edition, sixth paperback edition, Crecy Publishing, 2019, Manchester, p.142.

3   From Combined Report on The Dieppe Raid, 1942, Annex 7, Report by the Air Force Commander, Appreciation of the Enemy's Air Effort.

4   Of those 40, he had shot down 29 aircraft during the Battle of Britain. Norman Franks, *Dieppe: The Greatest Air Battle 19th August 1942*, Grub Street, London, 2010.

during the Battle of Britain. Because JG 26 was near the Dieppe area, it was the first of the two fighter wings to take part in the battle.[5]

JG 26 was organised into three Groups or Gruppen. The staff headquarters that commanded these three groups was at Saint-Omer/Wizernes. Hauptman Johannes Siefert, commanding 1 Gruppe, was based with his group at Saint-Omer/Arques, while II Gruppe, at Abbeville/Drucat, was under the command of Wilhelm-Ferdinand Galland. III Gruppe was based at Wevelgem/Courtrai and was commanded by Hauptman Klaus Mietusch.

JG 2 was also organised into three Gruppes and was under the overall command of Major Walter Oesau. JG 2 I Gruppe, based at Triqueville, was commanded by Oberleutnant Erich Leie. II Gruppe of JG 2, based at Beaumont-le-Roger, was under the command of Hauptman Helmut Bolz, while III Gruppe stationed at Maupertus was commanded by Hauptman Hans Hahn. As these were fighter groups the Focke-Wulf Fw 190 A-2 and A-3 were the main equipment. As for fighter-bombers, both groups used the Fw 190 A-3U1, the Messerschmitt Bf 109G-1 as well as some Bf 109Fs.

Some JG 26 pilots were highly experienced and had been with their respective organisations since before the war. Knight's Cross holder Hauptman Siefert had been with JG 26 prior to the war and like Schopfel had also racked up 40 victories. Also, in JG 26, Adolf Galland's brother, Wilhelm-Ferdinand, had 12 victories by the time of the Dieppe landings on 19 August 1942. Another experienced JG 26 pilot was Klaus Mietusch, who had been with the squadron since 1938.

Experienced fighter pilots of JG 2 included its leader, Walter Oesau, along with Erich Leie, who had 42 victories and also held the Knight's Cross. In May 1942 he had taken command of I/JG 2. Another highly experienced pilot from this group was Hans Hahn, who had one of the highest scores at 65 kills. He too held the Knight's Cross with the addition of Oak Leaves.

The German bomber force of the Luftwaffe at the time of the landings was heavily involved in attacking Allied shipping and the landing craft on the beaches. The majority of the bombers came from Kampfgeschwader 2 (KG2), which were primarily based in the Netherlands. The Dornier 217E was the main bomber that equipped KG2, while other units that were involved in the battle such as KG77 I Staffel flew Junkers 88 twin-engined bombers.

---

5   This information comes from Norman Franks, *Dieppe: The Greatest Air Battle 19th August 1942*, Grub Street, London, 2010.

Do 217s from II Gruppe KG40 were also involved in the operations of the day, as were the Heinkel 111s of III/KG53.

> Bombers were not actively engaged over the scene of the operation before 1000hrs, but from then onwards an average of about 20 LR Bombers kept up harassing attacks, mainly directed against our shipping standing off Dieppe. Formations varied in size from 3 aircraft to 12. There are no specific instances of them receiving special fighter escort but fighters in the target area provided local protection to their bombers as far as possible and received warning of this proximity in certain circumstances.[6]

Once the operation was under way the first of the German fighters to respond to the Allied landings came from JG 26. At 0600hrs on 19 August they had just ten serviceable aircraft and they were all scrambled to meet the threat from the Allies. Not much longer after this took place another 16 fighters were scrambled, eight from 2 and 3 Staffel respectively. These were all Fw 190 fighters. II/JG 26 was the first to draw blood when Oberfeldwebel (Ofw) Heinrich Bierwith[7] destroyed a Spitfire.

Norman Franks, author of the excellent *Dieppe The Greatest Air Battle, 19th August 1942*, suggests that the Germans had not maintained their fighter squadrons/Staffels in a state of readiness despite the fact that the tides were in a favourable condition for landings to take place. Low cloud and rain had been predicted for the day, so the assumption by the Germans was that the risk of an Allied attack on the French coast was low. In addition, several Luftwaffe pilots had been given leave and were not due back at their bases until after noon. However, once the alarm had been sounded and the Allied aircraft were over Dieppe in force, the rapid return of these pilots began in earnest.

> Early in the day, enemy air effort was confined entirely to fighters patrolling the area in small numbers. Occasionally, dive attacks on our ships were made from height. The German control merely

---

6   Combined Report on the Dieppe Raid, Annex F to Annex 7, Reactions of The German Air Force, Appreciation of the Enemy's Air Effort.

7   Ibid.

instructed his aircraft to go to the Dieppe area, where large numbers of British bombers and fighters were operating.[8]

Once these pilots were back and the Germans realised just how big the Allied operation was they began to scramble more and more aircraft (mostly fighters) to face the large numbers of RAF aircraft over Dieppe. Luftwaffe actions over this area were being monitored by British radar, which, according to Franks, monitored fifty German fighters from the Desvres and Saint-Omer sectors heading towards the building air battle. Radar also picked up another 12 German aircraft from Lille and 12 to 15 more from the Dunkirk area.[9]

In the Le Havre area, JG 2, led by Galland, were taking off around 0940–0941hrs. This was 11 Gruppe, who were joined later by a further number of fighters from Abbeville. Between 0930 and 1100hrs German fighter cover reached its peak, according to Franks, 'during the time they covered and escorted the Dorniers, an estimated 100+ being recorded'. More Luftwaffe bombers were escorted by fighters between 1200 and 1300hrs, while at 1400hrs British radar picked up more German aircraft heading for the battle zone from Belgium and Holland.

At 1030hrs, American B-17 heavy bombers pounded the German airfields in the Abbeville area, destroying several fighters on the ground as observed by the bomber crews and the pilots of their escorting Spitfires.[10] The Germans on the ground had only a three-minute warning of the attack and were unable to save many of their fighters. Several Fw 190s were destroyed and the airfield was out of action until 1500hrs, when British radar picked up activity in this sector once again. This activity was part of a raid on the beaches consisting of more than 80 aircraft.

The Luftwaffe was extremely active that day in defending the beaches and trying to stop the Allies. That day Do 217s and other bombers flew more than 145 sorties, while the fighters, Fw 190s and Bf 109s, flew almost 800.

---

8   See the Combined Report on The Dieppe Raid, 1942, Annex 7, Report by the Air Force Commander, Appreciation of the Enemy's Air Effort.

9   See Norman Franks, *Dieppe: The Greatest Air Battle, 19th August 1942*, Grub Street, London, 2010.

10   Ibid.

Some of the Luftwaffe fighter pilots engaged in the battle flew as many as six sorties during the day.[11]

Many Luftwaffe pilots excelled during the battle, either increasing their scores or racking up new victories. For example, Staffelkapitän Josef Sepp Wurmheller could be considered as the most outstanding Luftwaffe pilot of the air battle over the beaches of Dieppe. The reason for this consideration is that he had a broken foot on the morning of 19 August that was encased in a plaster cast. He already had 22 victories, ten of which he had shot down in May and the remaining 12 in June.

> Our first thoughts at the briefing were that we far preferred our own
> task in the air to that of the troops on the ground. We were pleased
> we were airmen and not soldiers, for some of us had flown over this
> part of France for almost two years and had a healthy respect for
> the German defences and gunners. Quite a few of our own pilots
> had been shot down in this area, to return with tales of bristling
> defences and a heavily fortified coastal belt. Our own opinion of
> Dieppe was hardly in accord with the official intelligence estimate,
> which indicated that the town was only lightly defended.[12]

On the morning of the 19th, when it was obvious what the Allies were up to, Wurmheller hobbled to his Fw 190 and was helped into the cockpit by a member of the ground crew. However, his machine developed engine trouble shortly after take-off and he force-landed in a field, hitting his head during the rough landing. With a raging headache he managed to get to a German post, where he was taken back to his airfield by car. Franks highlights this account in his book, *The Greatest Air Battle*.[13] Helped into another Fw 190, Wurmheller quickly took off and entered the fray over Dieppe. Two Spitfires and a Blenheim fell to his guns. Returning to base, his headache getting worse, he rearmed and refuelled and quickly took off. On this sortie he shot down three Spitfires and another on his fourth sortie over Dieppe. With his

---

11   These figures are from Franks' excellent book, *Dieppe, The Greatest Air Battle*, Grub Street, London, 2010.

12   Johnson (Johnnie), Air Vice Marshal, *Wing Leader*, Goodall paperback edition, Crecy Publishing, 2019, Manchester, p.142.

13   This entire account is documented in Norman Franks, *Dieppe: The Greatest Air Battle, 19th August 1942*.

headache so bad that his vision was now impaired, he had to fly with a veil over his eyes on his last sortie of the day. It was later discovered that he was suffering from concussion as a result of his forced landing. The victories he scored, however, brought his score up to 60 and he was the 146th Luftwaffe pilot to be awarded the *Eichenlaub* (Oak Leaves) to his Knight's Cross.[14]

> By now 20 to 30 enemy fighters were continuously on patrol in the area. During the main actions fought with the FW 190s at this stage of the battle, Flying Officer Cholewka of No. 317 (Polish) Squadron, particularly distinguished himself. Having fought a duel with two Fw 190s which were attacking a Spitfire, he was wounded in the right arm and right leg, lost consciousness twice and eventually landed holding the control column between his knees and operating the mechanism controlling the undercarriage with his left foot.[15]

Staffelkapitän Oberleutnant Siegfried Schnell, commanding 9 Staffel, 11 Gruppe, JG 2, also had a good battle. Unlike Wurmheller, he had already received his Oak Leaves to his Knight's Cross. While flying several flights over Dieppe he shot down five Spitfires, which increased his tally of victories to 70. By the time of his death over the Russian Front in early 1944 he had scored 93 aerial victories.

Other successful Luftwaffe pilots that day include Oberleutnant Kurt Ebersberger, of JG 26, who claimed victories 25 through to 28 of his personal tally, those being four Spitfires falling to his guns. Oberleutnant Fuelbert Zink, also of JG 26, shot down two Spitfires and a Mustang. No. 2 Staffel I/JG 26 had a hero in Emil Babenz, who claimed three Spitfires shot down that increased his total to 21. That day of this monumental air battle was the 25th birthday of Staffelkapitän of 7/JG 2, Oberleutnant Egon Meyer, which he celebrated by shooting down two Spitfires that brought his total up to 50. Sadly, he was shot down in March of 1944 but his total at the time of his death amounted to 102 victories, all gained in the west.

---

14 Franks, Norman, *Dieppe: The Greatest Air Battle, 19th August 1942*, Grub Street, London, 2010.

15 Operation Jubilee Combined Arms Report, The Dieppe Raid, Execution and The Air Battle.

Thirty Luftwaffe pilots made claims in the battle over Dieppe and one of those was the commander of 10 (Jabo) Staffel, JG 2, Oberleutnant Fritz Schröter. He was awarded the Knight's Cross for his outstanding leadership during the massive air battle of Dieppe. The list of claims made by his Staffel include one destroyer sunk by bombs plus two landing craft sunk, another destroyer, two trawlers and two landing craft damaged, with one RAF aircraft shot down.

> By 1100 hours, the activities of the enemy in the air had increased and the form of his attack had altered. Most of the enemy bombers were seeking to drop their bombs from between 10 and 12,000 feet, protected by escorts of Fw 190s at 15,000 ft. Two Squadrons of Spitfire units, Nos 402 and 611, were therefore sent to deal with this situation at a height of 23,000 ft, and this they did most successfully.[16]

> The German Bomber Force throughout confined its attentions to our convoy and did not harass our troops ashore. A bomber jettisoning its bombs crippled HMS *Berkeley* shortly before 1300 hours. She was later sunk by our own forces.[17]

Yet despite these successes the Luftwaffe fighter numbers had been substantially depleted by late afternoon on 19 August 1942. This was due to losses and battle damage, and this had virtually grounded the entire fighter complement, according to Franks. The Luftwaffe had only 18 spare Fw 190s available for the whole of its forces that day and these were from the Wevelgem Forwarding Centre.[18] Each of these aircraft were issued to various units during the day. By the end of the battle, stocks of ammunition for the 20mm cannon had been completely exhausted and were only available the following day by special airlift.

The Fw 190 pilots ran into the Mustang for the first time with mixed results. However, these were not the Mustangs that appeared with the

---

16   Ibid.

17   Operation Jubilee Combined Report, The Dieppe Raid. Annex 7, Report of the Air Commander Sir Trafford Leigh-Mallory.

18   These would have been fighters in reserve to cover losses.

daylight bomber raid over Europe two years later or the Mustangs that roamed the skies at will in 1944 and 1945. These were the early marks with the Alison engine, which did not give the aircraft its potency until this was exchanged for the Rolls-Royce Merlin.

German claims, however, would indicate that the Allies had lost far more aircraft during the operation:

> In August 1942 the British and Canadians carried out Operation Jubilee, a raid on Dieppe harbour. Fighter, Bomber and RAF Coastal Commands supported the Commando landings. JG 2 was based in northwest France under the command of Jafü 3. Stab and I. Gruppe were at Triqueville, II. Gruppe was at Beamont-le-Roger and III. Gruppe at Cherbourg-Maupertus. 11. (Höhen) Staffel, with high altitude Bf 109 G-1s acted independently at Ligescourt, nominally under the command of JG 26. The RAF did not succeed in forcing the Luftwaffe into a pitched battle over the beachhead and Fighter Command in particular, suffered heavy casualties. The British claimed to have inflicted heavy casualties on the Luftwaffe, the balance sheet showed the reverse; Allied aircraft losses amounted to 106, including 88 RAF fighters (70 Spitfires were lost to all causes) and 18 bombers, against 48 Luftwaffe aircraft lost. Included in that total were 28 bombers, half of them Dornier Do 217s from KG 2. JG 2 lost 14 Fw 190s with eight pilots killed and JG 26 lost six Fw 190s with six pilots killed. The Spitfire Squadrons, 42 with Mark Vs, and only four with Mark IXs were tasked with close air support, fighter escort and air-superiority missions. The exact number of Spitfires lost to the Fw 190 Gruppe is unknown. The Luftwaffe claimed 61 of the 106 RAF machines lost, which included all types: JG 2 claimed 40 and JG 26 claimed 21. Wing Commander Minden Blake was among the notable British casualties; the 130 Squadron leader was captured after being shot down by a Fw 190.[19]

---

19   From Jagdgeschwader 2, Wikipedia, 12 May 2021, Creative Commons Attribution Share-Alike License.

As we can see, there are some discrepancies in the numbers of aircraft shot down on both sides of the air battle over Dieppe. Digging deeper into the details of that fateful day may shed light on some of these.

RAF operations began with the North Weald Wing, which took off from their base around 0610hrs. According to Franks, 36 Spitfires got airborne led by Wing Commander F.D.S. Scott-Malden DFC, in charge of 242, 331, and 332 Squadrons. As Scott-Malden turned his wing out to sea the squadrons were stacked up, with 242 Squadron flying low at 3,000ft, 331 above them and 332 flying top cover.[20]

Up to this point no major Luftwaffe action had been seen except for small groups of Fw 190s and Bf 109s. However, by the time the wing arrived over the ships waiting off the Dieppe beaches they encountered the first large-scale Luftwaffe defensive attacks on the landings. Shortly after 0655hrs, both 331 and 332 squadrons were attacked by more than 30 Fw 190s and Bf 109s, resulting in a large battle of turning, diving, whirling dogfights. Three Fw 190s went down to the Spitfires of 332 and two more were damaged but two RAF pilots, Sergeant Per Bergsland and Sergeant Johnny Staubo, were shot down and taken prisoner.[21]

While the battle was building, radar stations along the southern coast of England began picking up a steady stream of German aircraft heading towards the battle area. Many of these plots were coming from the Saint-Omer and Abbeville sectors.

Scott-Malden's number two, Sergeant Bergsland, had been unable to keep up with his leader as the aircraft fought through cloud and the smoke from the landings below. He eventually lost sight of his leader and was then shot down and taken prisoner. 'Bergsland eventually wound up at Stalag Luft III at Sagan. He was one of the escapers in the Great Escape and one of the only three who succeeded in returning to England, in his case via Sweden.'[22]

The two Norwegian squadrons of the wing, 331 and 332, commanded respectively by Major Hedge Mehre DFC and Major Wilhelm Mohr DFC, had their share of the action. Mohr, for example, was hit early in the melee

---

20   This information comes from Franks, Norman, *Dieppe: The Greatest Air Battle, 19th August 1942*, Grub Street, London, 2010.

21   Ibid.

22   Franks, Norman, Dieppe: *The Greatest Air Battle, 19th August 1942*, Grub Street, London, 2010.

and was forced to break away from the battle. Major Mehre, commanding 331 Squadron, fared better. According to Franks, he managed to destroy two Fw 190s and damage another.

Also flying with the Norwegians was Captain Birkstead, a Danish pilot, who claimed the destruction of another Fw 190 and together with Sergeant Fredrik S. Fearnley shared another German fighter probably destroyed. The squadron claimed two more damaged in this action. Second Lieutenant Johannes Greiner, Major Mehre's number two, was hit by cannon fire from an Fw 190 and then again by flak, forcing him to spiral down until he managed to regain control. With shell splinters in his leg, he righted his stricken Spitfire and climbed to approximately 4,000ft, where he was able to safely bale out.[23]

> The enemy fighters were mostly Fw 190s and there were many brisk encounters with them in which, among others, No. 332 (Norwegian) Squadron distinguished itself under the command of Major W. Mohr DFC. This squadron shot down three of the enemy. Despite a fractured shin, Major Mohr remained on duty throughout the day and the squadron, led later by Captain F. Thorsager, made three sorties and claimed a total of seven enemy aircraft destroyed and eight damaged.[24]

Far below, No. 242 Squadron were not involved in the battle raging above them. At their height of around 2,000ft their visibility was good and the pilots spotted a blazing tanker in the harbour that subsequently exploded. German gunners north-east of the town of Dieppe were shelling Allied landing craft and troops that had managed to make it ashore.

Commanding 242 Squadron, Squadron Leader T.C. Parker radioed in to direct fire from the ships onto these German gunners. Two Fw 190s dived on the Allied positions, strafing the harbour area, the beaches and the landing craft. One of the Spitfires rolled into a dive and tore after the German

---

23   According to Franks, Greiner was picked up later by a motor launch: Franks, Norman, *Dieppe: The Greatest Air Battle, 19th August 1942*, Grub Street, London, 2010.

24   Operation Jubilee Combined Arms Report, The Dieppe Raid, Execution and the Air Battle, the Air Narrative.

fighters, firing, but this had no effect and the two German pilots managed to climb away out of range.

This initial large air battle also included twelve Spitfires from 403 Squadron, Canadians, who took off from Manston at 0645hrs. In command was Squadron Leader L.S. Ford DFC, who led the fighters towards Dieppe and they were immediately in the thick of the battle, tangling with Fw 190s and Bf 109s. Almost immediately two Canadian pilots attacked and destroyed a single Fw 190,[25] while Pilot Officer H.J. Murphy fired three bursts of machine gun and cannon fire at a Bf 109. Shells hammered into the German aircraft, which sent pieces flying in all directions. The stricken aircraft rolled onto its back, now in flames, and fell to earth out of control, crashing south-east of the town of Dieppe. While the Canadians had shot down two German aircraft, they lost three pilots who failed to return to base.[26]

More Canadians from 416 Squadron were also involved in this air battle, though at the tail end of it. Led by Squadron Leader Lloyd Chadburn, 416 Squadron had been assigned a patrol time of 0720hrs for them to arrive over Dieppe at around 12,000ft and begin their patrol above Red, White and Blue beaches. Upon arrival the pilots spotted several Fw 190s but did not engage them. Nearly 7,000ft below, 616 Squadron, led by Squadron Leader H.L.I. Brown, had begun their patrol over the beaches as well.

While all of this was taking place in the sky above, HMS *Calpe* moved towards the beaches to monitor the progress of the landings, specifically on Orange and Green beaches. Heavy fire from German shore batteries pummelling Red and White beaches were causing delays and problems with the landings there, while landings on Blue and Yellow beaches had completely failed.

There were many incidents of note during the air battle and one such, as described by Franks, took place in a conversation between Squadron Leader David Scott-Malden and Major Wilhelm Mohr as they drove around the airfield at Manston talking to pilots and aircrew. This was to decide which pilots and aircraft were fit to fly for the next sortie over Dieppe. When

---

25   The two Canadians from 403 Squadron who claimed this Fw 190 shot down were Flight Lieutenant George Hill and Sergeant M.K. Fletcher; Franks, Norman, Dieppe: *The Greatest Air Battle, 19th August 1942*, Grub Street, London, 2010.

26   According to Franks, the three pilots from 403 Squadron that failed to return were: Pilot Officers J.E. Gardiner, L.A. Walker and N. Monchier; Franks, Norman, *Dieppe: The Greatest Air Battle, 19th August 1942*, Grub Street, London, 2010.

Scott-Malden suggested that Mohr would be leading his section, Mohr said he could not. 'When the Wing Leader [Scott-Malden] showed some surprise, the Norwegian, with typical understatement said, "I am sorry but I am afraid I have a bullet in my body."'[27] Mohr had been hit in the right leg during a dogfight and had made no mention of it upon landing. He was quickly packed off to hospital.

Americans of the 308th Fighter Squadron based at RAF Kenley were thrown into the air battle as well, arriving over Dieppe around 0800hrs. They immediately ran into several German fighters and one Spitfire was quickly shot down in this first engagement.

Belgian pilots caught up in the dogfights over Dieppe managed to shoot down two Fw 190s and damage a third. No. 133 Eagle Squadron and 165 Squadron were also flying in the mix, battling it out with the Fw 190s and the Bf 109s over the beaches. No. 133, commanded by Flight Lieutenant Don Blakeslee DFC, patrolled at 7,000ft, where they quickly engaged several Fw 190s. Blakeslee managed to shoot down an Fw 190, which he shared with Pilot Officer W.H. Baker. At the same time, 165 Squadron were flying bottom cover and were low enough to watch Royal Navy destroyers laying a smokescreen to cover the beaches. They were also able to spot two Mustangs flying at high speed out of the smoke away from the French coast.

This brings us to the Mustangs that had been flying tactical reconnaissance sorties in pairs. From 239[28] Squadron two Mustangs had been covering the Fecamp–Yvetot–Totes roads, where they had spotted nothing of interest but had run into a curtain of heavy flak. The area from Longroy to Haute Forêt[29] was covered by two Mustangs flying fast and low from 414 Squadron, while the sector between Saint-Léger–Gauville–Amiens[30] had been covered by four other Mustangs. Of note are the two Mustangs flown by Horncastle and Stover. Horncastle hit a gull, which ripped a hole in the leading edge of his starboard wing. Stover, on the other hand, was attacked at low altitude by an Fw 190 and on his violent evasive action to get clear he hit a telephone

---

27   See Franks, Norman, *Dieppe: The Greatest Air Battle, 19th August 1942*, Grub Street, London, 2010.

28   According to Franks, this would have been Flying Officer D.A. Lloyd and Pilot Officer P. O'Brien.

29   Pilot Officer F.J. Chapman and Pilot Officer D.A. Berhardt from 414 Squadron.

30   These four Mustangs were flown by Flying Officer F.H. Chesters, Pilot Officer G.W. Burroughs, Flying Officer C.L. Horncastle and Pilot Officer C.H. (Smokey) Stover.

pole, ripping off 3ft of his starboard wing. Both pilots managed to get back home to their bases and landed safely.[31]

> At 0916 hours 175 Squadron, Hurricane bomber, and another of cannon-fighters, covered by two Spitfire squadrons, Nos 41 and 412, were ordered to attack the enemy positions on the West headland 'Hindenburg,' and did so. Between 1010 hours and 1040 hours several requests were made for maximum fighter support against the machine-gun positions on both headlands, which were sharp thorns in our flesh throughout the day. The enemy established upon them was never subdued despite all our efforts to do so. Three Close-Support Squadrons, Nos 3, 32 and 43, with two Fighter Squadrons, Nos 118 and 129, for cover, met these and other requests, which would probably have been fewer had the Military Force Commander been aware, at the moment he made them, that aircraft detailing the support about to be provided did not reach the Military Force Commander.[32]

The German heavy gun battery situated around Puys, code-named Rommel, had to be neutralised. It was decided that RAF Boston medium bombers would be the best way to accomplish this task so an order was sent to 88 Squadron at 0645hrs to carry out this mission. Squadron Leader Desmond Griffiths, flying Z2211 RH-L, led five other such aircraft to the target escorted by Spitfires. They attacked the battery at 5,000ft and then hit the deck once the bombs had been dropped as they were then attacked by a gaggle of 20 Fw 190s. Luckily for the Boston pilots and crews, the Spitfires managed to keep most of the Fw 190s otherwise occupied. However, some did get through to the bombers. One of the German fighters was hit by Griffiths' gunner, Pilot Officer Harold Stuart Jack Archer, who managed to cause enough damage that smoke began to pour from the German aircraft as its propeller stopped turning. The Fw 190 turned away while Archer kept up a running commentary over the radio to other Bostons and his own crew,

---

31   Franks, Norman, *Dieppe: The Greatest Air Battle, 19th August 1942*, Grub Street, London, 2010.

32   Operation Jubilee Combined Arms Report, The Dieppe Raid, Execution and The Air Battle, The Air Narrative.

directing fire and updating the progress of the Spitfires' battle against the Fw 190s. Archer was awarded the DFC for his actions.

This day was also the birthday of Griffiths' navigator, New Zealander, Alan Baxter. By the time of Operation Jubilee, he had completed 60 missions and flew two more this day, for which he gained his DFC. Griffiths also received a DFC for his part in the day's events.

However, another Boston was forced to ditch in the sea 15 miles from the French coast after being heavily damaged. Both gunners on board the stricken aircraft managed to bale out and were later rescued but the pilot, Warrant Officer Carl Adrian Beach, RCAF, and his observer, Sergeant D.F.J. Hindle, died before they could get out.

More Hurricanes, this time from 87 Squadron, attacked targets on the ground, strafing German positions in houses, machine gun posts and a tower on the cliffs. Fire from flak and German fighters against the Hurricanes was intense and one Hurricane was immediately shot down and destroyed. Another was hit and so badly damaged that the pilot was forced to bale out and was later rescued by the Royal Navy.[33]

Perhaps one of the best ways to get an idea of the chaos in the air over Dieppe is to turn to Squadron Leader J.E. (Johnnie) Johnson's account of his experiences leading his Spitfire squadron into battle over the beaches. Johnson's unit, No. 610 Squadron, was part of a larger wing from 12 Group based at West Malling. The wing was made up of three squadrons, Johnson's squadron flying top cover with Squadron Leader R.J.C. Grant DFM leading 485 New Zealand Squadron and Squadron Leader R.B. Newton leading 411 Canadian Squadron. All three of these Spitfire squadrons would run into the German Fw 190s and Bf 109s over Dieppe. Leading the entire wing was Wing Commander Pat Jameson, flying just ahead of Grant.

Initially, the wing came in at wave-top height, then once they reached the beaches began to climb to their allotted altitudes. No. 485 Squadron was to fly between 3,000 and 4,000ft, so Grant dutifully led his men to that height, seeing a huge melee of enemy fighters above them. Johnson's call sign was Red 1 and he took his squadron up to 7,000ft, where they were attacked by more than 50 Bf 109s and Fw 190s.[34]

---

33 Flying Officer Antoni Waltos was the officer killed in this attack, while Pilot Officer J. Baker managed to bale out.

34 The information in this paragraph and the preceding one comes from Johnson, *Wing Leader*, Goodall paperback edition, Crecy Publishing, 2019, Manchester, p.143.

In this battle he shot down one Fw 190 that fell into the sea and shared a Bf 109 with two other pilots. 'A 190 pulled up in front of my own section and I gave him a long burst from the maximum range. Surprisingly it began to smoke, the wheels dropped and it fell away to the sea.'[35] Wheeling away, he spotted more German fighters coming towards them from inland and immediately radioed this information to Wing Commander Jameson.

Let us now turn to Johnnie Johnson's account of the first battle of the day experienced by 610 Squadron over Dieppe. This account comes from his book *Wing Leader*. Johnson was one of the top aces for the RAF during the Second World War and went on to become Air Vice Marshal in the early 1960s. Officially, his score of victories stands at 34 German aircraft shot down.

> During a lull in the attacks my own section, which had been reduced to three aircraft, fastened on to a solitary Messerschmitt and sent it spinning down. Then they came at us again and we later estimated that we saw well over a hundred enemy fighters. Three of my Spitfires were shot down and I saw my own wingman, the Australian South Creagh, planing down streaming white glycol from his engine. It was impossible to protect him, for if we took our eyes off the enemy fighters they would give us the same treatment. They're bound to finish him off as he nurses his crippled Spitfire, I thought, I still had another Spitfire alongside, but I lost him when we broke in opposite directions. Then I was alone in the hostile sky.[36]

One thing to remember about the accounts of air battles during the Second World War is that when they were written down, for reports or for memoirs and so forth, they were memories of the individual who experienced them. While RAF pilots were debriefed right after each operation in order for other pilots to be able to corroborate claims of enemy aircraft destroyed, some accounts were written months later, or even after the war. Having said

35   Johnson, (Johnnie), Air Vice Marshal, *Wing Leader*, Goodall paperback edition, Crecy Publishing, 2019, Manchester, p.143.

36   Johnson, (Johnnie), Air Vice Marshal, *Wing Leader*, Goodall paperback edition, Crecy Publishing, 2019, Manchester, p.143.

that, these accounts are the only accounts of the aerial battles we have. In some instances, the German accounts do not completely line up with the RAF accounts.

> Ranging from ground-level to 20,000 feet and having a diameter of twenty-five miles, the air battle drifted and eddied over the coast and inland. The wing had lost its cohesion, but thirty-six Spitfires, or what was left of them, still carried out their task by fighting in pairs and fours and so achieved some concentration in the target area.[37]

It must be remembered at this stage that the majority of the Spitfires engaged in the battles over Dieppe were the Mark V variant. As Johnnie Johnson put it: 'Our Spitfire 5s were completely outclassed by the Fw 190s'.[38]

This could account for the high number of Spitfires claimed as shot down or destroyed by the Luftwaffe that day. The Spitfire Mk IX would redress the imbalance between the two fighters but only a handful of the new Spitfires were involved in the battle that day, the rest of them being the older Mark Vs.

From 610 Squadron, Pilot Officer Hokem was hit and barely managed to get his crippled Spitfire home, while two other pilots, Flight Lieutenant Peter Poole and Sergeant John Leach, did not return. Below 610 Squadron, the Canadians fought hotly against the German defenders and two of their number failed to return.

New Zealand pilots of 485 Squadron, flying well below the other two squadrons, engaged the German fighters at 3,500ft and managed to shoot down two Fw 190s and damage another. Also part of the wing led by Pat Jameson was 81 Squadron, flying high above the other three units. At 0825hrs they arrived over Dieppe and were immediately in the thick of the action, diving, wheeling and doing their best to keep the Luftwaffe from attacking the troops on the ground. This squadron scored one probable. Fuel exhausted, they headed back to West Malling. With the wing back home, Jameson and the rest of the pilots took stock of the situation they had just been involved with. All the squadron commanders agreed that 'they have never before experienced such an intensive battle with so many German

---

37   Ibid.
38   Ibid.

fighters. The battle had cost the wing five Spitfires, four pilots missing, another wounded plus three Spitfires damaged.'[39]

Earlier air attacks on the German machine gun positions that had been pinning down the Allied troops on the beaches had not inflicted the damage hoped for. These gun batteries were on the cliffs around Dieppe and in the houses on the cliffs and hills. HMS *Calpe*, the headquarters ship, made an urgent call for another attack on the German batteries and at 0735hrs 12 Hurricane MK IIc (each with four 20mm cannon) from 32 Squadron took off to mount the attacks. The German fire was coming from the cliff face, code-named Bismarck, that pinned the Canadians behind the sea wall on the promenade. After a quick radio call to HMS *Calpe*, Squadron Leader Thorn led the Hurricanes to their targets. They roared down 'experiencing heavy return fire but their 20mm cannons pounded the cliff face. As the Hurricanes roared away from Dieppe, two Fw 190s, dived through the Spitfire screen but failed to hit any of the Hurricanes.'[40]

> The close support operations of Hurricanes and Typhoons were not effective because tactical aircraft can rarely participate successfully in close-locked, hand-to-hand fighting of this nature. In later years we devised tactics and communications whereby our forward ground troops were able to indicate precision targets, and in Italy, attacks were successfully carried out against enemy troops occupying houses on the other side of the street from our own soldiers. But these facilities were not available at Dieppe. When Leigh-Mallory asked for a situation report, the reply was 'situation too obscure to give useful report'.[41]

Two Mustangs from 26 Squadron were sent out at 0800hrs to carry out tactical reconnaissance over Dieppe. Neither returned. Another two pilots from 239 Squadron carried out tactical reconnaissance flights over the beaches but became separated and only one of them managed to get back.

---

39   See Franks, Norman, *Dieppe: The Greatest Air Battle, 19th August 1942*, Grub Street, London, 2010, p.78.

40   Ibid., p.79.

41   Johnson, (Johnnie), Air Vice Marshal, *Wing Leader*, Goodall paperback edition, Crecy Publishing, 2019, Manchester, p.145.

Earlier, we mentioned the Spitfire Mark IX, the new mark of this remarkable aircraft. The Mk IX was the equal of the Fw 190 but as of this date there were not sufficient numbers to equip all the Spitfire squadrons. Franks details the experience of a Spitfire Mk IX pilot, Group Captain Broadhurst, who arrived back at Biggin Hill after his first flight over the target area. After speaking with his pilots from 222 Squadron, the US 307th 'Pursuit' Squadron and 602 Squadron, who had already been involved in the fighting over Dieppe, Broadhurst 'immediately telephoned 11 Group Operations Room and gave the Commander in Chief an outline of the situation as he had seen it, asking him to suggest to the AOC that patrols of Spitfire IXs in pairs be put up with the hope that these would be able to counter the Fw 190s as they approached the battle area. As it happened, the main Spitfire IX units available had been assigned as escort for a raid against Abbeville by the American 8th Air Force.[42]

The wing led by Pat Jameson was relieved by another three squadrons of Spitfires, this time from 130 and 131 Squadrons and from the US 309th Fighter Squadron. They were immediately engaged in the fighting throughout their patrol. Upwards of 50 German fighters of all types were in evidence almost continuously throughout the battle, the majority from JG 26. This replacement wing was led by Wing Commander M.G.F. Pedley, leading 131 Squadron, and when they arrived over Dieppe they formed a defensive circle to ward off the Fw 190s. However, the circle soon broke up into dogfights and the wing was split up.

Three American pilots from 309th Fighter Squadron were shot down into the sea, with one surviving while they managed to shoot down one Fw 190 and scored a probable. As with the Jameson wing, the Fw 190s in this instance were victorious, having shot down five Spitfires and wounded a sixth pilot while suffering possible losses of two fighters and more damaged.

Before we get into a detailed look at the main two German fighter units involved in the air battle over Dieppe, JG 2 and JG 26, it is worth looking at two differing opinions of the air operations. The first is from Johnson's book, *Wing Leader*, and comes from the perspective of a pilot in the thick of the fighting over the beaches.

---

42   See Franks, Norman, *Dieppe: The Greatest Air Battle, 19th August 1942*, Grub Street, London, 2010, p.80.

Tactically, the Dieppe raid must be regarded as a complete failure, for none of its stated objectives were achieved in full measure. It is a record of poor security, of faulty intelligence, of inadequate communications between air and ground, of a confused and bloody ground situation over which central co-ordination could not be exercised. It is a story of great gallantry and heavy loss of life, and the record of the (Canadian) Essex Scottish, who brought back 52 personnel, of whom 28 were wounded, out of a force of 553, gives some indication of the desperate situation on the ground. Perhaps Chester Wilmot made the best assessment of the operation when he stated: '[the] Dieppe raid yielded bloody warning of the strength of the Atlantic wall'.[43]

The second point below comes from a Combined Report, written after the fact (after the war) and researched from a series of reports from commanders and officers who were involved in some form in the air operations on 19 August over Dieppe.

Had the operation been extended over a period of two or three days, or been followed up immediately by a second similar raid in the same or some other area, the damage inflicted on the German Air Force Western Front forces might have been far reaching; the effect would have gone a long way towards expending the forces available and would, no doubt, have necessitated the withdrawal of units from probably the Russian Front or, possibly, the Mediterranean theatre.[44]

Neither view is right or wrong. They are written by different people with different experiences of the air battle. However, I suspect that when it came time to write the Combined Report there was a push by senior commanders of all the services to make the operations look less of a failure that Johnson and others have suggested it was.

---

43   Johnson, (Johnnie), Air Vice Marshal, *Wing Leader*, Goodall paperback edition, Crecy Publishing, 2019, Manchester, p.146.

44   Combined Report on the Dieppe Raid, Annex F to Annex 7, Reactions of The German Air Force, Appreciation of the Enemy's Air Effort.

Chapter 25

JG 26 Operations

The Allies mounted limited aerial activity over France for the first two weeks of august 1942 as preparations for the Dieppe raid were under way. JG 26 was kept in a state of readiness despite this reduced activity from the Allies over France. However, on the evening of the 17th, two days before the landings, this changed when a formation of American B-17 Flying Fortress bombers from the US Air Force 97th Bomber Group bombed the huge marshalling yards at Sottèville-les-Rouen. The bombers were escorted by a large formation of Spitfires and Fw 190s from II Gruppe JG 2 were scrambled to intercept them.

For the aerial battle over Dieppe for Operation Jubilee the RAF had massed 70 Squadrons, of which 48 were fighter squadrons comprising roughly 750 Spitfires.[1] By comparison, both JG 26 and JG 2 were able to counter with roughly 115 fighters each, giving the Allies a three to one advantage in the air for fighters. In numbers, therefore, the Allies should have won the day. But the story, as we have seen, was somewhat different.

At JG 26 Headquarters they were surprised by the sudden arrival of Allied aircraft over the beaches at Dieppe as well as by the reports of the landings under way there. 'Just a single word was to be heard all around – "invasion". Still nobody had any deeper knowledge.'[2] In order to see what was really going on, Oberleutnant (Oblt) Sternberg and Ulf Crump took off from Abbeville at 0620hrs. Once over the landings they contacted headquarters at 5/JG 26 and ten minutes later the rest of the squadron was up and heading for Dieppe. When they arrived, the pilots could see the Spitfires patrolling the skies at different altitudes covering the landing craft touching down on

---

1   Janowicz, Krzysztof, *JG 26 'Schlageter'*, *Vol. II*, Kagero, First Edition, Limited Edition, ISBN 83-89088-07-X. These figures may or may not be accurate as Janowicz does not appear to list a bibliography or sources. However, this could be misleading.

2   Ibid.

the beaches below. Almost at once they engaged the Allied fighters and the first victory of the day for JG 26 came from the guns of Ofw Bierwirth, who, at 0640hrs, shot down a Spitfire from 340 Squadron.[3]

From I and III Gruppen, several Fw 190s were immediately scrambled. Over Dieppe they arrived in loose formations carrying out unco-ordinated attacks that often resulted in dogfights with the Spitfires. Oblt Hermichen, commanding 3/JG 26, shot down a Spitfire upon his initial engagement in the fight, then then claimed a second destroyed shortly afterwards.[4] More kills were claimed by Fw 190 pilots of 3/JG 26 but they did not go unscathed. Three Fw 190 pilots were lost in this engagement – Ofw Czwilinski of 2 Staffel, Ofw Gerhardt and Unteroffizier (Uffz) Reider, both from 5 Staffel, were all shot down and killed.

Once the remaining pilots from this engagement returned to base, the engineers and mechanics serviced the Fw 190s, getting them ready for the next sortie over Dieppe. This time, however, the German defensive attack was going to be more co-ordinated and better prepared. The plan they made was that one group of fighters would attack the Spitfires at 6,000m, another at 7,000m and the rest would be high in the clouds flying top cover ready to dive down on the Allied airmen if needed.

Because of their planning, albeit quick and simple, the new tactics yielded better results very quickly. 'The powerful aerial cover over the landing beaches was breached in many places, which allowed the Jabos to strike.'[5] In this action, Uffz von Berg was killed when his Fw 190 crashed into the sea. So hectic was the action for the Fw 190 pilots that they only had time to refuel, rearm, perhaps eat something quickly, before climbing back into the cockpits of their fighters and getting airborne again to join the fight. It was not just Fw 190s that were involved in the air battle, the Germans also threw the Bf 109G-1s of 11 Staffel into the fray. From this group, Ofw Babenz shot down three Allied fighters, while the commander of 11 Staffel, Oblt Schmidt, claimed two destroyed. However, Schmidt was later shot down and died when his aircraft plunged into the sea.

---

3   Ibid., however, this cannot be fully corroborated as Janowicz does not seem to provide reference material for the facts of this account.

4   Janowicz initially states that Hermichen claimed this as an Airacobra but it turned out to be a Spitfire from the US Air Force 31st Fighter Group.

5   See Janowicz, Krzysztof, *JG 26 'Schlageter', Vol. II*, Kagero, First Edition, Limited Edition, ISBN 83-89088-07-X.

As the air battle continued, German bombers arrived over the beaches trying to disrupt the landings and cause havoc on the ground among the Allied troops. These bombers were escorted by fighters to try to stop the Spitfires and Mustangs from attacking the slower aircraft. Oblt Zink, commander of 2/JG 26, shot down a Mustang and two Spitfires in three sorties. Major Schopfel and Oblt Mietusch both destroyed two Spitfires in this action, while the commander of 9 Staffel, Oblt Ruppert, also claimed two.

Many Luftwaffe pilots that day claimed their first victories of the war. One of those was from 9/JG 26, Leutnant Otto Stammberger, who found himself above the mass of turning, rolling, whirling fighters in an opportune situation.

> He noticed two Spitfires flying stoically on a slight curve, as if unaware of all that was happening around them. He could not have wished for a better opportunity. Taking a convenient position, he put a good burst into one of them. On approaching the hit enemy, he saw that the Spitfire had lost its aileron and one of its wheels had been forced out of its landing gear lock. The aircraft was pouring smoke from its oil cooler. It was clear that it was in agony. In a moment it plunged down to hit the water.[6]

Stammberger watched the Spitfire go down and hit the water. The other Spitfire was nowhere to be seen but for Stammberger it was time to gain height. He roared over the sinking wreckage, pulled the stick back and began to climb, all the time wary about other Allied pilots that might have him in his sights. However, before he could do anything his fuel warning light came on and he knew it was time to return home. Pulling his stick round, he quickly headed for home base. While Stammberger was heading home, Feldwebel (Fw) Golub was shot down and killed.

> Fw 'Addi' Ghunz had also got his opponent, and later he told his comrades how he had gotten rid of a persistent Spitfire from his tail and pulled up to suddenly find himself near another one. He was looking at it, thinking his eyes were failing him – all down below they were fighting one another and this Spitfire here was flying above that bedlam straight, as if on parade. He must have

---

6   Ibid.

been either blind or completely stupid. 'Addi' looked in all directions to see if it was not an ambush, but the sky was clear – just the two of them over the whirlwind of racing machines. He quickly positioned himself behind the Spit and pressed the trigger at a distance of thirty metres. The Spitfire caught fire at once and plunged down. Later, he wondered how a plane could be all on fire from one wingtip to the other.[7]

JG 26 continued to fly and fight throughout the day until the last Fw 190 landed at 2132hrs. This was from 6/JG 26 and flown by Uffz Mayer. In all, JG 26 had carried out 36 missions and flown upwards of 377 sorties. At this point in the evening of 19 August, with the Dieppe operation over, the fighters of JG 26, those that remained, were in the hangars being serviced for the next round of aerial combat. The following excerpt from *JG 26 'Schlageter'*, *Vol. II* by Krzysztof Janowicz provides a unique insight into the workings of a Luftwaffe fighter group in Western France in 1942:

> Major Schopfel entered the hangar before midnight to see the technicians replace broken parts, stop holes, and test devices.
>
> 'How's it going?' he asked a mechanic hidden behind an opened lower part of a BMW engine cowling. He could only see part of his dirty overalls.
>
> 'Man, don't ask me how it's going – just give me No. 18,' he heard a tired voice from behind the cover and saw an extended hand.
>
> Surprised by this answer, he gave the wrench to the mechanic, when suddenly the feldwebel on duty appeared next to him.
>
> 'Herr Major, asking permission to report!'
>
> The mechanic working on the engine dropped the wrench and immediately jumped out from behind the cowling. Standing at attention, he spoke in one breath: 'Herr Major, please excuse me – I thought it was Klaus because he's continually talking, Sir.'
>
> Schopfel had wanted to give the soldier a good telling off at first, but seeing his soiled hands, smeared face and dirty overalls, he gave up. He just gave him a strict look and nodded his head.

---

7   Ibid.

The feldwebel was standing aside, not knowing what it was all about, but he resolutely remained silent.

'Work's going well. Only three machines will remain to be serviced in the morning,' the mechanic went on.

The major smiled slightly seeing the terrified soldier. He knew how much depended on these men, who lost much sleep to stitch as many aircraft as possible.

'Very well,' he replied. 'I'll have the cook prepare a meal for you.'

'Sir, this is the matter,' the feldwebel said, 'because the food store is locked for the night. I'm asking permission to open it.'

'Permission granted,' Schopfel said to the feldwebel. 'Please distribute the meal and then lock the store. The quartermaster will fill in the forms in the morning.'

He turned around and was going to depart when he turned back to the mechanic and said: 'You've dropped the wrench.'

The soldier immediately stooped to pick up the No. 18. Leaving, Schopfel knew he could rest assured – fine guys.[8]

In the end, who carried the day in terms of the air battle? Even though both sides exaggerated the claims of aircraft destroyed and damaged, the numbers provide us with an answer to that question. According to Janowicz, the Allies lost a total of 97 aircraft with a further 54 damaged. Of those lost, 59 were Spitfires.[9] Janowicz also claims that 31 Spitfires had to be sent for major repairs resulting from the damage inflicted during the fighting over Dieppe. However, the Luftwaffe claimed 141 Allied aircraft destroyed, which is an exaggeration. Closer to the mark is the claim of 103 aircraft destroyed in 945 sorties flown by the Luftwaffe throughout the day. The breakdown of aircraft destroyed is JG 26 claimed 38 Allied aircraft shot down or destroyed, while JG 2 claimed 69 had been destroyed in the battle. The Luftwaffe bomber crews also claimed six Allied machines brought down. In addition to this, the flak units on the ground claimed they had destroyed 30 British machines.

---

8   Ibid.

9   To be fair, Janowicz states that 59 Spitfires 'did not return to their bases', which does not necessarily mean they were destroyed. Some could have landed elsewhere, or some pilots could have run out of fuel and been forced to land at other bases.

Where this argument gets interesting is that the Luftwaffe only lost 48 aircraft: 23 fighters and 25 bombers. They suffered another 24 damaged. Based on these numbers, exaggerated or not, the victory for the air battle must go to the Germans, as did the victory on the ground. Yet this is despite the fact that the Allies had a three-to-one advantage in the air.

One of the reasons for this victory could be because the Germans were using their latest fighters, the Fw 190 and the Me 109G, both of which out-classed the Spitfire Mk V as Johnson stated in his book, *Wing Leader*. One has to wonder if the RAF had been fully equipped with the latest Spitfire MK IX, which was a match for the Fw 190 (perhaps with a slight edge), how much of a difference would that have made? Would the RAF have been victorious?

Chapter 26

JG 2

Pilots of JG 2 woke at dawn on the day of the landings to the alarm as the news of the Allied operations on the beaches of Dieppe spread through the airbase.

Because reports were confused and unclear, Hauptman (Hptm) Leie, the commander, ordered a reconnaissance flight over the area. Several Fw 190s, with Ofw Josef Wurmheller among them, took off from Triqueville at 0620hrs. They headed north. As we have seen in an earlier chapter, Wurmheller had a broken foot that had a plaster on it. With the help of his ground crew he managed to get into his Fw 190 and took off with the rest of the pilots.

First on the scene for JG 2 was a flight of two aircraft led by Unteroffizier (Uffz) Kurt Epsinger flying from south to north. Below they watched the Allied infantry troops landing on the beaches and the Allied warships shelling the landing area to keep the German infantry from attacking the landing craft. As there were so many RAF aircraft in the air Epsinger noticed a twin-engined bomber with an extended landing gear heading toward England. He easily caught up with it 5 km from Shoreham and holed its fuselage and wings with a long burst of fire, setting its right engine aflame. The burning bomber plunged to the sea, and hitting the surface broke in two and quickly sank.'[1]

After this attack, both German fighters pulled up and wheeled around heading back towards Dieppe. They spotted a single Spitfire from 129 Squadron and once again Epsinger went in for the attack. This time his attack was head-on and he poured his fire into the cockpit of the Spitfire, injuring the pilot, Sergeant Reeves. However, Reeves was able to return fire, his cannon shells peppering the Fw 190 as it came at him. A shell must have

---

1   Krzystof Janowicz, *JG 2 'Richthofen', 1942–1943*, Kagero, ISBN 83-89088-04.5. The aircraft shot down by Epsinger was a Boston of 418 Squadron under command of Sergeant Buchanan, according to Janowicz.

killed Epsinger because his fighter spun into the sea and disappeared under the surface. Although wounded, Reeves managed to fly his crippled Spitfire home. 'Epsinger was credited with two victories.'[2]

Two other Fw 190 pilots from 3 Staffel JG 2 managed to shoot down two more Spitfires, however, Uffz Rudolf Robbers was hit and had to force-land east of Dieppe, where he was taken to hospital to treat his wounds.

The commander of II Gruppe, Hauptmann Bolz, decided he needed to see what the situation was like over the beaches. He took off from Beaumont-le-Roger shortly after Epsinger was shot down. He spotted two Mustangs from 26 Squadron on a reconnaissance mission as he crossed the shore heading out to sea. Immediately, Bolz turned, positioning himself above and behind the first Mustang, flown by Flight Lieutenant Kennedy. Firing a long burst, the Mustang faltered, then fell to the ground out of control. Bolz then sent a long burst into the second Mustang, flown by Sergeant Cliff, destroying it. Both pilots were killed in this action.[3]

Pilots of 4/JG 2 led by Lieutenant Buhligen took off just after 0700hrs and quickly joined the aerial battle over the beaches. No. 332 Squadron (Norwegian) was attacked by several Fw 190s from this Staffel and three of the Norwegians were shot down. However, in this action Gefreiter (Gefr) Siegfried Eimer drowned after baling out of his Fw 190 and landing in the sea.

Meanwhile, Ofw Josef Wurmheller 1/JG 2 had been forced to crash-land due to engine failure. Because of his broken foot he had had to limp across a field towards a German gendarmerie station he could see in the distance. He had also suffered a concussion on crash-landing. Back at his base, suffering severe head pain, he managed to get back into a Fw 190, with the help of his colleagues, and took off:

> Partaking in the one-and-a-half hour long air battle, in which JG 2 claimed eleven shoot-downs, within five minutes Wurmheller shot down two Spitfires and one Blenheim.[4]

2   See Janowicz, *JG 2 'Richtofen', 1942–1943*.

3   Ibid.

4   Ibid: Janowicz suggests that the Blenheim was more likely a Boston twin-engined bomber.

However, for the victories they gained, three Fw 190s were lost. Janowicz tells us that by 1030hrs the RAF had lost 27 aircraft destroyed plus 13 damaged Spitfires, 'one Hurricane, two Bostons and six Mustangs. Due to such intensive actions on the part of JG 2 and 26 it is impossible in most cases to verify individual clashes.'[5]

II Gruppe of 9/JG 2 arrived over Dieppe at 1130hrs and immediately joined the swarm of aircraft wheeling and whirling about the sky. Battling it out with the Spitfires, Fw 190 pilots from this Gruppe claimed nine of the British fighters destroyed. This number included two from the guns of Hptm 'Assi' Hahn and two from Oblt Schnell. Fw 190s from I and II Gruppe, shortly after the previous action, carried out a head on attack, coming out of the sun, on Spitfires from 232 Squadron. Within seconds Oblt Herbert Bottcher 'shot down Flight Lieutenant Strong and his wingman Sergeant Walker, killing them both'.

Other German pilots from JG 2 were very busy throughout the day in the air battle. During a series of ferocious aerial dogfights and battles, twelve Spitfires were shot down.[6]

Two Fw 190s, armed with bombs, managed to get through to the ships and bombed HMS *Berkeley* at 1400hrs. One half-ton bomb smashed into the stern of the destroyer, disabling it. Royal Navy ships later destroyed it, ensuring that it sank.

> On that day the Jabo attacked warships, torpedo boats, freighters and beaches themselves, gaining great success.[7]

Throughout the day pilots from JG 2 took off constantly, landing only to rearm and refuel. That day saw Oblt Erich Leie gain his 43rd victory when he shot down a Spitfire.

> The British operation was being heavily supported by the RAF. The English pilots flew in groups of 30–40 fighters, while

---

5   Ibid., Janowicz, *JG 2 'Richthofen', 1942–1943*.

6   This is from Janowicz, although he does not provide detail of these battles. Perhaps these were battles with Spitfires against JG 26?

7   See Janowicz, *JG 2 'Richthofen', 1942–1943*.

Blenheims, Whirlwinds and Hurricanes were attacking our coastal fortifications.

In the beginning JG 2 flew only in a strength of single Schwarms and did not achieve any significant successes, whereas the English were flying constantly and covered their ground troops so efficiently that they managed to fight off all attacks. During my third flight at 1150 I shot down one Spitfire five kilometres north of Dieppe, and it fell down burning like a torch next to a landing barge. In my attack I was certain of my wingman's cover from the other Spitfires but I was hit in the fuselage and wings. I cringed in the cockpit. On looking behind, I saw a Spitfire turning right.

I decided to force-land and directed toward the nearest field, but everywhere steel English helmets I could see. I still had some reserve of altitude. Twenty kilometres from Abbeville my plane was already smoking well and the ammo started to explode. The machine burned ever stronger so in the blink of an eye I ejected the canopy and jumped out at 500 metres. My face and right hand were burned. I had come through a real thermal shock. Now I was waving over fields of crops. At 200 metres the parachute lost some tension because I had seized the lines too high and the canopy had too much weight to carry.[8]

More victories went to pilots of JG 2, according to Janowicz. Oblt Schnell shot down three Spitfires, while Oblt Egon Mayer claimed two and Lt Erich Rudorffer also accounted for two, bringing his score to 45 victories.

Throughout the day, Wurmheller continued to fly despite his pounding headache and his broken foot. He would land, stay in his cockpit while the ground crew rearmed and refuelled his aircraft, then he would take off. This he did over and over again and ended up shooting down four Allied aircraft until he could no longer operate the controls because his vision was so blurred. He had to be lifted out of the cockpit and carried to the medics, where he was diagnosed and treated for concussion. During the battle Wurmheller scored seven victories, shooting down and destroying seven Allied fighters. This brought his total up to 60 victories and earned him the Oak Leaves to

---

8   This is a quote from Oblt Eric Leie cited in Janowicz, *JG 2 'Richtofen', 1942–1943*.

his Knight's Cross on 13 November 1942. He was also promoted to Leutnant (Lieutenant). He was just 24 years old.

The last victories of the day for JG 2 took place around 1900hrs when Lt Kurt Buhligen shot down two Spitfires, his 24th and 25th. The five victories of the day by Oblt Schnell brought his total score to 70, while Oblt Egon Mayer reached a total of 50 that day having shot down two Spitfires himself.

Pilots of JG 2 flew a total of 423 combat flights in the air battle over Dieppe. They claimed 71 victories. Of those, Janowicz states that seven were never confirmed and five went unclaimed. At the same time, 10 (Jabo)/JG 2 'was very highly esteemed for sinking one destroyer and causing damage to another, and also for bombing one trawler and two landing barges, plus shooting down one Spitfire. Its commander, Oblt Schröter, was awarded the Knight's Cross for that.'[9]

While in previous chapters we have seen the statistics of aircraft and personnel lost on either side, there have always been discrepancies depending on the source material. Since most of the material on JG 2 has been taken from Krzysztof Janowicz's book, *JG 2 'Richthofen', 1942–1943*, we will use some of the statistics relayed in that publication. This should give the reader an idea of how costly the entire Dieppe landings were on the land, the sea and in the air. Janowicz states that 68 per cent of the Allied ground forces were lost, which breaks down as 1,179 dead, 600 wounded and 2,190 taken prisoner by the Germans. These were mostly Canadians. He also suggests that the British lost 28 Churchill tanks while the Royal Navy lost the destroyer HMS *Berkeley* along with 33 landing craft and 550 personnel killed. By contrast, the Wehrmacht lost 311 troops killed and 280 wounded.[10]

In the air, the RAF suffered casualties that amounted to 'an experience of the greatest losses suffered on a single day during the whole war'.[11] The RAF carried out 2,955 combat sorties, of which 2,494 were flights by fighters of various types, mostly Spitfires. In total, the RAF lost 97 aircraft and 54 damaged. Fifty-nine Spitfires were destroyed or shot down by the Luftwaffe pilots and another 31 were badly damaged and required extensive servicing. The RAF lost 81 pilots killed and 29 wounded. On the other hand, the

---

9   See Janowicz, *JG 2 'Richtofen', 1942–1943*.

10 Sadly, Janowicz does not indicate what his sources are for this information. We can only assume that the statistics he publishes here are from multiple sources.

11 See Janowicz, Krzysztof, *JG 2 'Richthofen', 1942–1943*.

Luftwaffe lost 23 fighters and 25 bombers for a total of 48 aircraft destroyed and an additional 24 damaged. JG 2's losses amounted to 13 Fw 190s and BF109Gs destroyed, with seven others damaged. Eight JG 2 pilots lost their lives while another six were wounded.

> The British intelligence estimated that on the following day the Luftwaffe had been reduced to about seventy aircraft. In truth, at the French airbases 194 fighters waited ready to go since most of the damaged planes had been repaired during the night in airbase workshops.[12]

Perhaps, in this instance, the last word should go to the Allied Air Commander, Air Marshal Trafford Leigh-Mallory, from his report on the Dieppe Raid:

> The very low rate of casualties suffered in all types of Squadrons during such intensive daylight operations in close support of a combined expedition are of particular interest.[13]

And again:

> The operations showed that such expeditions can be successfully supported and protected by home defence Fighters operated by the normal Home Defence Fighter Organisation, assisted by forward direction through R/T in ships. This efficient organisation is fully capable of so operating Air Forces to the limit of present fighter range and is bound to be superior to any alternative forward control scheme which could never provide anything like equal facilities.[14]

From the same Combined Report, the following conclusions were reached by the author of Annex 7, who wrote the short piece on the Reactions of the German Air Force:

---

12   See Janowicz, Krzysztof, *JG 2 'Richthofen', 1942–1943*.

13   Operation Jubilee Combined Report, The Dieppe Raid, Annex 7, Report of the Air Commander.

14   Ibid.

a) That, from an air point of view, the operation was highly successful, because it forced all available German Air Force aircraft to operate and thus enabled the Royal Air Force to inflict considerable casualties on the enemy's forces on the Western Front, and draw on his already depleted reserves;[15]

b) That, although the operation was satisfactory, it was not of sufficient duration to deplete the enemy to a point where he was no longer able to make good his losses from his reserves.

c) As it was, the wastage inflicted on the German Air Force on the Western Front by Fighter Command during the operation, was greater than during a normal month of recent offensive sweeps.[16]

Clearly, from the quotes above there are differences between the perceptions of the raid by the Allies and by the Germans, who saw it as an abject failure on all fronts, land, sea and air. It is up to the reader to form their own conclusions in this instance.

---

15 We have seen earlier that the number of fighters available after the battle was more than the Allies were prepared to admit.

16 Operation Jubilee Combined Report, The Dieppe Raid, Appendix F to Annex 7, Reactions of the German Air Force.

Part 4
After the Battle
and Legacy

Chapter 27

The German View of the Battle

> If the British attack us again on the same scale, or on a broader
> front, it is to be expected that they will attempt to penetrate weak
> spots and try to encircle the harbours. They are not likely to repeat
> a massed frontal attack against a strongly fortified area, as in the
> Dieppe attack of August 19th 1942. It is therefore most important
> that we have mobile reserves ready for a counterattack. These
> mobile reserves must be equipped with the many motorised anti-
> tank weapons, some of which are still lacking.[1]

After the Dieppe raid the Germans realised that their regimental and sector reserves needed to be held in close support and be supplied with heavy
weapons and artillery as much as possible. It was thought that the reserve
battalions then held in separate billets needed to be assembled by the very
latest after the second stage alarm had been sounded. 'These reserves must
start counterattacking promptly and automatically and not wait for orders
in unclear situations. The quickest way to clarify the situation is to initiate a
forceful attack to prevent the enemy from consolidating his position.'[2]

Experience from Dieppe showed to the Germans that quick counterattacks
by their reserves would leave the reserves from higher formations free to
support units that had been unable to cope with the battle. This point is
illustrated in the experience of the 571st Infantry Regiment. The battalions
had been informed at 0710hrs that the attack at Quiberville by the British
and Canadians had been stopped but the Allies had managed to successfully
land at Pourville. The regiment was ordered to then launch its attack from
Hautot but the situation was unclear, the country close in and everywhere the

---

1   Battle Report of the German Commander-in-Chief West (G.H.Q. Army Group D) on
     the English Landing Attempt at, and on Both Flanks of Dieppe, 19 August 1942.
2   Ibid.

patrols went they ran into British and Canadian fire. It was the German view, after Dieppe, that had a determined attack towards Pourville been launched 'it would have probably cleared up the situation more quickly and would have helped wipe out even larger numbers of the enemy near Pourville'.[3]

The Germans realised that although their corps reserves had been alerted without difficulties, their assembly had taken too much time. Transport columns were not concentrated in the reserves area and they realised that they should be distributed much closer to the troops. They also realised from their experience defending Dieppe that artillery had to be assigned to the corps reserves at all times. 'Part of their artillery must always be limbered up to permit rapid commitment with the corps reserves.'[4] The artillery battalion of the corps reserves situated on the coast came into action too late because of the time it took to limber up and embark on the transport. 'It would be desirable to have corps reserves closer to the coast and to attach certain reserve units to Divisions as in the past. This would be possible if the corps, in case of an enemy attack, could count on the support of one motorised or armoured division.'[5]

Dieppe showed the Germans that the Allies were capable of landing tanks on the beaches from landing craft very quickly, which meant that they needed greater anti-tank defences 'even in the small ravines through which paths run down to the coast, e.g. near Criel-Quiberville-Saint-Aubin-Veulettes, etc.' At the time of the Dieppe landings the beaches were heavily gravelled and while the Germans realised that the gravel made landing of tanks difficult, it did not stop them from landing. 'Several tanks were moved over the gravel without difficulty after they had been repaired. Witnesses reported that many more tanks (probably 16) had reached the promenade along the beach, but that they turned around and re-crossed the gravel to find more protection against the heavy defensive fire behind the gravel bank.'[6]

The Germans also realised that passive anti-tank defence such as the anti-tank walls were successful. It was important for the walls to be situated in such a way so that their flanks could be covered by machine gun fire that would prevent Allied engineers from using the walls as cover, in order to

---

3   Ibid.
4   Ibid.
5   Ibid.
6   Ibid.

plant charges and destroy them or punch holes in the walls. The Germans realised that they should stagger the walls in depth in case the first one or two were breached.

As far as active anti-tank defences were concerned, the Germans quickly discovered, through examining the Churchill and other captured armoured vehicles, that the armour was not penetrated by the German 37mm shells in most cases. While they had found evidence of several hits, they had found few places where the shells had managed to penetrate the Churchill's armour. Only in two places were their anti-tank shells able to punch through – in the rear and the side. However, they did find that the tracks of the Allied tanks were vulnerable to anti-tank fire.

The Germans were pleased with the artillery beach defences, although Dieppe indicated that many more would be needed should the Allies invade again. 'If these weapons were to be provided, war establishments would have to be changed because the infantry does not possess sufficient personnel to man them.'[7]

The experience of Dieppe showed the Germans that their coastal guns should be employed into defence sectors as close to the infantry strongpoints as necessary. When it came to pounding the landing craft with artillery fire, the Germans found that independent fire was much more superior to controlled fire. Crucial to the success of artillery was the co-ordination between artillery and other branches of the armed forces.

Contrary to what the British thought of the effect of their air attacks, which they believed had made a difference, the Germans found that 'they did not produce the expected effect on our batteries and AA positions. The reason probably was that the British themselves, in order to blind the defences, had laid such a heavy smokescreen that the accuracy of their own weapons and target recognition was considerably reduced.'[8]

For the Germans, the Dieppe experience illustrated how effective their co-ordination with all branches of the armed forces and with the Todt Construction Organisation had been. They described it as 'excellent and frictionless', with everyone carrying out their duties seamlessly. Co-ordination with the fighters was undertaken by German Corps Headquarters between Jafs 2, Jafs 3, IX Fliegerkorps and Luftflotte 3 Army Liaison officer at Army

---

7   Ibid.
8   Ibid.

Group West. In the future, the Germans felt that a single command post that co-ordinated all air force and army operations would be highly useful. 'This command post, with sufficient communications facilities, would be the only one to make enquiries at corps and would help to avoid in overcrowding of signal channels.'[9]

The Germans discovered that some of their minefields, particularly those in the ravines, were not effective as the British and Canadians were able to bypass them. They realised that for another amphibious assault by the Allies, minefields would need to extend beyond the ravines and that no wires should be visible on the seaward side. 'The first wave of the British attacking Puys was caught in a minefield. This made it possible to kill 50 to 60 men by machine gun fire.'[10]

During the battle the Germans found that their communications functioned well. Division and Corps headquarters were continuously informed of developments and how the battle was progressing. However, they realised that while the British did not try to destroy German communications posts, they needed to have message centres established in a line parallel to the coast for about 10km. 'These message centres must be at junctions of main roads leading to the shore and should be on a single telephone network with Divisional and Corps Headquarters. This would make it possible to reach reserve units committed in the combat zone by telephone at all times.'[11]

Such a network would also make it easier for reserve units approaching from either the rear or the flanks to stay in touch. The Germans also believed that the batteries should have a third radio set since those forward observers using the telephone network made for slow fire control. On the other hand, radio communications between 770th Army Coast Artillery Battalion and the 813th Battery functioned continuously and satisfactorily.

The Germans also realised that in the case of a second stage alarm they needed to stop all civilian traffic in the combat zone right away. 'French motor vehicles were actually going into and out of Dieppe during the battle.'[12]

---

9   Ibid.
10   Battle Report of the German Commander-in-Chief West (GHQ Army Group D) on the English Landing Attempt at, and on Both Flanks of Dieppe, 19 August 1942.
11   Ibid.
12   Ibid.

Chapter 28

Dieppe and the Media

To say it clearly; due to the losses sustained on the Eastern Front the Germans had already lost the war by June 1944. D-Day did not alter the outcome of the Second World War, although it accelerated the decline of the Third Reich.[1]

Well before the Dieppe landings Hitler had ordered a defensive belt be constructed that stretched along the French and Belgian coasts bringing all of the threatened ports into one large impregnable fortress. This was known as the Atlantic Wall. Construction of this was started early in the war and as such was not a direct result of the Dieppe raid. Indeed, a German report published on 25 April 1941 stated that ports such as Le Tréport and Dieppe likely would 'not be attacked directly by the enemy but would be assaulted by means of landing attempts at nearby points'.[2]

Everybody agreed that the so-called Atlantic Wall alone would not stop an invasion. The design for the defensive battle was characterised by a two-step approach: The troops deployed along the coastline were to slow down the enemy, thus buying time for the more powerful reserves to be brought up to the battlespace in order to defeat the landed enemy.[3]

---

1 Strohn, Dr Matthias, An Absolutely Harrowing Organisation, *British Army Review* No. 175, Summer 2019, CHACR, Camberley, Ministry of Defence.

2 Henry, The Planning, Intelligence, Execution and Aftermath of the Dieppe Raid, 19 August 1942, cites Campbell, Dieppe revisited, p.199; Stacey, Six years of war, p.352 (German report).

3 See Strohn, An Absolutely Harrowing Organisation, *British Army Review* No. 175, Summer 2019.

That means that it was not necessary to capture a port initially as the first part of the operation in order to land men and materiel. However, to sustain an invasion a deep sea port would be needed for the transfer of war materials from ships to shore. Penetrating weak spots between defended areas was the key.

> An invading army would 'try to take the harbours by an encircling movement. They are not likely to repeat a massed frontal assault against a strongly fortified area', as at Dieppe. For this reason, the report continued, that mobile reserves, including a large component of armour and motorized anti-tank weapons, be prepared for a counterattack role, were considered essential.[4]

A report of 1955 held in the Cabinet Office Historical Records, based upon as much available Allied and German documentation as possible, concludes that Hitler wanted to strengthen the defensive positions in the west, especially around the port areas, in order to thwart an Allied invasion.[5]

The report continues by saying that Hitler had realised before Operation Jubilee took place that there was a pressing need to deny the western ports to the Allies and 'the raid seems merely to have confirmed him in this intention'.[6]

However, 1944 saw a reversal of German strategy where they began to reorganise based on defeating any invasion on the beaches instead of their strategy at Dieppe of using mobile reserves to counterattack any attempt by the Allies to invade in the west. This reversal did not come from the Germans' experiences at Dieppe; remember that they believed they had

---

4   'Note on the attempted British landing at Dieppe 19 August 1942 and Its lessons from the German point of view', *c.* August 1942, p.3, DHist 594.003 (Dt) 'whereas until']; Theatre Intelligence Section Report No. 86, 'German Lessons from the Dieppe raid', 8 March 1944, p.6, NAC, RG 24/10702/2125C1.981 (D298) ('try to take harbours']. 322.

5   Führer Conferences of 2 and 13 August and 29 September 1942 as cited in Shelley, James, German Lessons and Influence on Strategic Thinking as outlined in Henry, The Planning, Intelligence, Execution and Aftermath of the Dieppe Raid, 19th August 1942.

6   Wheatley, R., Cabinet Office, to Dr. G.W.S. Friedrichsen, British Joint Services Mission, Washington, 'Dieppe raid and Allies' need for invasion ports', 21 December 1955; and Notes by R. Wheatley on Dieppe raid in file ll/4/I 13 November 1963, Cabinet Office, Historical and Records Section (COHRS), CAB 146/349 [closed until 1998].

soundly defeated the Allies there. Instead, it came from their experience of the Allied landings in the Mediterranean theatre.[7]

The Combined Report on Operation Jubilee, written by the Allies, indicated that the landings at Dieppe had forced the Germans to mount significant movement of troops from the eastern theatre to the western fronts to counter the threat. 'Only one SS motorized division, Das Reich, and one SS motorized brigade, Adolf Hitler, were actually transferred.'[8]

A little more than three months before D-Day, on 26 February 1944, the Allied Supreme Headquarters received a bundle of German documents that Allied Intelligence had managed to steal from the German High Command. These were a godsend for the Allies as they provided a detailed picture of the German view of the Dieppe raid. They were intelligence reports from 81st Corps dated 22 August 1942, the 81st Corps operations report dated 25 August 1942, the German Corps commander's action report dated 2 September 1942, the 320th Infantry Division operations report 2 September 1942 and divisional orders concerning coastal defences that were sent from 81st Corps to 320th Infantry Division on 11 September 1942.[9]

These reports were excellent for helping the Allies refine their plans for the D-Day invasion that took place on 6 June 1944. The Germans expected that if the Allies attacked the coast of France again on a similar or larger scale across a broad front that they would try to penetrate the weak spots in the German defences. At the same time, the Germans expected that the Allies would try to capture or, at the very least surround, the harbours, then cut them off as they moved inland.

Looking at the critique from the 81st Corps report we can see that:

---

7   Campbell, Dieppe revisited, p.221, as cited in Henry, The Planning, Intelligence, Execution and Aftermath of the Dieppe Raid, 19th August 1942.

8   Basil H. Liddell Hart states Dieppe led Hitler to order the despatch of two of the best Panzer divisions – at a crucial moment of his drive for Stalingrad. So even in failure, the Dieppe raid created a valuable distraction in aid of the Russians, *The Tanks, Vol. 2* (London; Cassell, 1959), p.320; J.R.M. Butler and J.M.A. Gwyer, 'Anglo-American strategy reconsidered: the decision for Torch', in *Grand Strategy*, June 1941–August 1942, 3(11) (London: HMSO, 1964), p.646. 323; cited in Shelley, James, 'German Lessons and Influence on Strategic Thinking'.

9   Shapiro, L.S.B., 'Dieppe As The Enemy Saw It', *MacLean's Magazine*, 1 March 1946, London.

On the whole the transmission of orders and reports functioned satisfactorily. It must be borne in mind, however, that the British (Canadians) did not attempt to destroy command posts and message centres of divisional and lower headquarters. This calls for the establishment of message centres along a line running parallel to the coast at a distance of about 10 kilometres. These message centres must be at junctions of main roads leading to the shore and should be on a single telephone network with Division and Corps headquarters . . .[10]

The Allies now knew what kind of reaction they could expect when they set foot on the beaches of Normandy. Because the Germans would move their mobile reserves to the beaches to try stop the invasion, the Allies, where they could, quickly moved inland causing confusion, 'thereby completely confusing German mobile reserves who rushed down [to the beaches] expecting us to mass for defence'.[11]

From the hundreds of Allied prisoners of war captured by the Germans on 19 August 1942 after the raid ended, the Germans were able to understand the British plan of attack. This and much more is laid out in the following extract from the 81st Corps report on the Dieppe raid. According to this report the Allies were to:

a) Land at 0610 in Dieppe itself and on both sides of the city under the *Mission*: protection of the Air Force and the Navy; (b) to occupy the city and fortified area of Dieppe; (c) to push through with infantry and armoured units to Arques-La-Bataille, where it was assumed that a division command post was located . . . After completing their mission, they were to re-embark by 1530 hours.[12]

Also, the report listed the Allied commanders involved in the landings. The Germans believed that the Allied Commander-in-Chief was Lord

---

10   Ibid.

11   See Shapiro, 'Dieppe as the Enemy Saw it', *MacLean's Magazine*, 1 March 1946, London.

12   Ibid.

Mountbatten, that Major General Roberts was the ground forces commander; that Brigadier Lett was the commander of 4th Brigade and that Brigadier Southam was commanding 6th Brigade. They knew that the Allies used 58 tanks of the Calgary Regiment for the operation. They also knew that the British used two Commando units: 3rd Commando and 4th Commando.

The report goes on to outline the Allied preparations:

> The undertaking was prepared most conscientiously. The operation order is very detailed (121 typewritten pages) and therefore difficult to visualize as a whole. The planning, down to the last detail, limits the independence of action of the subordinate officer and leaves him no opportunity to make independent decisions in an altered situation.
>
> The enemy had very good maps dated Aug. 1, 1942, with fortifications clearly inserted, presumably the results of the evaluation of aerial photographs . . . Corroboration by secret agents was evidently not carried out (e.g. the strength of the tank barriers in Dieppe was not known). It was assumed that the 110th Infantry Division was in the sector and that division headquarters was located in Arques-La-Bataille. There was a general lack of knowledge as to the location of [our] regimental and battalion command posts.[13]

The German report continues looking at the combat efficiency of the Allies:

> The Second Canadian Division had lain for quite some time in the south of England, most of the time in camps . . . The Canadians on the whole fought badly and surrendered afterward in swarms. On the other hand, the combat efficiency of the Commandos was very high. They were well trained and fought with real spirit. It is reported that they showed great skill in climbing the steep coastal cliffs.[14]

From here, the Germans then outlined the record of events that took place on the morning of the 19th as the Allies were landing. They specifically

13   Ibid.
14   Ibid.

outline the short naval engagement between the Allied attacking force and the German convoy that alerted the German defences up and down the coast:

> While the defensive forces were still in doubt whether the ships in front of Dieppe were friendly or enemy, a series of concentrated air attacks began at dawn. While bombing and strafing attacks were still in progress, swarms of landing craft in waves of 40 to 50 headed for shore out of the protection of the natural morning fogs and artificial smokescreens laid down by the attacking planes.[15]

From this point in the report the German authors then outline the disposition of their own division that was involved in the defence of the Dieppe coast – 571st Infantry Regiment of the 302nd Infantry Division, 'headquarters with two infantry battalions; two engineer companies; Third Battalion of the 302nd Artillery Regiment'.[16]

It is the following point that is most important for our purposes, which is the German view of the success of the Dieppe landings. In particular, why the Germans felt the raid was a failure:

> The operation failed primarily because: in Puys the landing was repulsed, in Dieppe the tanks did not succeed in crossing the anti-tank wall, and near Pourville the British (Canadian) battalions did not continue their advance . . .

They believed the cause of the Allied failure was their basic miscalculation of the German defences and that they tried to:

> 'Grab the bull by the horns' by landing the main body of their invasion forces, particularly the tanks, right in front of Dieppe. They persisted with this plan, although they were aware of the strength of the Dieppe street defences, concrete constructions, antitank walls, machine-gun positions and coastal guns. This we know from their maps. It is also inconceivable why they did not support with tanks the battalions which landed near Pourville. An attack with tanks

---

15   Ibid.
16   Ibid.

from Pourville against the hill west of Dieppe and against the '4 Vents Farm' might have been successful, although it would have been most difficult to overcome the antitank walls, the pier and the Scie dam.

Contrary to all expectations, the British (Canadians) did not employ parachutists and airborne troops. If they had attacked Puys simultaneously with airborne troops and from the sea, the initial position of the defenders of Puys would probably have been critical.

The British (Canadians) must have expected that the massed employment of the Air Force against the coastal defences of Dieppe would shatter the German defences to such an extent as to enable the assault battalions to break through the coastal defences. It is probable that the heavy smokescreen over Dieppe considerably diminished the accuracy of hits and the effect of the British air attacks.

They did land light and heavy mortars, but their entire combat order mentioned only one light battery and one light anti-aircraft section, which was to be landed near Puys. As this landing failed, this artillery was not actually employed. A few light assault guns would probably have been more use to the British (Canadians) in their first attack than the tanks. Since fire control observation on the big ships was poor because of the smokescreen, the landing force had no artillery support whatsoever.

The Germans did not understand why the Allies underestimated their defences when they had such detailed intelligence reports and aerial reconnaissance photographs. They also found it surprising that the Allies expected to carry out the operation in less than a day:

The British (Canadian) operational order fixed every detail of the action for each unit. This method of planning made the failure of the whole raid inevitable in the event of unexpected difficulties.

Therefore, the Germans were convinced that the operation was doomed to failure before they arrived at the beaches. The Allies suffered significant losses as the Germans state in their reports.

'By Aug. 24, 475 dead were buried . . . Total enemy losses amount probably to at least 60 to 70 per cent of the landing force.'[17]

But what of the German High Command, the German newspapers, the German people and so forth. What was their view of the Dieppe raid? To answer this question, we must look at what was going on in Germany just before the landings took place as they influenced the German reaction:

> Difficult decisions over the allotment of increasingly scarce resources, the perplexing military complications thrown up by multiple and simultaneously active theatres of operations, fears over wavering morale on the home front, and an increasingly fractious relationship between Hitler and his army generals (particularly his Eastern Front generals) were all affected by the sudden and unexpected events of the Dieppe raid on 19 August 1942.[18]

These tensions were being played out in 1942 and can be seen in key German newspapers such as *Völkischer Beobachter*, the official newspaper of the Nazi Party, the War Diary of the High Command of the Armed Forces OKW, the Diaries of Joseph Goebbels and the German Weekly News, which were newsreels played in local German cinemas across the country at that time:

> Hitler's speeches, directives, proclamations, and table talk, offer a rich history of the interplay of these tensions and the impact of the Dieppe raid on their resolution by the autumn of 1942. These sources also reveal that the German reaction to and analysis of the Dieppe raid is very different from the more familiar Anglo-Canadian narrative.[19]

In the summer of 1941, von Rundstedt was becoming increasingly concerned about a possible Allied invasion in the west. These concerns he relayed to Hitler who, finally, in December 1941, after Operation Barbarossa had stalled,

---

17   See Shapiro, citing the 81st Corps' Intelligence Report on the Dieppe Landings.

18   David Ian Hall, 'The German View of the Dieppe Raid August 1942', *Canadian Military History*, Vol. 21, Iss. 4, Article 2.

19   Ibid.

ordered the construction of the Atlantic Wall, an impregnable fortified coast-line of France and Belgium that faced Britain across the English Channel. At the time, Hitler had committed 75 per cent of the German war machine to the terrible fighting on the Eastern Front against the Soviet Union and as such, he did not want a major diversion in the west that would reduce this commitment. Hence, the Atlantic Wall.

> Hitler's concerns seemed justified in early July 1942 when German intelligence warned that an Anglo-American decision on where and when the 'second Front' would be launched was imminent.[20]

Decisions regarding the Atlantic Wall were made during two conferences that took place on 2 and 13 August 1942, both chaired by Hitler. These meetings took place at his military headquarters, Werwolf, at Vinnitsa in Ukraine.[21] When news of the Allied landings at Dieppe reached Hitler, who was still at his HQ in Vinnitsa, his mood was one of confidence and calm rather than panic. 'Hitler was visibly pleased with the response of the German garrison in Dieppe but also with the fact that the raid appeared to confirm his strategic view of the war in 1942. Churchill had tried an audacious attack and it had been thwarted with speed and conviction.'[22]

The Norwegian German Radio Service was the first media outlet to announce the Dieppe landings. The OKW (High Command of the Armed Forces) issued a special bulletin outlining the Allied actions and how the operation had been thwarted by the German forces. The bulletin was reasonably accurate and it included a speculative editorial on Churchill's motivations for mounting the invasion. It concluded that Churchill had approved the landings as an appeasement to Stalin who, as we know, wanted a second front opened up as soon as possible. The raid was reported by the OKW along two lines. The first was that it was a well-prepared plan that had taken months to create and ended with the landing force pushed into the sea after only nine hours. The second was that the raid was quickly created five days after

---

20   Ibid., 'The German View of the Dieppe Raid August 1942, *Canadian Military History*, Vol. 21.

21   Ibid.

22   Ibid., David Ian Hall, citing Horst Boog, Werner Rahn, Reinhard Stumpf and Gern Wegner, *Germany and the Second World War*, in his article, 'The German View of the Dieppe Raid August 1942', *Canadian Military History*, Vol. 21, Iss. 4, Article 2.

Churchill had visited Stalin in Moscow. 'Both lines were developed in the following days with each reinforcing the other as confirmation of Churchill's desperation and stupidity.'[23]

The day after the landings, Goebbels joined Hitler at Werwolf in order to discuss the lines to take for the media and press for an official response to the Dieppe raid. Goebbels shared Hitler's view that the landings had been a rash decision on the part of the British under pressure from Stalin. The next day, the failure of the British attack at Dieppe due to the successful German defence filled the front pages of newspapers across Germany.

> The leading articles addressed the main themes that Hitler and Goebbels had decided on in Vinnitsa: Churchill's invasion catastrophe, Stalin's displeasure with his western Allies, and the folly of the Second Front.[24]

As far as the German media was concerned, no doubt aided and instructed by Goebbels, Dieppe was proof positive that mounting an invasion in the west in 1942 was beyond the abilities of the Allies. The media coverage of the Dieppe raid pleased Goebbels, as did the reaction of the public.

> The weekend ended with the first screening of a newsreel that showed the results of the Dieppe raid. Images of shattered tanks and landing craft shrouded in the smoke of battle filled the screen. The beaches were littered with the debris of beaten and demoralised soldiers: hundreds of discarded helmets, rifles and other weapons, and a few remaining bodies of the dead that had not yet been removed for burial.[25]

Dieppe featured heavily in the 26 August 1942 newsreels and included a section of a map taken from a captured officer that outlined the British execution and plan for the landings. The cameras depicted large swathes of Canadian prisoners being marched through Dieppe to prisoner of war camps.

---

23   See David Ian Hall, 'The German View of the Dieppe Raid August 1942', *Canadian Military History*, Vol. 21, Iss. 4, Article 2.

24   Ibid.

25   Ibid.

Scenes of destruction on the beaches showed Allied military equipment from tanks, landing craft, trucks to weapons littering the shore. 'Regardless of whether it was a raid or an invasion, the film images could not be denied: it was an unmitigated disaster for the British and their Canadian Allies who provided the main body of troops for the attack.'[26]

The Sunday, 30 August edition of *Völkischer Beobachter* (*VB*) ran the final feature on Dieppe. The article personally attacked Churchill by bringing up his previous military catastrophes such as the evacuation of Dunkirk. 'Churchill's military naivety and strategic subservience to Stalin, the poor planning and tactical incompetence evinced in the execution of the invasion attempt, and English willingness to let Canadians die in a fiasco',[27] featured heavily in two sub-articles to the main article within the edition.

> Very little new information was provided in the Dieppe articles but there was accurate and substantial detail on the full plan of the operation, the order of battle, intercepted radio reports made by the landing forces throughout the day, and the enemy's losses. Extensive excerpts from OKW's official and final report on Dieppe were also published, citing the main reasons for the attack's failure – insufficient fire support, failure to deploy airborne troops to 'hold the ring,' an overly detailed plan and inflexible execution, and the amateurish way the British waged war.[28]

The successful defence of Dieppe by the Germans was an important public relations and military victory for Hitler because it proved that the Atlantic Wall was strong enough to repel any Allied attack from the sea. This meant that Hitler could use the majority of his military might to destroy the Soviets in the East. The victory of the German forces over the Allies at Dieppe provided the German people with an optimistic view of the future, especially

---

26   Ibid.

27   Ibid.

28   See David Ian Hall, 'The German View of the Dieppe Raid August 1942', *Canadian Military History*, Vol. 21, Iss. 4, Article 2 citing *VB*, Sonntag, 30 August 1942, pp.1–2.

when the Wehrmacht had achieved some real successes against the Soviet Army in September of that year.[29]

At the end of August 1942, the message from the German media, especially from *VB*, to the German people was optimistic, that victory was around the corner and all they had to do was stay focussed and have faith in Hitler.

However, this air of optimism quickly disappeared by the beginning of September as Rommel and his Afrika Korps mounted an offensive in Egypt that quickly ground to a halt due to lack of ammunition and fuel. In this instance, the RAF had complete control of the air, which meant that Rommel lost his element of surprise, and by 5 September 1942 he and the Afrika Korps were right back at their original starting point having abandoned Alam el Halfa. Elsewhere, the tide was turning against the Germans. The Soviets were beginning to take control as winter approached and German offensives were beginning to stall.

On 28 September 1942, Hitler met with his commanders in the west. He told them his belief was that the next attempt the Allies would make for opening up a second front in the west would rely on overwhelming air power. 'We must realise that we are not alone in learning a lesson from Dieppe. The British have also learned. We must reckon with a totally different mode of attack and at quite a different place.'[30]

Well before the Dieppe raid Hitler and his generals were fully aware of the increasing possibility of an invasion from the west by the Allies. By December 1941 they had begun the construction of the Atlantic Wall to meet the threat from the west. Dieppe was not a sudden surprise for the Germans and the High Command did not fall into a panic the moment the alarm was raised. Instead they handled it with confidence and coolness. For political and strategic reasons, the German press portrayed Dieppe as a victory for Germany and failed attempt by the Allies in opening up a second front. Its propaganda value was immense and this was used to great affect by Goebbels' media machine:

---

29   These are the victories at Rxhev and Kaluga, reported in *VB*, where the Soviet attacks had stalled with the Red Army suffering severe losses.

30   See David Ian Hall, 'The German View of the Dieppe Raid August 1942', *Canadian Military History*, Vol. 21, Iss. 4, Article 2 citing Record of Hitler's Secret Speech to Western Commanders, 29 September 1942, First Army War Diary, Annexes T312/23/9706 et. seq. (Microcopy T312/Roll 23/Pages 9706 onwards) as outlined in David Irving's *Hitler's War*, pp.410, 860.

The ongoing pressures in concluding the campaign at Stalingrad and in the Caucasus led eventually to a complete breakdown between Hitler and his generals in September 1942. The generals demanded more men and more resources at a time when resources were limited and strategic pressure on a number of fronts – the Battle of the Atlantic, the air war, the Mediterranean, and the defence of the West – all demanded Hitler's attention and more of the Nazi war machine's severely stretched resources. Most importantly, the Dieppe raid did not alter German strategic thinking about the conduct of the war or defence against an invasion in the west. Russia was the key to both – victory and preventing a successful invasion. When D-Day finally came on 6 June 1944, Hitler and the Germans had already, by their own logic, lost the war.[31]

---

31   See David Ian Hall, 'The German View of the Dieppe Raid August 1942', *Canadian Military History*, Vol. 21.

Chapter 29

Dieppe and its Influences on D-Day

Some call Dieppe an experiment, a prelude to D-Day, but it is important to emphasize that it was a raid, a complex one, but a raid nonetheless. Starting in 1942, the British Combined Operations Headquarters under Lord Mountbatten carried out several raids to boost public morale and to convince the Soviets that the Allies were serious about opening a second front. Bruneval and St. Nazaire had shown the efficacy of raid operations, Dieppe was the next iteration.[1]

What then of the influences of Dieppe on the D-Day landings and what lessons did the Allies learn from the disaster that was Dieppe? Indeed, with D-Day, Allied ground attack fighters and bombers pounded, strafed and destroyed German communications centres that were situated a few miles inland from the beaches, instead of concentrating solely on German defences such as heavy gun batteries as they had done at Dieppe. This strategy meant that the Germans could not set up an organised counterattack of the invasion using their coastal communications network as they had done at Dieppe because Allied air power had destroyed it.

As for the influence of Dieppe on the D-Day Invasion, some scholars would argue that it made little difference, or, not as much as has been previously thought. Dr Matthias Strohn of the Centre for Historical Analysis and Conflict Research suggests that the Germans had already lost the war by the time of the invasion:

---

1   Jonathan Carroll, 'The 1942 Dieppe Raid and its influence on D-Day', Stephen Ambrose Historical Tours, https://stephenambrosetours.com/the-1942-dieppe-raid-and-its-influence-on-d-day

The tank reserve was the perceived trump card of the German army in the west. In contrast to the rather sorry state of the rest of the army, it was well-equipped: The tank force comprised of 10 divisions, four of which were Waffen-SS divisions (at the end of June two further Waffen SS tank divisions were deployed from the Eastern Front: 9th 'Hohenstaufen' and 10th 'Frrundsberg'). In addition, there were three heavy tank detachments of battalion size, two of which came from the Waffen-SS. In total, this force had about 1,600 tanks and tank destroyers.[2]

Unlike in 1942 when the Germans were capable of putting up a co-ordinated and well executed defence against the Allies' landing at Dieppe, in 1944, it was a different story:

The [tank] divisions were supposed to turn the tables and ensure that Germany would win the campaign in the west. Unfortunately for the Germans, reality would prove different. The command structure, Allied air superiority and re-supply issues meant that the divisions were brought up to the front-line piecemeal. The envisaged powerful knock-out stroke with an iron fist in reality turned out to be a mere number of slaps in the enemy's face.[3]

The Germans believed that Dieppe was a failed cross-Channel invasion but as we have seen it was part of a series of raids designed to take the pressure off the Soviet Union. It was the strongly prepared German defences at Dieppe that ultimately defeated the British and Canadians at Dieppe, not the second-rate German troops manning those defences. A key lesson, therefore, was not to attack heavily defended fortifications but, instead, to go for the wide open beaches of Normandy that were not as heavily defended as Dieppe was. This gave the Allies the space to land large numbers of troops and materiel quickly. 'Supplying any cross-Channel invasion was of course critical, but Dieppe showed that attacking a defended port was simply too

---

2   See Strohn, 'An Absolutely Harrowing Organisation', *British Army Review*, No. 175, Summer 2019.

3   Strohn, Dr Matthias, 'An Absolutely Harrowing Organisation', *British Army Review*, No. 175, Summer 2019, CHACR, Camberley, Ministry of Defence.

costly and risked destroying the port facilities themselves. Having learned this, the Allies solved the vital need for port facilities by the subsequent development of the portable Mulberry Harbours.[4]

Dieppe also enabled the Allies to learn and change their way of conducting armoured warfare. The Canadian tanks had been unable to deal with the gravel and shale on the beaches and the obstacles the Germans had built there. A solution was needed and this came from Major-General Percy Hobart, who examined the experiences of the tanks at Dieppe in order to develop special armoured vehicles that could handle beach obstacles.

> The result, dubbed 'Hobart's Funnies', was a series of vehicles designed to breach the fortifications of the Atlantic Wall. Hobart modified existing Churchill and Sherman tanks to create flame-thrower, anti-mine, and bridge-laying/bunker busting tanks. As such, when the British and Canadians landed at Gold, Juno, and Sword beaches on June 6th 1944, Hobart's Funnies proved decisive in allowing a swift breach of the German defences – with a corresponding reduction in casualties. The Canadians at Juno fought ferociously, penetrating the farthest inland on June 6th, to avenge their defeat at Dieppe.[5]

Viewing the Dieppe raid through the lens of history, it is easy to point fingers and claim that the high loss of life led to little or no gain for the Allies. Since 1942 those that were involved in the raid in one way or another have had a difficult time in justifying the failure that it was.

> Regardless of their spin, Dieppe was an unmitigated disaster showcasing how unprepared the Allies were in 1942 for any large amphibious operations. However, the law of unintended consequences meant that a raid on the coast of France designed to boost morale not only had the opposite effect, but also ended up shaping the eventual invasion of France in 1944. Lord Mountbatten, an architect of the raid, claimed that 'the battle of D-Day was won on the beaches of Dieppe'. While certainly trying to justify the

---

4   See Jonathan Carroll, 'The 1942 Dieppe Raid and its influence on D-Day'.
5   Ibid.

disaster, there is a certain truth in his claim. Many operational elements of the Overlord planning can be traced back to the costly lessons unintentionally learned at Dieppe in 1942.[6]

We can see that the Allies learned the lessons of Dieppe and applied them to D-Day, but by comparison it would appear as if the Germans did not. For what was lacking in the German reaction to the invasion was a sense of urgency. They had not built up their supplies of fuel, ammunition or moved their communications network further inland or even designed an alternate communications system knowing that the Allies would use superior air power. We know that Hitler warned his generals in the west that the Allies would land in a different place. We also know that German military resources in 1944 were stretched thinly. Does that mean, therefore, that the Germans could not provide enough divisions in the west to counter an invasion or enough air power in the west to defeat Allied air power, or does it mean they did not have the urgency to do so?

This book has been about the German view of the Allied landings at Dieppe. Ultimately, the core question has to be asked: given what the Germans learned from Dieppe, or what they thought they had learned, why weren't they able to mount an effective defence at Normandy and stop the setting up of a second front in the west by the Allies? What happened to their mobile reserves they used so effectively at Dieppe, why weren't they as effective in Normandy?

It is the belief of this author that the Germans viewed Dieppe as a failed invasion attempt by the Allies, not as a raid, and because their strong fortifications were able to stop the advances of the Allies they became complacent when it came to D-Day. They still believed the Atlantic Wall would save them.

---

6   Ibid.

Part 5
Appendices

Appendix 1

Von Rundstedt's Final Report

In this appendix it is only fitting that the last word should come from Field Marshal Karl Rudolf Gerd von Rundstedt, the Commander-in-Chief West of the German forces. His evaluation of the British and Allied raid on Dieppe provides an interesting summary of the overall German impression of the operation.

Much of von Rundstedt's views of the operations are based upon documents taken from captured PoWs as well as from hourly operational reports coming in from the fighting. Having studied these captured documents, von Rundstedt believed that the magnitude of the operation and the 'almost too precise planning, in accordance with so rigid a scheme, as well as in view of the forces employed – one Canadian division, reinforced by Commandos and special troops – the operation at Dieppe cannot be considered a local raid.'[1]

Indeed, he believed that the expenditure in men and materials was far too great for the operation to be classified as a raid. 'One does not sacrifice 29 or 30 of the most modern tanks for a raid.'[2] Von Rundstedt felt that by employing such a large force, the British wanted to quickly seize the 'Dieppe bridgehead', after its defences had been destroyed, in order to use the excellent port facilities for landing 'floating and operational reserves'.

> For with the floating reserve alone there were 28 tanks, certainly of the same types. An expenditure of 58 such tanks cannot be reconciled with a short destructive raid. Nor, however, can it be established without contradiction by the captured operational

---

1 From Report No. 10, Historical Section, National Defence Headquarters, Operation Jubilee, The Raid on Dieppe, Information From German War Diaries, Report of the Commander-in-Chief West, (Field Marshal von Rundstedt) on the Dieppe Raid, 19 August 1942.

2 Ibid.

order, whether the operation was of a local character or – in the event of success – was to be the beginning of the 'Invasion'.[3]

The captured British operational orders clearly stated there was to be withdrawal and re-embarkation. 'It is, however, no proof of the enemy's final intention, that withdrawal and re-embarkation were planned in detail.'[4]

Von Rundstedt knew that after the completion of their tasks and re-embarkation, Nos 3 and 4 Commando were ordered to wait before returning to England to see if they were to take their place in the reserve force due to land behind the main force if the landings had been successful. They were to return to England without delay only in the case of not succeeding in their tasks.

Also, the hint in the captured order that the troops are not to destroy the gasworks at Dieppe, but to leave them going until the Engineers arrive, leaves open the possibility of issuing new orders at a given time. It appears certain that, had Dieppe fallen, these orders would have been given.[5]

Given the extent of the forces used, the Germans found the deployment and tactics of the RAF difficult to understand. For example, why was the Dieppe bridgehead not isolated by a heavy aerial bombardment in order to either delay or prevent the Germans from deploying their local reserves against the landings? Baffled by this lack of aerial effectiveness, it only made sense to von Rundstedt 'if the Englishman wished to save his massed bomber formation for employment in a second phase – namely the commencement of the 'Invasion£ – after the capture of Dieppe.'[6] Another reason why von Rundstedt believed the Dieppe landings were not a raid but a major operation that failed.

The British knew where the 10th Panzer Division were, that they were in reserve and could be deployed quickly into the battle. 'It may be that this was

---

3   Ibid., Paragraph 2.
4   Ibid.
5   Ibid., Paragraph 4.
6   Ibid., Paragraph 5.

decisive in inducing him to refrain temporarily from the use of his bomber formations. He will not do it like this a second time!'[7]

Field Marshal von Rundstedt's Chief of Staff, Kurt Zeitzler, visited 302nd Infantry Division at Dieppe the day after the landings took place, 20 August, to get a personal impression of the battlefield. His observations were relayed back to von Rundstedt. On his arrival he ordered that Alarm Scale II be cancelled for all units involved as there was clearly no imminent threat of another Allied landing any time soon. He also placed 10th Panzer Division under the command of 81 Corps.

At 0800hrs this day the first casualty reports began arriving at 302nd Infantry Division HQ that showed the losses to the German army were moderate, 'even though the figures were not yet final because all the hospitals, etc., had to send in their returns'.

However, Naval Group West reported that one of three port defence craft had been sunk in the harbour without its crew, likely as a result of a direct hit during the height of the battle.

At 1200hrs on the 20th 3rd Air Fleet reported that the number of enemy aircraft shot down during the battle was now at 112. This message was confirmed along with figures of British and Allied naval vessels sunk or damaged:

Total sinkings:

> 5 merchant ships of about 13,000 tons
> 1 destroyer
> 1 escort
> 1 S-boat (probable)

Damaged:

> 4 cruisers
> 4 destroyers
> 5 merchant ships 15,000 tons
> 3 S-boats
> Sea rescue boat
> 1 assault landing craft
> 1 towing boat

---

7   Ibid.

Probably damaged:

4 merchant ships 12,000 tons
1 S-boat[8]

When Zeitzler returned to C-in-C GHQ he provided his personal impressions of the battlefield to von Rundstedt. He stated that British losses were high and that there were still bodies everywhere even though many had already been buried. 'In front of an MG position covering from the flank a narrow sector of beach between the sea and the bluffs, there were mountains of dead bodies.' Zeitzler estimated the number to be over 100 at this one point on the beaches alone. There was a large quantity of modern Allied weapons that had been either destroyed or abandoned on the beaches, these being mostly light and heavy infantry weapons. Zeitzler stated that: 'The English fought well. Canadians and Americans not so well, the latter quickly surrendered under the impression of high bloody losses.'[9]

In his report to von Rundstedt, Zeitzler stated that the beach 'west of Dieppe harbour presents a picture like Dunkirk. Three large transports burned out beached during low tide with some landing craft between them. There was much destroyed equipment and about 20 tanks all of which were dealt with immediately on landing.'[10] In other areas of the beaches landing craft, tanks and masts could be seen protruding from the water at low tide.

At specific points in the town of Dieppe damage was heavy but for the most part it was moderate.

During the battle the civilian population behaved well. No incident of sabotage or obstruction of military measures. At noon of the day of the battle the shops in Dieppe were already open again. In the main areas of battle civilians still made a confused impression but the quick arrival of the Panzer Division made a strong impression amongst the population.[11]

---

8   Ibid.
9   Ibid., Section II, Evaluation, 1945hrs.
10   Ibid.
11   Ibid.

Zeitzler then added his personal impression of 813th Artillery Troop, who were positioned roughly a kilometre from the coast, in front of a bluff, with all-round protection for close-quarter defensive fighting that included barbed wire. The guns pointed out to sea and during the battle they fired on many naval targets. 'Then fighters fired at the troop in low-level attacks and with tracers set the cartridges at nearly all the guns on fire. The gun crews had to extinguish the fires.'[12]

At the same time the 813th position was attacked by Allied infantry and after two hours of fighting the position was overrun. At this point the guns were still intact and the last fired at 250m range. The strength of 813 Troop at the guns was an establishment of 112 but in this battle, '30 were killed, 21 wounded and recovered by their own units, amongst them was the gravely wounded troop commander'. At the time, Zeitzler stated that there were ten men missing who he believed would have been picked up by relieving troops coming to the rescue of the 813th. Two appeared to have been taken prisoner.

> It is doubtful whether these have been taken along to the ships. A telephone operator in the telephone building did not allow himself to be overrun. He held the bunker until relieved, threw back a hand grenade which was thrown in and is now badly wounded in hospital. The guns were damaged by air attack and are partly burned out.[13]

Finalising his report to von Rundstedt, Zeitzler claimed that Allied losses amounted to 2,095 prisoners, of those there were 617 wounded. He believed that more than 600 Allied soldiers and officers had been killed and the number of drowned could not be calculated at that time.

On 21 August 1942 von Rundstedt received a message from the Führer and Supreme Commander of the German Forces, Adolf Hitler:

> Thanks to the careful preparations made by command and troops, an English landing attempt on a grand scale was completely broken up in the shortest of time.

---

12 Ibid
13 Ibid., Section II, Evaluation, 2010hrs.

I beg you, Herr Field Marshal, to express my thanks and my appreciation to all participating units of the three armed services. I know that in the future too I can rely on the Commanders and the soldiers of the Armed Forces in the West.[14]

The message was duly passed on by von Rundstedt's staff to all participating units and all three services. As the battle came to an end von Rundstedt ordered that a set of basic lessons from the battle be compiled and sent out by 23 August 1942 to the General of Artillery Alfred Jodl, Chief of the Armed Forces Operations Staff, to the High Command Army within von Rundstedt's own command as C-in-C West.

Von Rundstedt finished his evaluation of the Dieppe landings with the following observations:

I have had the captured English operation order for Dieppe translated and mimeographed. According to German ideas this order is not an order, but an aide-memoire or a scheme worked out for a map exercise. Nevertheless, it does contain many points of value to us.

First, how much the enemy knows about us.

Second, the peculiarities in his method of landing and fighting. For that reason, this order is to be thoroughly studied by all staffs, to collect lessons for our coastal defence and for the training and education of our troops.

But it would be an error to believe that the enemy will mount his next operation in the same manner. He will draw his lessons from his mistakes in planning and from his failure and next time he will do things differently.

The Commander-in-Chief West

Von Rundstedt

Field Marshal

Von Rundstedt finished his report with some details of German losses. The total number of casualties for all the three German armed services amounted to 591 men. The Army lost 115 killed, 187 wounded and 14 missing. The Navy lost 78 missing or killed and 35 wounded, while the Air Force suffered 104 killed and missing, and 58 wounded.

---

14   Ibid., Section II, Evaluation, 21 August 1942.

Appendix 2

Operation Cauldron (Varengeville)

On 19 August 1942, 4 Commando consisting of 252 all ranks as well as seven Allied personal mounted an assault on a German 6 gun battery near Varengeville. There were roughly the same number of Germans defending the position who had the advantage of knowing the ground, concrete, wire and mines, hidden machine guns, mortars and dual purpose flak guns. They'd had two years to perfect their defences yet within 100 minutes of the Allied landings their position was overrun and the battery, all its works, outbuildings, pill boxes and so on were totally destroyed. More than 150 Germans lay dead. British casualties amounted to 45 dead and wounded and of the wounded, 12 were back on duty within two months.[1]

The detailed analysis of the destruction of the gun battery at Varengeville comes from *Notes from Theatres of War, No. 11, Destruction of a German Battery by No. 4 Commando During the Dieppe Raid* and it focuses on why this action was as successful as it was. The notes and analysis, written in 1942, were used as a study guide for the infantry. Indeed, the introduction states that to realise its full value, 'officers and NCOs should first study it as an indoor exercise and then be told what happened on the day'.[2]

Known as Operation Cauldron, it was an outstanding example of what can be achieved by a small force of troops armed with light infantry weapons with sound planning and thorough training.

---

1   Notes from Theatres of War, No. 11, Destruction of a German Battery by No. 4 Commando During the Dieppe Raid. Originally printed in British Army Review No 158 Autumn 2013.

2   Ibid., Introduction, War Office February 1943, p.3.

It is a model of fire and movement tactics. Frontal fire pinned the enemy to the ground while the assault troops moved around their flank to the forming up position, the assault itself being preceded by a final crescendo of fire. The principle of this attack and that of the battle drill taught at the School of Infantry are the same.[3]

At the very beginning of the account the author states that the reason for publishing was so that everyone could learn from 'the story of a stimulating achievement'.

Planning

Cauldron's plan was simple, flexible and understood by all ranks. Its thoroughness was based on a detailed study of information and aerial photographs of German positions. There was a determination to carry out the plan, a will to gain surprise and a confidence that the task of destroying the battery could be achieved. However, good plans are not a guarantee of success; they must be completed by skilful and determined execution.

The key elements of the training regime for the operation were:

- Accurate prediction of the nature of the various actions on the day.
- Sound training programme that enabled the soldiers to meet the sudden challenges on the day with the confidence of highly trained athletes.
- Implicit confidence of the troops in their weapons, the culmination of months of practice in all phases of the fire-fight.[4]

Most operations require some form of special training and this was no different. Throughout the training special attention was paid to cliff climbing, use of scaling ladders, the use of Bangalore[5] torpedoes in unusual circumstances and measures for embarkation and re-embarkation were all practised until

---

3   Ibid.

4   See Notes from Theatres of War, No. 11, Destruction of a German Battery by No. 4 Commando.

5   The Bangalore torpedo is essentially an explosive charge inside one or more metal connected tubes and is mostly used by combat engineers for clearing obstacles that would otherwise need to be cleared by closer contact while under fire.

perfection was reached. Elaborate care was taken on the seating arrangements in the landing craft to ensure that once on the beaches there would be no need to reorganise under heavy enemy fire. Several trials took place until a solution was found.

The Objective

Cauldron Force's orders were to destroy the German gun battery at Varengeville with all speed and cost. Since the battery covered the Dieppe approaches it had to be silenced before any of the large landing craft were sent in, making this preliminary operation absolutely essential to the larger plan. Cauldron Force were set to land after 0450 hours.

The position of the battery was 3½ miles west of Dieppe near Varengeville and 110 yards from the sea front. Except at Beach One and Beach Two, the cliffs were very steep. At Beach One two precipitous gullies led up to the wooded area 300 yards from the battery. Beach Two, situated near the mouth of the River Saâne, was the next possible landing place after Beach One.

Air photographs showed no indication of defences along the cliffs or at Beach One.

- **Beach One**: In the battery area, wire could be seen on all sides except to the west. The guns were located at (3) and (4). Only one MG position (5) was definitely located, but it was expected that others were similarly placed to cover the re-entrant angles of the wire and the road approaches. An overhead cable (6) led from the battery position to the lighthouse. This was thought to be an OP. Last-minute reconnaissance reported two light AA guns in the lighthouse area. This battery area was considerably built over and consequently difficult to interpret. Subsequent events, however, revealed that the intelligence, in general, was correct. Additional information is shown on the sketch map and is described in the narrative.[6]
- **Beach Two**: At Beach Two bales of wire were seen on the beaches at the western extremity of the cliff line, were two pillboxes covering the beaches plus the flat ground at the mouth of

6   See Notes from Theatres of War, No. 11, Destruction of a German Battery by No. 4 Commando During the Dieppe Raid, Introduction, War Office Feb 1943.

the River Saâne. Inland of Beach Two is a complicated network of trenches and wire and MG posts could be seen on the high ground to the right of the village of St Marguerite covering the valley of the River Saâne.[7]

The intelligence reports showed that the battery and its protective troops were part of the German 110 Division, a crack formation that had seen hard fighting on the Eastern Front. Reports also suggested that there were infantry units stationed in the Sainte-Marguerite battery area and the Quiberville areas respectively.

The plan of Commander Cauldron Force was to hold the enemy with covering fire from the coastal side of the battery while assaulting it from inland. He divided his command into two groups, with Group 1 providing covering fire and Group 2 carrying out the assault.

- **Group 1**, a total of 88 all ranks, consisted of:
  - Group HQ
  - C Troop 4 Commando
  - Fighting Patrol A Troop, 4 Commando
  - Signal mortar detachment
  - Signal Section
  - IO, MO, RSM
  - R Naval Beach Master, Allied Personnel,
  - Reserve ammunition carrying party
- It was to land at first light on Beach One and:
  - form a bridgehead above the cliff, both for the advance and to cover the withdrawal
  - engage the battery frontally with small arms fire as soon as the alarm was raised or the battery itself had opened fire on the main landing at Dieppe. They were not to close with the battery until Group 2 had captured the battery position.[8]

---

7   Ibid.
8   Ibid.

A ten-man reinforcement team carrying additional 3in mortar ammunition was to be landed after daylight and they were also to lay down light No. 18 smoke generators on the beach to cover the withdrawal.

- **Group 2**, with a total of 164 all ranks, was to land on Beach Two in two waves consisting of:
  - CO Cauldron Force
  - Force Headquarters
  - A Troop (less fighting patrol) 4 Commando
  - B Troop 4 Commando
  - F Troop 4 Commando
  - Allied personnel

- A Troop, less one section, was to land on Beach Two to the left of the River Saâne and its tasks were to cover the assault on the battery from the west and to protect the flank from attack from the west during the withdrawal.[9]

The plan called for the first wave of a section of A Troop to land in a Landing Craft Assault (LCA) [10] under covering fire from a Landing Craft Support (LCS)[11] at the left end of Beach Two with the immediate goal of taking out any opposition to the landing of the second wave, especially from the two pillboxes. From there this section was to move as quickly as possible to the double crossroads area to ensure the enemy in Sainte-Marguerite could not interfere with the assault on the battery.

Using four LCAs, the remainder of Group 2 were to land on Beach Two, with the second wave consisting of B and F Troops and Force HQ following after a three-minute interval, slightly farther up to the right on the beach. This force was then to move as quickly as possible up the valley of the Saâne

---

9   Ibid.

10   Landing Craft Assault – a flat-bottomed boat approximately 35ft long by 9ft wide, drawing about 3ft at the stern. It carried a maximum of 35 soldiers. The crew consisted of one naval officer and three ratings. Square bows lowered to form ramp for disembarkation.

11   Landing Craft Support – a flat-bottomed boat same size as LCA. It was not meant to carry troops, so had no disembarkation ramps. It was armed with Oerlikon and/or 3in mortar for smoke and twin, dual-purpose, Lewis guns.

into a wooded area. In the meantime, the LCS was to lie off Beach Two and fire on any attempt by the enemy to bring up reinforcements from the Quiberville area along the coast road.

If the landing was delayed alternate plans had been drawn up to shorten the approach to the objective if the landings took place in daylight. However, if the delay was slight the main force was to take the same direct route as the section of A Troop but if the delay was considerable then the entire force was to land on Beach One.

B and F Troops were to attack the battery from the wooded area. Ninety minutes were allowed for the approach from the beach to the forming up position. C Troop and A Troop were to provide covering fire and a squadron of four-cannon Hurricanes were to sweep in and shoot up the battery positions. Three white Very lights with radio messages were the signals for the assault to begin.

- **Notable Points in Planning:**
  a) The landing craft were to provide covering fire for the initial landing if required. This responsibility was jointly that of the military personnel with their automatic weapons and of the naval crews with stripped Lewis guns.
  b) Personnel were to remove all papers and identification other than identity discs.

- **Weapons and Equipment:**
  a) All troops carried their normal weapons except C Troop, who carried two extra LMGs and an anti-tank rifle, together with four discharger cups and four snipers' rifles with telescopic sights.
  b) The day before the operation all grenades were to be primed, magazines filled and equipment checked in daylight.
  c) Considerable ammunition and explosives were to be taken and so had to be widely distributed but no rations or water bottles could be carried. 1,000 rounds of. 45 and 1,000 rounds of. 303 reserve were to be landed on Beach One, plus 3,000 rounds of reserve. 303 remained in LCAS. No. 36 grenades were carried by all riflemen, and a useful number of No. 77 (phosphorus) grenades were taken. Incendiary

bombs and bullets were also carried. Made up charges were to be carried for destroying the guns and installations.

- **Communications:**
  a) Radio communications were to be set up between both Group HQs and all Troops. Intercommunication between Group 1, C Troop, Beach Signal Station, and LCA was by No. 18 Sets; between Group 1, Group 2 and within Group 2, by No. 38 Sets. In addition, various links manned by attached personnel were established from Beach One to the beach used by the Canadians on the left flank, with Force HQ and with the naval landing craft.

The Narrative

As with the preceding section, the details for the narrative of the action by the Commandos on the Varengeville gun battery come from Notes from Theatres of War, No. 11, Destruction of a German Battery by No. 4 Commando During the Dieppe Raid, Introduction, War Office Feb 1943. We begin here with Group 1.

As Group 1 approached Beach One at 0930hrs the lighthouse was flashing when it suddenly cut off and moments later some white star shells went up from the semaphore tower by the lighthouse, meaning the landing had been spotted by the Germans. The LCA commander was then asked to increase speed. It was difficult to see the beach but the flare from the lighthouse served as a navigational guide and it was possible for the two white houses on the cliff to be seen and recognised from the aerial photographs all ranks had memorised.

The LCAs went in according to plan and arrived within a yard of the correct place. Because of the pre-arranged seating plan in the LCAs, no reorganisation of troops took place as they disembarked. Indeed, they landed in waves onto dry land. Previous experience had shown that automatic weapons are likely to jam after a wetting and one Bren gun that had been pointing over the bows of one of the LCAs had been splashed by a wave and was very sluggish until the lubricants warmed up.

Although it was high tide, the whole of Group 1 was under the cliffs in less than a minute. The leading sub-section of C Troop began moving up the left-hand cleft but returned quickly, reporting it was impassable because it was partly filled by fallen rocks and was heavily wired. They then tried moving up the right chimney and blew two Bangalore torpedoes in the wire but this choked the exit. With time being paramount, the troops used explosives that enabled them to scale the cliffs. It was realised that this was likely to sacrifice surprise, but progress otherwise was impossible.

Fortunately, the explosions coincided with heavy firing further down the coast and the enemy manning the battery did not hear them. With the group having scaled the cliff, they pushed on quickly with their first task. After searching some houses on the way, 1 Section, C Troop, arrived at the front edge of the wood facing the battery. A sub-section from 2 Section searched all the remaining houses and ground in the immediate vicinity of Beach One, while another sub-section guarded the bridgehead around the gulley.

After cutting the telephone cable from the lighthouse, A Troop's fighting patrol worked their way round to the right of the battery. As C Troop went into action, A Troop's patrol engaged the gun sites from windows of adjoining houses with accurate small arms fire at 250 yards. This patrol also silenced the west flak gun, killing three successive guns crews. C Troop's No. 1 Section entered a small salient strip of scrub facing the forward wire of the battery 250 yards in front of them and they could see some of the enemy, including what appeared to be a cook in a white suit standing around unconcerned, suggesting that they'd achieved complete surprise.

The time was now 0530hrs. The mortar Observation Post (OP) had been established and the corporal in charge made an error in judgement and moved the mortar too far forward. He ordered the linesman to go back uncoiling the wire so time was lost and they were only able to open fire just before the final assault. While line communications failed, communication from the OP from the Group Commander's radio to C Troop worked as it had been thoroughly practised and anticipated.

By 0540 hours C Troop's No. 2 Section were in position and the battery was being heavily engaged by small arms fire. The three Bren guns fired in short bursts one by one on a prearranged plan. Each gun had 16 magazines, of which about 12 were fired. One Bren gun set up in long grass about 150 yards from the target and began firing continually without being observed.

Three snipers did excellent work keeping the enemy pinned down. One of them, his face and hands painted green, and wearing suitable camouflage, crawled forward to a position 120 yards from the battery. These snipers had been issued with incendiary bullets as well as standard ammunition to fire at the wooden battery buildings. However, the incendiary bullets were a mistake as they did not set a house on fire and also drew enemy fire. Three enemy MG positions were successively silenced by the accurate shooting of these Bren gunners and snipers.

To silence enemy fire from buildings, the anti-tank rifle was used and the gunner fired 60 rounds in rapid fire at the flak tower at the rear of the gun emplacements, which were out of range, but a 68 grenade was fired through the window of a house to silence a sniper. A short time after the enemy had been engaged with small arms fire the 2in mortar team arrived and began firing. The first bomb fell short, but the second hit one of the cordite dumps behind the guns resulting in a blinding flash. The time was now 0607hrs and the battery was silenced.

Other cordite dumps were hit and exploded, severely burning the German gun crews as the mortar fire continued. The 2in mortar continued to give accurate fire behind the gun emplacements. Small arms fire and mortar fire (with smoke just before zero hour for the assault) continued until the assault signal went up at about 0630hrs. A few minutes later a German 80mm mortar, firing from east of the battery position, got the range just as the party was beginning to withdraw and the first three casualties occurred. Hitherto, enemy fire (mortar, heavy MG, and horizontal flak) had been consistent but inaccurate, being mostly too high. It is thought that the 2in mortar position was given away when it started to fire smoke by the trails that these bombs leave while passing through the air.

Meanwhile, the remainder of C Troop had searched all the houses above the beach and the surrounding cover, killing enemy snipers. The overhead cable from the lighthouse OP to the battery had been destroyed. The five or six salvos fired by the battery at the shipping off Dieppe all fell short; their failure was probably due to the cutting of this line.

The story of the attack on the Varengeville gun battery by British Commandos continues with Group 2.

The five LCAs and one LCS containing Group 2 also increased speed when the white star shells went up from the lighthouse at 0430hrs. As A Troop (less one section) disembarked and began to cross the heavy breach wire they came under mortar and MG fire and had four casualties. The remainder of the group immediately went ashore 150 yards further up the beach, using rabbit netting to get across the wire. They also came under fire and received eight casualties. The enemy used a concentration of tracer ammunition, which, in the half light, had a very unpleasant effect on men not accustomed to it. There seems to be some doubt whether this fire was coming from high ground west of Sainte-Marguerite or from the Quiberville direction or both. Most of the casualties were from the mortar – which fortunately, soon lifted and continued firing at the retreating landing craft.[12]

Two medical orderlies, who were brothers, remained with the wounded. One was taken prisoner with them, the other escorted three walking wounded along the clifftop to Beach One, two of whom were unfortunately killed on the way. One officer, leaving his boat, was hit by mortar fragments, his right hand becoming useless. Nevertheless, he led a charge in the final assault on the battery, using his revolver and grenades, with his left hand accounting for a number of the enemy dead. He subsequently received a bar to his MC. A lance corporal of the Royal Signals was stunned by the same bomb. He recovered consciousness ten minutes later and knowing the plan and, as the only signaller in his section, that he was of major importance, he managed to re-join his section in the wood. He arrived in time to give Force HQ the necessary situation report before the assault signal. A private soldier, under heavy fire, climbed a telegraph pole and with his wire cutters cut lateral communications along the coast; he was awarded the MM.

As the troops were getting over the wire, three Boston aircraft passed overhead and drew enemy fire from the command who crossed the Quiberville–Sainte-Marguerite road, proceeding at the double along the east bank of the River Saâne, in accordance with the plan. B Troop was in the lead closely followed by Force HQ, then F Troop. This advance was to be covered by smoke if they were fired on from the high ground near Quiberville. With the river on their right, the going, mostly through long grass, was heavy, since the river had overflowed its banks. The bend in the river where the force was to swing east was also easily identified, though by this time it was 0515hrs and daylight.

The ground from the river to the south-west corner of the wood was more exposed, though not devoid of cover. As Group 2 crossed the open spaces by bounds they could hear the heavy volume of small arms fire as C Troop engaged the battery. Suddenly, they heard the roar of the first cordite

---

12   See Notes from Theatres of War, No. 11, Destruction of a German Battery by No. 4 Commando.

explosion and clearly saw sheets of flame above the trees, which increased their confidence that all was going well.[13]

Reaching the wood, B and F Troops divided according to plan and made their way towards their forming up areas.

B Troop moved forward inside the southern edge of the wood and then filtered through the orchard by sub-sections. Using cover, they approached the perimeter wire, where they came under inaccurate fire from a MG position, the flak tower and from various buildings. From thereon they advanced by fire and movement with covering smoke. One MG was stalked and silenced with a grenade. They reached their assembly positions, just short of the main battery buildings reporting to HQ they were ready for the assault.

F Troop advanced under the cover of smoke due north on either side of the road, to the corner of the perimeter. Here a sergeant records that a number of Germans were surprised in a farmyard while organising a counterattack on C Troop and were shot up with Tommy guns.[14] From the buildings and enclosures just inside the perimeter they encountered vigorous opposition and sustained several casualties. The troop commander was killed by a stick grenade, and one of the section officers was mortally wounded. The sergeant took cover but was also killed. The third officer was shot through the hand, the bullet lodging in his wrist, but he closed with his opponent and killed him.

This officer took over command of the troop, and in the final assault on the battery, though shot through the thigh, led his men in bayonet charges from one gun site to another. He was subsequently awarded the Victoria Cross. The troop sergeant major was also badly wounded in the foot, but continued to engage the enemy in a sitting position; he received the DCM. Fighting their way forward and overcoming resistance, F Troop reached their start line under cover in a ditch along the road immediately behind the gun emplacements.

Force HQ, consisting of the commander, adjutant, two runners three signallers with No. 38 sets, and a protective section of four Tommy gunners from the Commando orderly room, had moved forward to the north-west corner of the wood, where a heartening situation report was received from

---

13   Ibid.
14   Ibid.

the commander of Group 1.[15] A Troop reported that they were in a position west of the battery position and had inflicted heavy casualties. Force HQ now moved behind and between B and F Troops near the track where the commander contacted officers commanding B and F Troops.

At Z+90, exactly on time, the four-cannon Hurricanes swooped in, strafing the gun sites and battery positions but this was only partly successful as they were bounced by a formation of German Fw 190s.

The assault signal was given at about Z+100. B Troop rushed the building to the right of the gun sites and F Troop the gun sites themselves. The charge of F Troop went in across open ground under fire, overrunning strongpoints, and finally ended on the gun sites themselves, where all the crews were bombed, shot or bayoneted. B Troop had a somewhat easier task in the assault. Odd enemy groups were despatched in underground tunnels, in the battery office, in the cookhouse and outbuildings. Two German officers were killed after a rousing chase from one house to another. The guns, both barrels and breech blocks, instruments, and most of the subterranean stores and ammunition dumps, were blown up by F Troop.

Mopping up and all-round defence was done by B Troop. Dead Germans were piled high up behind the sandbag breastworks that surrounded the guns. Many had been badly burned when the cordite was set alight in the early stages of the operation. Other bodies of men who had been sniped by C and A Troops lay all around the area, in and out of bunkers, slit trenches, or buildings. Isolated resistance from pillboxes caused a further half-dozen casualties, since all strongpoints were enfiladed from one section of the wire to another (the perimeter covered some 50 acres); when one position was stormed and the crews killed, the Command personnel engaged came under heavy fire from the next position. Isolated German snipers continued to resist from outside the gun emplacements, picking off single men moving by themselves, but were not willing to unmask their positions during the mopping up operations by going after multiple targets that might expose their positions.

At this stage the groups made good use of smoke generators and the No. 77 phosphorus grenades, which explode on impact, proved especially successful. Union Jacks for captured positions proved useful as recognition signals.

---

15   See Notes from Theatres of War, No. 11, Destruction of a German Battery by No. 4 Commando for details.

At the time Cauldron Force commander felt that the success of the operation was down to the excellence of junior leadership and superior weapons training.

Withdrawal

While the guns were being blown up, the force commander ordered the medical officers and stretcher bearers by RT to come up from the beachhead to the battery position. Once the demolitions and mopping up operations were finished, F Troop, Force HQ and B Troop headed swiftly down to Beach One, carrying their wounded while being guided by elements of C Troop, who were covering the withdrawal.

Meanwhile, on the left flank, A Troop ambushed and shot up an enemy patrol coming from Saint-Marguerite. It is worth noting here as an example of bad training that the enemy advance points were too close together and that the shot that started the ambush passed through the two leading Germans.

However, it took some time to get the wounded through the gaps in the wire and time could have been saved had the gaps been widened while the operation was under way. Suddenly an enemy mortar began firing as the withdrawal was in progress but it was quickly silenced by the Commando 3in mortar that had been mounted on the beach to cover such an eventuality. The mortar crews judged the distance by the line of flight of the Germans' bombs and returned fire.

Forming the rearguard, C Troop were the last to withdraw and did so in accordance with a frequently rehearsed drill whereby the LMGs in pairs leapfrogged one another, while the rear elements put up a smokescreen from haversacks containing smoke grenades, which had been dumped for this purpose at the top of the gulley on the troop's way up. The withdrawal across the rocks to the LCAs was made through a lane of smoke some 200 yards wide from No. 18 generators placed in position during the operation. The lane was extended for about 50 yards into the sea by naval smoke floats put out by the LCS and LCAs. When LCAs were a few hundred yards out, and no longer under the lee of the cliffs, they came under inaccurate MG fire from the vicinity of the lighthouse, and further use was made of smoke until out of range.

The total casualties of the operation were 45:

> Officers killed – 2
> Officers wounded – 3
> Other ranks killed – 10
> Other ranks wounded – 17
> Other ranks wounded and missing – 9
> Other ranks missing – 4

No casualties were suffered during the withdrawal. Of the 20 men wounded and evacuated, several had carried on right through the action and 12 were back on duty within two months.

This operation showed how a small group of infantry with infantry weapons can inflict heavy enemy casualties at a relatively low cost due to sound understanding and appreciation of infantry firepower, team work, efficiency and discipline:

- The high number of Germans killed by infantry weapons while they were behind cover is down to the special training in accurate shooting
- One of the key lessons of this action is the application of successful mortar fire throughout the operation; the 3in from 800 yards in front of the base plate and the 2in in its correct role
- A just reward for the careful training prior to the operation was the high number of German casualties scored by the rifles and Bren guns fired from the hip at close range during the assault.[16]

---

16   See Notes from Theatres of War, No. 11, Destruction of a German Battery by No. 4 Commando During the Dieppe Raid, Introduction, War Office February 1943 for further details.

Bibliography

Reports

Report No. 100, Canadian Military Headquarters, Operation Jubilee, The Raid on Dieppe, 19 August 1942, Part 1 The Preliminaries of the Operation.

Report No. 10, Historical Section, National Defence Headquarters, Operation Jubilee, The Raid on Dieppe, Information From German War Diaries, Report of the Commander-in-Chief West, (Field Marshal von Rundstedt) on the Dieppe Raid, 19 August 1942.

Report No. 116, Operation Jubilee, The Raid on Dieppe, 19 August 1942, Additional Information from German Sources, Directorate of History, National Defence Headquarters, Ottawa, Canada.

Report No. 101, Operation Jubilee, The Raid on Dieppe, Part 2, The Execution of the Operation, Paragraph 15, Canadian Military Headquarters.

Report of Group 5 Commander D.B. Wyburd, Appendix 7 to Enclosure No. 13, Report of Naval Force Commander, Report No. 101.

Battle Report of German Commander-in-Chief West (GHQ Army Group D) on the English Landing Attempt at, and on Both Flanks of Dieppe, 19 August 1942, Historical Section, Army Headquarters, Ottawa, November 1946.

Report of 302 German Infantry Division, Operations Section -1a, on the Dieppe Raid.

Notes from Theatres of War, No. 11, p.15.

Report of Naval Force Commander, cited in Report No. 108, Operation Jubilee, The Raid on Dieppe, 19 August, Part II, Execution of the Operation, Section 2, The Attack on the Main Beaches.

Lecture Notes, The Combined Service Raid on Dieppe, 19 August 1942.

H.Q. 81 Corps report to G.H.Q. West at 1249hrs.

Combined Report on the Dieppe Raid, 1942, Annex 7, Report by the Air Force Commander, Appreciation of the Enemy's Air Effort.

Operation Jubilee Combined Report, The Dieppe Raid. Annex 7, Report of the Air Commander Sir Trafford Leigh-Mallory.

Report No. 86, 'German Lessons from the Dieppe raid', 8 March 1944, p.6, NAC, RG 24/10702/2125C1.981 (D298).

Articles

Carroll, J., 'The 1942 Dieppe Raid and its influence on D-Day', Stephen Ambrose Historical Tours, https://stephenambrosetours.com/the-1942-dieppe-raid-and-its-influence-on-d-day

Hall, D.I., 'The German View of the Dieppe Raid August 1942', *Canadian Military History*, Vol. 21, Iss. 4, Article 2.

Henry, H.G., 'The Planning, Intelligence, Execution and Aftermath of the Dieppe Raid, 19 August 1942'.

'Jagdeschwader 2', Wikipedia, 12 May 2021, Creative Commons Attribution Share-Alike Licence.

Shapiro, L.S.B., 'Dieppe As The Enemy Saw It', *MacLean's Magazine*, 1 March 1946, London.

Shelley, James, 'German Lessons and Influence on Strategic Thinking' as outlined in Henry, 'The Planning, Intelligence, Execution and Aftermath of the Dieppe Raid, 19 August 1942'.

Strohn, Dr Matthias, 'An Absolutely Harrowing Organisation', *British Army Review*, No. 175, Summer 2019, CHACR, Camberley, Ministry of Defence.

Wikipedia, 'HMS *Queen Emma*', entry https://en.wikipedia.org/wiki/HMS_ Queen_Emma

Globe and Mail, Toronto, 22 August 1942.

Books

An Official History, *The Dieppe Raid: The Combined Operations Assault on Hitler's European Fortress August 1942*, Frontline Books, ISBN 978-1-52675-291-8.

Caldwell, D., *JG 26 Luftwaffe Fighter Wing War Diary, Vol. One: 1939–42*, Stackpole Military History Series, Grub Street, 1996.

Ford, K., *Dieppe 1942, Prelude to D-Day*, Illustrated by Howard Gerrard, Osprey Publishing, 2003, Oxford.

Franks, N., *Dieppe: The Greatest Air Battle, 19th August 1942*, Grub Street, London, 2010.

Janowicz, K., *JG 26 'Schlageter', Vol. II*, Kagero, first edition, limited edition, ISBN 83-89088-07-X.

Janowicz, K., *JG 2 'Richthofen', 1942–1943*, Kagero, ISBN 83-89088-04.5.

Johnson, J., Air Vice Marshal, *Wing Leader*, Goodall paperback edition, sixth paperback edition, Crecy Publishing, 2019, Manchester.

Thompson, R.W., *Dieppe At Dawn, The Story of the Dieppe Raid*, Hutchinson and Co., London, 1956.

Index